PAUL STORR

PLATE I

PAUL STORR

From an attributed portrait in the Stapleton-Champneys Collection

PAUL STORR

1771-1844

Silversmith and Goldsmith

N M PENZER

Spring Books

London · New York · Sydney · Toronto

First published 1954
and © 1954 by B T Batsford Ltd, London

This edition published 1971 by
The Hamlyn Publishing Group Ltd
London · New York · Sydney · Toronto
Hamlyn House, Feltham, Middlesex, England

Printed and bound in Great Britain by
Hazell, Watson & Viney Ltd, Aylesbury, Bucks

ISBN 0 600 37960 4

CONTENTS

ACKNOWLEDGMENT

To Her Majesty The Queen I tender my most respectful thanks for permission to reproduce plate from the Royal Collection at Windsor Castle.

My thanks are due also to H.R.H. The Princess Royal and the Earl of Harewood for a similar favour in respect of the Harewood Plate. His Grace the Archbishop of Canterbury has most kindly allowed me to reproduce the Portuguese reliquary. To the following I owe a debt of gratitude for permission to include specimens of Storr plate from their collections: the late Duke of Bedford, Their Graces the Dukes of Portland, K.G., and the Duke of Wellington, K.G., the Most Hon. the Marquesses of Anglesey and Londonderry, the Earl Spencer, Lord Fairhaven, Doctor Anthony Storr, the Misses Storr, Mrs. Vernon Faithfull Storr, Mrs. L. M. Kaye, Mrs. Jean Rhodes, Mrs. Edward Munves and Francis Stonor, Esq.

To my old friend Edward Parker Stapleton and his son Henry Champneys I am indebted for much laborious research work and the discovery of the painting of Paul Storr. Laurence Whistler has kindly given his opinion on this painting. I am under great obligation to Sir Charles Bird Locock without whose expert genealogical help the inclusion of the pedigrees of Storr and Beyer would have been impossible.

The reproductions of examples of Church plate are due to the kindness and help so readily given by the Reverend W. P. Baddeley, Vicar of St. Pancras, Euston; the Reverend A. W. S. Holmes, Rector of Churchill and Sarsden, Oxfordshire; the Reverend H. A. McCann, Rector of Begbroke, Oxfordshire; and the Reverend D. G. R. Taylor, Rector of St. Mary's, Otley, Suffolk. My thanks are due to the following goldsmiths and silversmiths for sending photographs of pieces used in the present work: Messrs. Carrington and Co. Ltd., Corbell & Co. Ltd., Garrard & Co. Ltd., Harman & Lambert, Lewis & Kaye, Ralph Hyman of New York, James Robinson of New York, S. J. Shrubsole of London and New York, and D. and J. Wellby Ltd.; Messrs. Crichton Bros. have given much expert advice and help on many occasions.

For permission to reproduce plate belonging to colleges, corporations, museums, and so on, I am indebted to the Principal and Fellows of Brasenose College, Oxford; the Master and Fellows of Trinity College, Cambridge; the Lord Mayor and Corporation of London; the Chamberlain's Court, Guildhall House; the Mayor and Corporation of Dover; the Worshipful Company of Goldsmiths; the Trustees of the National Maritime Museum, Greenwich; the National Coal Board; the Victoria and Albert Museum; the Wellington Museum, Apsley House; the Art Institute of Chicago; and the Cleveland Museum of Art.

ACKNOWLEDGMENT

Throughout my work at Windsor Castle I received every kindness and help from Sir Owen Morshead, K.C.V.O., D.S.O., M.C., the Librarian.

I should also like to acknowledge the help so unstintingly given by the staffs of all libraries in which I have worked—especially the British Museum, the Society of Antiquaries and the Cambridge University Library.

To Mr. A. G. Grimwade, of Messrs. Christie, Manson and Woods, I owe especial thanks for the vast amount of trouble he has taken in compiling Appendix A of the present work in which the sale of all Storr pieces has been tabulated with such care and patience. My friend Mr. Charles Oman, Keeper of the Department of Metalwork at the Victoria and Albert Museum, has given me the benefit of his great knowledge throughout the whole period of my work.

As I trust is self-evident, my publishers, Messrs. B. T. Batsford Ltd., have spared neither time nor expense in making the format of the volume worthy of its subject—the work of a Royal goldsmith.

Lastly I want to acknowledge my great debt to my friend, the late E. Alfred Jones, not only for the continual use I have made of his numerous publications but also for the inspiration he has given me in my work.

Cambridge, 1954   N. M. PENZER

LIST OF ILLUSTRATIONS

LIST OF ILLUSTRATIONS

13

LIST OF ILLUSTRATIONS

PEDIGREE I

BEYER

Adam Beyer,
1729–1804
m. Ann Lewis,
b. 1735

Catherine Beyer,
d. unmarried

Lorence Beyer,
1733–1789
d. unmarried

Sarah Beyer
m. John Reid

Mary Ann
Beyer, 1767–1851
m. James Bird,
1768–1850

Elizabeth Susanna
Beyer, 1770–1843
m. Paul Storr,
1771–1844
(See Pedigree II)

Catherine Beyer,
1760–1817
m. Richard Hunt,
1754–1824

John Samuel
Hunt, 1785–1865
m. Elizabeth
Gunning, d. 1877

Three
others
d. inf.

Henry Peale
Bird, 1799–1882
m. Emily
Barnes, d. 1878

Frances Jane
Bird, 1804–1842
m. Thomas Pitman
(Canon) 1801–1890

Two other
sons, three
other daus.

Fanny Bird
Pitman, 1837–1889
m. Sir Charles
Brodie Locock,
2nd Bart., 1827–1890

One
other
son,
two
other
daus.

Sir Charles
Bird Locock,
3rd Bart., b. 1878
m. Christine Maria
Bennett, b. 1881

John Hunt,
1811–1879
m. Emma
Smith
d. 1889

Eleven
others

Thomas Pitman
(Rev.), 1828–1863
m. Mary Bedgegood
1819–1905

Henry Barnes
Pitman, 1831–1872
m. Mary Eliza
Pitman (1st cousin),
1841–1917

Margaret Abbie
Locock, 1872–1925
m. Sir Charles
Montague Lush,
Judge of the
High Court,
1853–1930

Four
other
daus.

One son, two daus.

One son, two daus.

Two sons, three daus.

John Mortimer
Hunt, 1844–1897
m. Eliza Henderson,
d. 1924

One
other
son,
two
other
daus.

Four sons, two daus.

Keziah Elizabeth
Hunt, 1840–1918
m. Henry Francis
Makins, 1841–1914

Wilfrid Mortimer
Hunt, b. 1871
m. Anne
Henrietta Hornet

Hilda Margaret
Hunt, b. 1873
m. Sir Arthur
Wallace Pickard-
Cambridge
1873–1952

Two
other
sons,
one
other
dau.

One son,
three daus.

Pauline
Makins
m. Nigel
Christopher
Walsh (Hon.)
1867–1931

Isabel Makins
m. Sir James
Gilbert Mellor,
Brig.-Gen.,
K.B.E., C.M.G.

Constance
Makins
m. Hastings
Rashdall
(V. Rev. Dean),
1858–1924

Sir Ernest
Makins, Brig.-
Gen., C.B.,
K.B.E., D.S.O.,
b. 1869
m. Florence
Mellor

Sir Roger Mellor
Makins, K.C.M.G.,
K.C.B., b. 1904
m. Alice Davis

One
other
son

Beatrice Makins
m. Charles
Cameron
Leveson-Gower,
Col., C.M.G.,
b. 1866

Two daus.

Two
other
sons,
one
other
dau.

One
son,
one
dau.

One son, four daus.

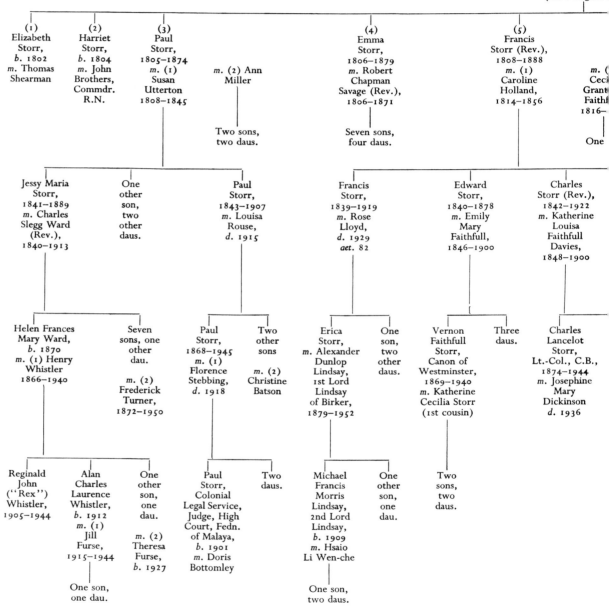

Paul Storr, 1771–
m. Elizabeth Susa
Beyer, 1770–18
(See Pedigree I

| (1) Elizabeth Storr, b. 1802 m. Thomas Shearman | (2) Harriet Storr, b. 1804 m. John Brothers, Commdr. R.N. | (3) Paul Storr, 1805–1874 m. (1) Susan Utterton 1808–1845 | m. (2) Ann Miller | (4) Emma Storr, 1806–1879 m. Robert Chapman Savage (Rev.), 1806–1871 | (5) Francis Storr (Rev.), 1808–1888 m. (1) Caroline Holland, 1814–1856 | m. (Cec Gran Faith 1816– |

Two sons, two daus.

Seven sons, four daus.

One

| Jessy Maria Storr, 1841–1889 m. Charles Slegg Ward (Rev.), 1840–1913 | One other son, two other daus. | Paul Storr, 1843–1907 m. Louisa Rouse, d. 1915 | Francis Storr, 1839–1919 m. Rose Lloyd, d. 1929 aet. 82 | Edward Storr, 1840–1878 m. Emily Mary Faithfull, 1846–1900 | Charles Storr (Rev.), 1842–1922 m. Katherine Louisa Faithfull Davies, 1848–1900 |

| Helen Frances Mary Ward, b. 1870 m. (1) Henry Whistler 1866–1940 | Seven sons, one other dau. m. (2) Frederick Turner, 1872–1950 | Paul Storr, 1868–1945 m. (1) Florence Stebbing, d. 1918 | Two other sons m. (2) Christine Batson | Erica Storr, m. Alexander Dunlop Lindsay, 1st Lord Lindsay of Birker, 1879–1952 | One son, two other daus. | Vernon Faithfull Storr, Canon of Westminster, 1869–1940 m. Katherine Cecilia Storr (1st cousin) | Three daus. | Charles Lancelot Storr, Lt.-Col., C.B., 1874–1944 m. Josephine Mary Dickinson d. 1936 |

| Reginald John ("Rex") Whistler, 1905–1944 | Alan Charles Laurence Whistler, b. 1912 m. (1) Jill Furse, 1915–1944 | One other son, one dau. m. (2) Theresa Furse, b. 1927 | Paul Storr, Colonial Legal Service, Judge, High Court, Fedn. of Malaya, b. 1901 m. Doris Bottomley | Two daus. | Michael Francis Morris Lindsay, 2nd Lord Lindsay, b. 1909 m. Hsaio Li Wen-che | One other son, one dau. | Two sons, two daus. |

One son, one dau.

One son, two daus.

16

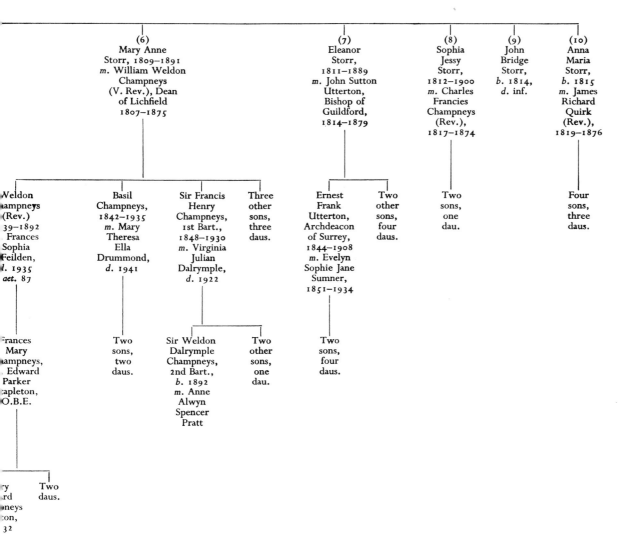

(6)
Mary Anne
Storr, 1809–1891
m. William Weldon
Champneys
(V. Rev.), Dean
of Lichfield
1807–1875

(7)
Eleanor
Storr,
1811–1889
m. John Sutton
Utterton,
Bishop of
Guildford,
1814–1879

(8)
Sophia
Jessy
Storr,
1812–1900
m. Charles
Francies
Champneys
(Rev.),
1817–1874

(9)
John
Bridge
Storr,
b. 1814,
d. inf.

(10)
Anna
Maria
Storr,
b. 1815
m. James
Richard
Quirk
(Rev.),
1819–1876

Weldon
Champneys
(Rev.)
39–1892
Frances
Sophia
Feilden,
d. 1935
aet. 87

Basil
Champneys,
1842–1935
m. Mary
Theresa
Ella
Drummond,
d. 1941

Sir Francis
Henry
Champneys,
1st Bart.,
1848–1930
m. Virginia
Julian
Dalrymple,
d. 1922

Three
other
sons,
three
daus.

Ernest
Frank
Utterton,
Archdeacon
of Surrey,
1844–1908
m. Evelyn
Sophie Jane
Sumner,
1851–1934

Two
other
sons,
four
daus.

Two
sons,
one
dau.

Four
sons,
three
daus.

Frances
Mary
Champneys,
Edward
Parker
Stapleton,
O.B.E.

Two
sons,
two
daus.

Sir Weldon
Dalrymple
Champneys,
2nd Bart.,
b. 1892
m. Anne
Alwyn
Spencer
Pratt

Two
other
sons,
one
dau.

Two
sons,
four
daus.

ry
rd
neys
:on,
3 2

Two
daus.

17

CHAPTER ONE

THE MAN AND HIS WORK

IN any attempt to assess the value of a man's work—in whichever of the Arts—in a fair and unbiased manner, as is only his rightful due, it is necessary to put it in its true perspective, to take into account the times in which he worked, to allow for the dictates of passing whims and fashions, to note any extraneous influences, to gauge aright the standard of technique displayed, and finally to consider if the dictum of posterity be right and just.

History can offer many examples of personal initiative and genius being stifled by poverty and lack of opportunity, by prejudice and jealousy, or by misunderstanding and ignorance. This, of course, was not the case with Paul Storr, but one wonders how his technique would have developed had his working life not coincided with one of the great periods of English history, and, above all, had there been no Philip Rundell to inundate him with orders for the Royal Family, for the celebration of a fresh victory, or to fulfil a contract for one of the great houses of a wealthy and aristocratic England.

Considering, then, the degree to which circumstance played a part in Storr's life we can but wonder at the high standard of his work—even when repetition of design got dangerously near that *coup de grâce* of all craftsmen—mass production. It is impossible to point to any piece by Paul Storr as an example of faulty workmanship. We may not approve of the design, we may dislike the proportions, we may criticize unnecessary elaboration of detail, we may consider a piece more suited to marble or bronze than to silver—but bad workmanship: never!

Storr was working from designs drawn by men to whom the nature of gold and silver was practically unknown. Thus Tatham was an architect, Flaxman a sculptor, Stothard a painter and Theed both painter and sculptor. Their *métier* was stone and marble, pottery and porcelain, and classical line-drawings. To transmute from one medium to another demands great skill, and in this Storr was a master. If in judging his work we had to depend solely on his massive and "grand" pieces we might dismiss him merely as a fine and clever craftsman, but if we examine his earlier products and some of those simpler domestic objects which appeared from time to time—*parva componere magnis*—we shall see more than the craftsman—we shall see the artist. Paul Storr was the last of the great goldsmiths.

THE CLASSICAL REVIVAL

When in 1792 Storr had completed the period of his apprenticeship almost the first article he produced, in conjunction with William Frisbee, was a two-handled vase of Greek form. When in 1799 he made an oval tea-pot and placed it on a stand upheld by fluted pilasters surmounted with goats' heads joined by floral swags, he was but copying what he had learned from his Anglo-Swedish master, Andrew Fogelberg. In both cases he was following the current taste of the age—the age of the Classical Revival. In the middle of the eighteenth century the last vestiges of the rococo in architecture and furniture were being swept away by the onslaught of the Adam brothers. As always, the shape and decoration of silversmiths' work was equally affected.

The asymmetry caused by the introduction of rocks, shells, foliage and the broken line was now to give place to the straight line, the symmetrical garland, the pendant rings or masks, the oval and the arabesque. To say, however, that silversmiths produced nothing rococo in the second half of the eighteenth century would be the very reverse of fact as countless extant pieces prove. The enormous influence, and undoubted charm, of so much of Huguenot rococo had an appeal that was not to be so easily effaced. Although the introduction of the "Adam style" and the accession of George III were practically contemporary, it was only forty years later, in 1800, that His Majesty remarked: "I am a little of an architect and think that the old school is not enough attended to—the Adams have introduced too much of neatness and prettiness. . . ." Walpole had already (in 1785) scoffed at "Mr. Adam's gingerbread and sippets of embroidery", and now his decoration was considered "feminine" and out of tune with the age. The Roman versus Greek battle had been waged for years—Piranesi champion of the Roman and the Abbé Winckelmann of the Greek. While the discoveries at Pompeii and Herculaneum and the writings of Sir William Hamilton and others had evoked an enormous interest in Roman art, the foundation, and especially the publications, of the Society of Dilettanti had pointed the way for a Greek revival. This Grecian flame had been fanned by the publication in 1806 of *Designs for Ornamental Plate* by Charles Heathcote Tatham, an almost exact contemporary of Storr. The work must have been well known to him, for not only do many of the drawings find an echo in much of his work now in the Royal Collection, but the Preface, praising as it does the work of the silver-chaser—Paul was the son of a silver-chaser—and championing the "massive" as against the "light and insignificant", would have a special appeal. In view of the scarcity of the volume in question, and of the effect it was to have on the design of plate largely illustrated in the present work, no apology is made for quoting from the Preface.

To encourage and facilitate the study of the Antique, in its application to that species of Ornament commonly called Plate, has been my principal motive for this publication. It has been lamented by Persons high in Rank, and eminent for Taste, that modern Plate had much fallen off both in design and execution from that formerly produced in this Country. Indeed, the truth of this remark is obvious, for instead of *Massiveness*, the principal characteristic of good Plate, light and insignificant forms have prevailed, to the utter exclusion of all good Ornament whatever. If we consult the Works of the celebrated Italian Chasers, we find that richness of design was a principle ever regarded by them; in Skilfulness of Execution they indeed stand unrivalled. . . . Good Chasing may be considered as a branch of Sculpture, and as it is well known that excellence in this Art is only to be obtained by indefatigable study and labour, so it is constant application to Modelling alone that will form a good Chaser; when this is not steadily regarded, the Art must inevitably decline, and instead of Objects fitted to excite the admiration of Persons of real taste, nothing is to be expected but Sconces, Girandoles, and Candlesticks, fit only for the dazzle of an Assembly House, or of a County Ball-Room.

The very next year (1807) appeared Thomas Hope's *Household Furniture and Interior Decoration*, which, although adversely reviewed in some journals,[1] had an influence on public taste. It consisted of drawings largely by himself, showing how classical ornamentation and line could be adapted to the English home, not only in furniture but in such domestic utensils as the casserole-dish, the ice-pail, the sugar basin and the tea-urn. On Plates 47 and 52 will be seen several designs used in later years by Storr.

It was not long before the Greek designs depicted in the above-mentioned works —and particularly in Stuart and Revett's *Antiquities of Athens*, 5 vols., 1762–1830— were to influence the neo-Classic School of architects. Such names as John Nash, William Wilkins, Sir Robert Smirke, George Basevi, Professor Cockerell, Sir Charles Barry and several others will at once come to mind. But perhaps the most thoroughly "Greek" architect of this time was William Inwood, whose chief work, built in conjunction with his eldest son, was the New Church of St. Pancras, Euston. It is, moreover, this church which is of especial interest to us owing to the fact that Paul Storr was commissioned to make the Communion plate in a style to suit the building. As we shall see later, this was by no means the only church plate he made, but in all other cases the designs were either copies of the antique or else conformed to the usual type of Communion cup, flagon and paten made in the early nineteenth century.

The Church of St. Pancras. As we are chiefly concerned with the Classical Revival, it may be of interest to give a brief history of St. Pancras Church.

In 1811 Parliament voted large sums of money for the erection of new churches as a thank-offering for victories in the Napoleonic wars. For years the little Church of St. Pancras, with the Kentish Town Chapel, had fought a losing battle in its efforts to supply the spiritual needs of a rapidly increasing borough population. But now seemed the time to act, and it was proposed to erect a new parish church, capable of seating some 2,000 people. At first, in 1812, opposition led to the temporary shelving of the proposition, but in the summer of 1815 a committee, selected by

[1] *Edinburgh Review*, Vol. X, p. 478. See art. *Dictionary of National Biography*. For a modern appreciation see Lord Wellesley, *Burlington Magazine*, May 1937, pp. 233–40, and M. Jourdain, *Regency Furniture*, 1934 (2nd edit., 1948).

nearly 200 principal householders, proceeded to obtain the necessary Act of Parliament. This Act was passed on 31st May 1816 by which the Trustees were empowered to raise the sum of £40,000—although its ultimate cost was over £76,000. It would appear that the Committee had a neo-Classical style in mind, for of the thirty plans submitted in 1818 it was that by William Inwood, based entirely on Athenian models, which was chosen. It should be remembered that the long and bitter quarrels about the famous Elgin marbles had just ended satisfactorily.[1] The sculptures had been exhibited in 1817 and at long last they had been hailed as the marvel of the Ancient World. Greek art was now the vogue, and the St. Pancras Committee were nothing if not up to date!

Inwood's eldest son, Henry William, had returned in 1819 from his architectural studies in Greece, fired with the enthusiasm that his work on the Acropolis had kindled. He had brought back with him not only innumerable plans and sketches, which were later to be used in a work on the Erechtheum, but a complete set of casts of the ornamentation round the doorways of that lovely Ionic temple. Father and son worked together, and the casts were used for the doorways under the hexastyle portico on the west front, while the lateral vestries (entrances to the catacombs[2]) were copied from the famous Caryatid portico.

The steeple presented a problem, but a daring two-story version of a copy of the Tower of the Winds at Athens, surmounted by another one of smaller size, got over the difficulty—with what success was a matter of opinion.[3] The foundation-stone of the church had been laid by H.R.H. Frederick Duke of York on 1st July 1819 when he offered to present such altar plate as would be in keeping with the Greek *motifs* as shown in Inwood's design. Paul Storr was duly consulted, and it was agreed that the capitals of the north porch of the Erechtheum would provide all necessary ornamentation—the anthemion, the ovolo and the astragal beading.

The acanthus would be useful for enriching the upper curves of the flagon handles, and possibly for the concave sweep of the feet—but that was all. Accordingly the plate was duly made, and presented in 1822. Although it was somewhat massive in size, the sole use of the Grecian ornamentation mentioned above produced a most impressive result. The cups proved to be too high ($9\frac{1}{2}$ in.) for general use, and it was decided in 1853 to have two of them melted down by Storr's successors, Hunt and Roskell, and so four smaller cups, $8\frac{1}{2}$ in. high, were produced.[4] The complete list of the plate as originally made is as follows:

[1] For a clear and highly interesting account of the whole matter see Adolf Michaelis, *Ancient Marbles in Great Britain*, Cambridge, 1882, pp. 132–51.

[2] This is why the figures carry water ewers and inverted torches to symbolize their functions as guardians of the entries to the vaults.

[3] For an adverse criticism see James Fergusson, *History of the modern styles of Architecture*, 2nd edit., 1873, pp. 334, 335. The best general account is probably that by J. Britton and E. W. Brayley, included in Britton and Pugin's *Illustrations of the Public Buildings of London*, Vol. I, 1825, pp. 145–66, with three Plates. For the most recent account see the L.C.C. *Survey of London*, Vol. XXIV (Pt. IV), 1952, pp. 1–4 and Pls. 7–10.

[4] See Edwin Freshfield, *Communion Plate of the Parish Churches in the County of London*, 1895, p. [29] with the Plate opposite, Pl. VII (the verger's wand), and Pl. VIII (one of the beadle's staves).

Altar Plate — Silver-gilt

Two Flagons	height 18 in.
Four Cups	height 9¾ in.
Three Patens	diam. 8½ in.
Three Dishes	diam. (2) 14½ in. 24 in.
Two Spoons	one with perforated bowl
Knife	silver-gilt handle
Verger's wand	silver 28½ in.

Further details will be found in the text of the present work, pp. 210, 212. Of interest are two beadle's staves, which probably came from the old church. They are dated 1774 and 1812 respectively, and have metal heads—an orb surmounted by a Roman soldier to represent St. Pancras.

As mentioned above, the St. Pancras plate was by no means the only Church plate made by Storr. As a matter of fact it was among the very first things he made, as is proved by an alms-plate of 1792 at St. Michael's Begbroke, Oxon (J. T. Evans, *Church Plate of Oxfordshire*, 1928, pp. 17, 18). For St. John the Baptist Church at New Windsor he made two chalices, from secular cups, in 1817 (J. W. and M. I. Walker, *Church Plate of Berkshire*, 1927, p. 345), while in 1826 and 1827 he supplied the Oxfordshire villages of Churchill, Sarsden and South Newington with similar sets of Communion plate (Evans, *op. cit.*, pp. 42, 150 and 113). In 1834 Queen Adelaide, wife of William IV, ordered from Storr a chalice, paten, flagon and alms-dish for Holy Trinity, Hermitage (Walker, *op. cit.*, pp. 150–1). A few years after Storr's son, Francis, had become Rector of St. Marys, Otley, Suffolk, in 1837, he made an exact replica of their Elizabethan chalice as well as a standing-paten to match. It seems highly probable that this far from exhausts Storr's ecclesiastical work, but as few books on County Church plate contain indexes of makers' marks, and several counties have no published lists of plate whatever, it is impossible to furnish a complete list. Mention may be made of the fine restoration work done by Storr in 1836 to the seventeenth-century Portuguese reliquary now in Lambeth Palace (see further pp. 240, 242).

THE NELSON PLATE

But long before Inwood and his son had built St. Pancras Church in the Greek style, the demand for plate of classical design had been steadily increasing for patriotic reasons. The brilliant series of British naval victories, beginning in 1794 with Howe's victory on "The Glorious First of June", led to the raising of funds to provide gratuities for the wounded and dependants of the killed, and to reward the officers for deeds of valour. Large sums were raised at Lloyd's Coffee House for these purposes, and with every fresh victory a new fund was launched. After the Battle of the Nile (1798) and again after the Battle of Copenhagen (1801) similar funds were raised, and on each of these occasions the Committee at Lloyd's, wishing to offer Nelson a personal tribute of gratitude, voted the sum of £500 for the purchase of a service of silver plate. The order for all this plate was given to Messrs. Rundell & Bridge, and to Paul Storr, as head of their manufactory, fell the task of carrying out the order. Considerable delay was caused by the fact that the actual items were to be selected by Nelson himself. But so close did one victory follow on the other that after the "Nile" service had been delivered, the "Copenhagen" was not really *another* service, but consisted of additional items selected by Nelson to supplement the first. It is not surprising, therefore, to find the separate items of the two sets have become muddled. The British Museum possesses a document[1] entitled "Inventory of sundry Plate belonging to The Right Honble Lord Viscount Nelson furnished by Rundell & Bridge November 1800". The date is obviously wrong as Nelson was not a Viscount in 1800.[2] The Inventory, which contains plate from both services, is as follows:

		oz.		dwt.
10 oval dishes	weight	703	,,	7
4 round do	,,	119	,,	19
4 oblong do	,,	230	,,	4
4 deep Cassarole	,,	136	,,	16
4 Comport & Covers	,,	234	,,	—
1 Tureen & Cover to match	,,	128	,,	6
8 Sauce Boats to suit	,,	170	,,	12
8 Salts to do.	,,	35	,,	16
2 Oval Vegetable dishes	,,	178	,,	8
4 polishd Ice pails	,,	307	,,	—
1 Tureen Ladle	,,	6	,,	6

Folio 8 verso.

		oz.		dwt.
8 Sauce Ladles to weight	,,	15	,,	3
8 Sauce Ladles	,,	3	,,	1
6 doz Pad plates	,,	1,287	,,	19
18 Soup Plates	,,	363	,,	19

No details as to the makers are given, and as the whereabouts of the pieces to-day is, with but few exceptions, unknown it is impossible to say exactly which items were made by Storr and which were entrusted to other hands. A few pieces, however, have luckily come back to Lloyd's, including two fine entrée dishes and a vegetable dish by Storr, and a breakfast dish and four soup plates by Timothy Renou.

Apart from the personal plate delivered to Nelson,[3] Rundell & Bridge made no

1 Add. MSS. 34, 990, fol. 7.
2 For full details of the question of dates, as well as copies of letters to and from Nelson, see Warren R. Dawson, *The Nelson Collection at Lloyd's*, 1932, pp. 3–14. For the Backhouse Urn, see his *Treasures of Lloyd's*, 4th edit., 1930, p. 157; and C. Wright and C. E. Fayle, *History of Lloyd's*, 1928, pp. 181–2—also see Plates facing pp. 208, 212 and 228.
3 For details of the Battle of the Nile Cup, see p. 106.

less than sixty-six Trafalgar Vases between 1804 and 1809. They were all designed by John Flaxman and are now scattered all over the world. Here again it is impossible to say how many were made by Storr. Finally, mention may be made of the Backhouse Urn, a massive piece made by Storr in 1806 and presented by the Committee on American Captures at Lloyd's to Thomas Backhouse, their Chairman, for his "able, zealous and indefatigable attention to the object of their concerns for the last ten years".

THE WELLINGTON PLATE

As visitors to the Wellington Museum at Apsley House are aware, the objects of fine and applied art connected with the 1st Duke, and presented to the nation in 1947 by the 7th Duke, include plate, porcelain, batons, orders and decorations, apart from pictures, furniture and personal relics. The plate can be conveniently divided into two groups: presentation plate and ambassadorial plate.

Of the presentation plate, the earliest is a table service of 125 pieces of silver, parcel-gilt, known as the Deccan Service. It was made by William Fountain, Joseph Preedy, John Moore and John Edwards in 1805–6 and 1806–7, and presented to the Duke on his return to England by the Army of the Deccan which he had commanded at the Battle of Assaye in India. The *motifs* employed in the design include the cobra, the elephant and finials of turbaned natives. A small selection from this service is shown in the Portico Room. In the Waterloo Gallery on the original banquet table is the huge centre-piece of the Portuguese Service presented to the Duke in 1814 by the Prince Regent of Portugal. It includes some ninety pieces, made in 1811–16 by Vicente Pires de Gama and João Teixeira Pinto from designs by D. A. de Sequeira. Two hot-plates with stands were made by order of the Duke to go *en suite* with other items in the service. They were the work of Storr and bear the date-letter for 1820–1. Four years later Robert Garrard made a lamp and dish for them. In the Striped Drawing-Room are two fine centre-pieces by Storr presented respectively by the field officers of the Army in Portugal and the general officers originally landed at Figueria in 1808. They are both reproduced in the present work (Pls. XXXIII and XXXIX).

The next piece of presentation plate is the Waterloo Vase, made in silver-gilt in 1824–5 by Benjamin Smith. The upper part shows the French cavalry attacking a British infantry square. The merchants and bankers of the City of London presented the Duke with a huge pair of candelabra as well as the silver-gilt Wellington Shield designed by Thomas Stothard. They were both made by Benjamin Smith, originally one of Storr's assistants. We now come to the so-called Ambassador Service of some 650 pieces of silver and silver-gilt.

On 5th July 1814 the Duke was, most unexpectedly, appointed Ambassador to Paris and occupied the house of Princess Borghese, at that time used as the British Embassy. Entertaining was on the grand scale and this enormous service had to be hastily assembled. The work was entrusted to Rundell, Bridge & Rundell and Paul

Storr himself was responsible for over a hundred pieces. These pieces, all silver-gilt, were as follows:

Two fruit-bowls and stands	272 oz.
Seventy-two dessert plates	1,208 oz.
Twelve bottle stands	240 oz.
Two ice spades (11″)	13 oz. 5 dwt.
Six ice spades (8½″)	21 oz. 10 dwt.
Four sugar ladles	7 oz. 10 dwt.
Four cream ladles	7 oz. 10 dwt.

Of these, the most important pieces are the fruit-bowls and bottle stands, which are duly reproduced and described on pp. 144 and 180 and Pls. XXXIV and LI. With such a large service, wanted at such short notice, it was necessary to put most of the work "out". It may be of interest, therefore, to record the names of the other makers, so far as they are known, together with some indication of what they made:

Paul Storr (as listed above)	102
William Fountain (dishes and ice-pails)	14
William Pitts (dishes)	18
William Eaton (table plates)	75
Robert Hennell (soup plates)	36
James Collins (?) (ice-pails)	2
John Moore (waiters)	6
Mary and Elizabeth Sumner (spoons and forks)	173
William Eley, Wm. Fearn, and Wm. Chawner (serving forks, soup ladles and grape-scissors)	16
Robert Garrard (table spoons)	2
Benjamin Smith (salvers and fruit-baskets)	4
Benjamin & James Smith (dishes and sugar vases)	34
Mark Bock (dessert and table knife handles)	78
Unmarked (wine labels)	24
Unidentified (spoons and forks)	72

Total: 656

The only Wellington plate by Storr still in possession of the 7th Duke are four massive silver-gilt candlesticks, with baluster stems chased with acanthus, on octagonal bases, two being fitted with triple branches for lights. They are engraved with the arms of the 1st Duke. They are 19 in. in height and 12 in. in width. The London date-letter is that for 1811–12.

The 7th Duke possesses a remarkably fine "Flaxman Cup" by Storr which was exhibited at the 1952 Regency Exhibition at the Royal Pavilion, Brighton (No. 67 in the catalogue). It is described in detail on p. 196 and Pl. LIX of the present work.

In concluding this brief account of the Wellington plate it is of interest to mention that the 1st Duke was a fine judge of plate and liked acquiring it. When British Ambassador at Paris he was a frequent visitor at Odiot's shop, and his account books, still preserved, record the purchase in Waterloo year of a large pair of silver candelabra for 8,584 francs. His Grace was also attracted to large dishes embossed with fruit and flowers, of which he had good examples. Unfortunately he kept his purchases to himself, destroyed all correspondence and never talked about the subject to his friends.[1]

THE HAREWOOD PLATE

The large part Paul Storr played in supplying the kind of plate demanded by the Regency age was evident to anyone who saw the Regency Exhibition at the Royal Pavilion, Brighton, in 1951. By far the most striking thing was the magnificent scene in the Banqueting Room where the table was laid for twenty-four guests reproducing the well-known painting in Nash's *Views of the Royal Pavilion*. The banquet is supposed to have reached the dessert stage, and the great table glitters with the truly wonderful silver-gilt dessert service of over fifty pieces which was made by Paul Storr between 1806 and 1816 for Edward Lascelles, who was raised to the peerage as Lord Harewood in 1812.[2] Owing to the kindness of H.R.H. the Princess Royal and the Earl of Harewood, the finest examples from this service are reproduced in the present work (see Pls. XLIV, LI, LII, LIV and LVII) and so need no description here.

In the Regency Exhibition of 1952 the place of honour on the great table was taken by a magnificent *épergne*, the joint work of Paul de Lamerie and Paul Storr, the property of the Corporation of London.[3] Other important Storr pieces were lent by the Duke of Wellington, the Marquess of Londonderry and the Lady Berwick, and the National Trust.[4]

THE WARWICK VASE

Of all the classical objects brought to this country from Italy in the eighteenth century the most spectacular, if not the most important, was undoubtedly the huge white-marble two-handled vase, which, after its purchase in 1774 by the Earl of Warwick, became known as the Warwick Vase. Four years later Piranesi published three very fine engravings of it, and in 1800 an account of it appeared in the *Gentleman's Magazine*. The very shape of the vase, quite apart from the classical masks and Bacchic emblems with which it was enriched, suggested endless possibilities to the silversmith, and Storr was soon producing ice-pails, soup tureens and centre-pieces based on the original. Of all these, the most important was a set of twelve silver-gilt

[1] I am indebted to the present Duke, who has given me most of this information in the course of correspondence.

[2] *Souvenir Programme and Catalogue of the Regency Exhibition in the Royal Pavilion, Brighton, 1951*. The dessert service is catalogued on p. 20, Nos. 53–63. See also H. Clifford Smith, "The Harewood Plate at the Regency Festival Exhibition at Brighton", *Apollo*, Aug. 1951, pp. 41–4; and Clifford Musgrave "The Regency Exhibition at Brighton", *Connoisseur*, Oct. 1951, pp. 90–5.

[3] For this see Pl. XXXVIII and p. 145.　　　　[4] *Catalogue*, 1952, p. 15.

ice-pails made by him in 1812–14 for the Prince Regent. In 1812 he had also made a pair for Edward Lascelles,[1] which forms part of the dessert service to which we have already referred. Copies of the Warwick Vase were made in materials other than silver—including the full-size bronze facsimiles at Windsor Castle and Cambridge (cast by Charles Crozatier in Paris) and the iron one at Birmingham—and its shape became known and recognized in a large variety of articles.

THE ROYAL COLLECTION

It is almost impossible to over-estimate the great losses of gold and silver plate which England has suffered over the centuries. The wanton destruction of priceless ecclesiastical vessels at the time of the Reformation was enormous, and the melting-pot, like a voracious dragon with an insatiable appetite, was always dangerously near —ready in times of trouble to consume the plate of ruler and subject alike. If we consult the old Royal inventories (many printed,[2] some soon to be published,[3] and others still in manuscript[4]) we can get a good idea of the size and richness of the collections, detailed descriptions and weights of the individual pieces, and an appreciation of the great variety of objects listed. Such jewels and plate of Elizabethan and Jacobean date as remained at the outbreak of the Civil War in 1642 were either sold or consigned to the melting-pot. Of the sacrifices demanded, and duly made, by Oxford and Cambridge as well as by so many of the London Livery Companies, we are only too well aware. Gold and silver plate was no longer regarded as having any artistic or aesthetic value, a heritage of our forebears to be preserved at all costs. It was nothing but potential coin with which troops could be paid and battles won. Even the plate and jewels pawned in Holland were ultimately dispersed. With the Restoration, save for a few pieces still preserved in the Tower, the Royal collection was practically non-existent,[5] and even the coronation of Charles II was postponed partly because there were no regalia to complete the ceremony.[6]

As time went on the Royal collection was gradually built up by presents and purchases, and when the inventory of George I was made in 1721 it was once again

[1] *Souvenir Programme and Catalogue of the Regency Exhibition, 1951.* No. 55.

[2] For these see the great work of F. de Mély and E. Bishop, *Bibliographie Générale des Inventaires Imprimés*, 3 vols., Paris, 1892/4/5. The "Tables" in Vol. III are indispensable. A further volume, bringing the work up to date, is badly needed.

[3] The 1574 Inventory of Queen Elizabeth (Stowe 555) has been edited by A. J. Collins, Keeper of the MSS. Brit. Mus., and is to be published by the Museum in the near future.

[4] For several important MSS., apart from 555, see *Cat. of the Stowe MSS. in the Brit. Mus.*, Vol. I, 1895, Class XI, "Royal Household, Wardrobe Accompts, Inventories, etc.", pp. 447–52. There are two important Henry VIII inventories: Harl. MSS. 1419 at the Brit. Mus., and the two MS. volumes at the Society of Antiquaries, *King Henry VIII's Jewel Book*. With these cf. the printed article with the same title by Edward [Trollope] Bishop of Nottingham in the *Associated Architectural Societies' Reports and Papers*, Vol. XVII, Pt. II, 1884, pp. 155–229. For other interesting lists see *Letters and Papers—Henry VIII*, ed. J. S. Brewer and (later) J. Gairdner, Vol. III, Pt. I, No. 463; Vol. IV, Pt. I, No. 1907; Vol. IV, Pt. III, No. 6789; Vol. V, No. 1799; and Vol. VI, Nos. 338, 339.

[5] See J. A. Bennett, "Account of the Royal Jewel-House Papers of the 16th and 17 cents. in the possession of Capt. H. G. St. John-Mildmay", *Archaeologia*, Vol. XLVIII, 1884, pp. 201–20; and also *Seventh Report of the Royal Commission on Historical MSS.*, Pt. I, 1879, pp. 590–6.

[6] The new regalia were made by Sir Robert Vyner, the "Prince of Goldsmiths", at a cost of nearly £32,000. He also lent Charles II the necessary plate for ceremonial functions. See Robert Cole, *Archaeologia*, Vol. XXIX, 1842, pp. 262 et seq.

of considerable size and importance.[1] In all 266 items, with their weights, are recorded, but this number gives little idea of the quantities as some items contain many pieces. For instance, there were "30 candlesticks", "46 knurld dishes and 115 others", "15 doz^n of white Plates", "10 doz^n Spoons, 9 doz^n fforks, 9 doz^n knives" and so on. Much of this plate remains to-day, but succeeding Hanoverians were in the habit of melting down "old-fashioned" plate, so that considerable losses have occurred in this way. The first Hanoverian "collector" of plate was George IV when Prince Regent, and after he had got rid of quantities of "old-fashioned" plate, first in 1817 and again when King in 1823, the Royal collection was, to a very great extent, "modern". The Royal Goldsmiths, Rundell, Bridge & Rundell, supplied the great majority of the new plate, and, as was only to be expected, Paul Storr's work excelled all others both in quantity and quality. In 1911 E. Alfred Jones published his fine work on the *Gold and Silver of Windsor Castle*, which, amongst its 103 Plates, and many unillustrated items, contained numerous examples of Storr's work. But Jones selected only the more elaborate pieces and thus a mistaken idea of Storr's work as represented in the Royal collection is obtained. It actually includes every type of object required by a royal household, and the numbers made by Storr run into thousands. Some idea of the quantity can be obtained from the fact that in the 1914 Inventory his name appears as maker in over 300 numbered entries, many of which include hundreds of separate pieces.

It has often been stated that Storr hardly ever made small table plate, but the Royal collection proves the contrary to have been the case. I have been permitted to inspect His late Majesty George V's special fully illustrated copy of the 1914 Inventory which contains no less than 339 Plates on which are included examples of every piece made by Storr in that great collection. Among his sets of small plate may be mentioned the "Boar Hunt and Mask pattern" set, made between 1811 and 1814, which consists of over 1,300 pieces, while the "Honeysuckle" set of slightly earlier date runs to well over 2,000 pieces! By gracious permission of Her Majesty I have been permitted to include in the present work a selection of Plates from this special copy of the Inventory (see Pls. XXVIII, XL, XLV, L, LXXII and LXXIV).

Another point of interest in this Royal copy is the fact that the text is interleaved in order to give the dates and prices of every piece purchased by the Prince Regent (nearly all in 1811) and as George IV in 1824, 1825, 1826 and 1827. By far the most expensive item was the enormous wine-cooler of 8,000 oz. which cost £8,500, while other large purchases included sixteen candelabra at £4,374, the Warwick Vase ice-pails at £3,470 and the four "Ephesian Diana" soup tureens at £4,498. Never before has the work of a single craftsman—from the most massive centre-piece to the humble wine-label and salt-spoon—been so completely represented in any collection. And the fact that it is the collection of our beloved Queen adds a new glory to the name of Storr.

[1] This MS. inventory is to be seen at the Public Record Office (Treasury Board Papers (T.I.), Bundle 235, No. 25) where others, such as those of Anne and George III, yet undiscovered, may lie hidden.

CHAPTER TWO

FAMILY HISTORY

THE YORKSHIRE FAMILY OF STORR

IT would appear that Paul Storr was a member of the London branch of the family who for centuries had lived around Hilston and Owstwick in the East Riding of Yorkshire. No detailed history of the English[1] family of Storr exists, and the information contained in the "Pedigree of Storr of Hilston" given in Vol. II, pp. 79–80, of George Poulson's *History and Antiquities of the Seigniory of Holderness,* Hull, 1841, is both incomplete and faulty. Of more use is the thirteen-page monograph, *Notes on the Families of Storr of Hilston and Owstwick,* compiled by A. B. Wilson-Barkworth for private circulation in 1890. Unfortunately the author's interests are almost entirely confined to Yorkshire, and as soon as a member of the family moves away he is disregarded. As we shall see shortly, it was a Marmaduke Storr who settled in London, and although he appears in Poulson's "Pedigree", dates are sadly lacking and any hint as to profession or business is completely ignored. However, several interesting facts about these early London members of the Storr family have come to light which, if they fail to show a definite connection with Paul Storr himself—as I fear they do—may at least provide material for further research. The Storr pedigrees of Hilston and Owstwick go back to three brothers—Joseph and Marmaduke of Owstwick and John of Hilston, and their sister Frances. They were all members of the Society of Friends, commonly called Quakers, and all three brothers suffered imprisonment for their faith. Joseph died in 1657 leaving his property to his brother Marmaduke, and it is with him and his descendants that we are chiefly concerned. John is of interest to us only because his great-grandson, also a John Storr, became a rear-admiral of considerable renown, and, if family tradition be reliable, knew both Paul and his uncle John well. We shall have occasion to refer to him later.

Marmaduke Storr seems to have spent most of his life at Owstwick. He married twice, firstly to Dorothy (surname unknown) by whom he had three children— Dorothy, Isaac and Marmaduke, and secondly (Dorothy dying in 1668) to Ann, widow of William Stringer of Ulrome. There are no children recorded of the second marriage. Marmaduke died in 1678, and Ann in 1680.

His eldest son, Isaac, also married twice and died in 1728. The younger son, who for the sake of clarity we will call Marmaduke (2), was born in 1667 and was in business as a tanner at Selby. He married Elizabeth Batty by whom he had four sons

---

[1] In *The Storrs Family, Genealogical and other memoranda,* published in New York, 1886, the author, Charles Storrs, considers the Storrs and Storr families to be of common origin. He quotes Poulson's work, but adds nothing of importance. Members of the Storrs family in England deny having any connection with that of Storr.

—William, John Marmaduke (3) and Batty. It was Marmaduke (3) who decided to move to London where he took up his residence in the Parish of St. Olave's, Southwark, and carried on the business of a goldsmith and watchmaker.[1] On 28th September 1724 he was registered as an apprentice of the Worshipful Company of Clockmakers to Stephen Horseman for a period of seven years—Horseman himself had been apprenticed to the famous Daniel Quare from 1701 to 1708 and must have been a maker of considerable repute, as in 1709 he was admitted as an honorary Freeman. The Clerk of the Clockmakers tells me that there is no trace of Marmaduke having been admitted to the Freedom, the reason being that he probably failed to submit his "masterpiece". The date of his entry into the Goldsmiths is not recorded, but he received the Freedom of the Company by Redemption on 30th April 1741, when he was entered as a watchmaker. He married Hannah Smith in 1728 and had by her four children—Marmaduke (4), b. 1733; Elizabeth, b. 1736; Hannah, b. 1738; and Caleb, b. 1743. In 1748, at the age of fifteen, Marmaduke (4) was apprenticed as a goldsmith to his father, who died in 1750. He must have found another master to complete his apprenticeship, and in October 1755 he received the Freedom of the Company by service. He was elected to the Livery on 7th July 1763, but resigned in April 1785. Directories show that for twenty years (1755–75) he was at 20 Lombard Street, although the actual number was not added until 1767. F. J. Britten (*Old Clocks and Watches and their Makers*) gives him as a watchmaker of 20 Lombard Street, 1760–74. This latter date was doubtless determined by the fact that in 1774 Marmaduke Storr was declared bankrupt.[2] He appears to have been discharged soon after, as in 1776 we find him installed at 47 Lombard Street and described as a broker in 1780. From a note attached to a bond in the Commission of Civil Lands it is clear that Storr got into financial difficulties again, and we hear no more of him. The date of his death has not been ascertained. Meanwhile, Marmaduke (3)'s brother, Batty Storr, had married a Miss White by whom he had three sons—Isaac, William and Jonathan. Isaac died unmarried and was buried in the Quakers' ground in York. His two brothers both became watchmakers, and are duly recorded by Britten. Jonathan worked in York (1765–80), but William moved to London where in 1765 his address is given as Jermyn Street, and as 44 St. James Street from 1779–94. Kent, however, shows him still there in 1796.

[1] The London Marriage Register (Friends' House) gives Marmaduke (3) as born in 1702; married at the Bull and Mouth, Southwark, on 13th Dec. 1728 to Hannah, daughter of Caleb and Elizabeth Smith of Stockton; and (now of St. Mary Woolnoth, Lombard Street) died of fever on 16th July 1750, being buried in the Quaker burial-ground in Long Lane, Bermondsey.

[2] *Gentleman's Magazine*, Vol. XLIV, 1774, p. 288. Great care and patience has to be exercised before quoting from London directories, as the editors of some record changes of address and the abandonment of premises much sooner than others. Thus in some cases a directory will merely copy the previous year's entry without making any check. For instance, in 1774 Kent duly records Marmaduke Storr as being at 20 Lombard Street, but as in that year he became bankrupt, he is not entered in 1775. But the *New Complete Guide* of 1775 still gives him at Lombard Street (misprinting No. 20 as 26). Throughout this work I have checked and re-checked all directory dates, using first all the famous collection at Guildhall Library, then those at the British Museum and the Cambridge University Library, with reference, where necessary, to Sir Ambrose Heal's collection and other odd editions in both public and private hands. In all this work my guide has been the excellent publication by Charles W. F. Goss, *The London Directories 1677–1855*, London, 1932.

It is clear that William gained the respect of the Clockmakers Company, for when it was decided in 1781 to enrol among the Fellowship, as Honorary Freemen, "men whose practical knowledge of the Art would be valuable in the protection of the rights and privileges of the Craft, and whose social position would enable them to render useful service in the defence of its interests . . . ", we find that the list issued on 2nd April of that year (S. E. Atkins and W. H. Overall, *Some Account of the Worshipful Company of Clockmakers*, 1881, p. 184) includes the name of William Storr.

He married Mary (surname unknown) by whom he had several children, most of whom appear to have died in infancy. We have now arrived at a date contemporary with the early working life of Paul Storr, but before dealing with what little is known of his immediate ancestors, we should consider for a moment the one remaining member of the Yorkshire Storrs who was the most distinguished of them all. I refer to John Storr, Rear-Admiral of the Red, who, according to family tradition, was an uncle of Paul and wanted him to follow his footsteps and go into the Navy. I can find no proof of this whatever.

As neither the *Dictionary of National Biography* nor other modern biographical works make any mention of John Storr, a few notes on his career may be of interest.[1] His possible relationship to Paul will be discussed later. John Storr was the son of Joseph Storr, J.P. for East Riding (d. 1753), the grandson of Joseph Storr of Hilston (d. 1729), and the great-grandson of John Storr of Hilston (d. 1657), after whom he was named. According to his monument in Westminster Abbey, to which we shall refer later, he was born on 18th August 1709. Entering the Navy as a midshipman, probably about 1721, he was promoted to be commander of a sloop of war on 3rd July 1746. He was advanced to be Captain of the *Gloucester* by commission dated 1st November 1748. We next hear of him early in 1755 when he was made Captain of the *St. George*, a second-rater of ninety guns. In September 1756 he was appointed to the *Revenge*, in which ship he greatly distinguished himself on 28th February 1758 when Admiral Osborne defeated the French Admiral M. Duquesne near Cape de Gata, off the Almerian coast of SW. Spain. Captain Storr attacked and took the *Orphée*, a large French ship-of-war mounting sixty-four guns. In this encounter he was wounded in the leg, his calf being torn away by a splinter. He soon returned to England and was employed during 1759 in the main or Channel fleet under the orders of Sir Edward Hawke.

In November of that year he again distinguished himself when Hawke routed the French fleet under M. de Conflans off Belle Isle, south of Quiberon Bay. Storr took a prominent part in the capture of the *Formidable*, and although driven out to sea on the night of the action, got in again without having sustained any material damage. He quitted the *Revenge* not long afterwards, and does not appear to have held any subsequent commission till 1762, when he commanded the *Monmouth*, of sixty-four guns,

---

[1] Apart from Poulson's *History of Holderness*, both the *Westminster Abbey Register*, p. 434, and John Charnock's *Biographia Navalis*, Vol. VI, 1798, pp. 92, 93, have been consulted. For this latter reference I am indebted to the Library of the Admiralty.

on the North American Station. After the conclusion of the war Storr held no further commission. On 19th March 1779 he was advanced to be Rear-Admiral of the White, and promoted to the same rank in the Red Squadron on 26th September 1780. In 1773 he had married a Mrs. John Norris Fisher (formerly Gordon) to whom he bequeathed all his Yorkshire estates, for life, and all his personalty. Admiral Storr died at Bath (some accounts say London) on 10th January 1783. He was honoured by a burial in Westminster Abbey and is represented by a white marble bust,[1] by William Tyler, R.A., in the east aisle of the North Transept (St. John the Evangelist Chapel). Originally it was flanked by naval trophies and had a pyramid behind, but these have since disappeared.

And so concludes what evidence I can find on those members of the Storr family of Yorkshire who sought their fortunes in London or overseas.

W. & J. STORR, HATTERS

The problem which now presents itself is just where Paul Storr fits in, and what relation—if any—he was to the Yorkshire Storrs. The one remaining descendant of the Admiral has, alas, no family papers which help us. The difficulty is increased by the fact that none of the early London Storrs were of sufficient importance to find a place in biographical works of reference. As we have already seen, even the Admiral is not given in the *Dictionary of National Biography*! How, then, can we expect the lives of insignificant goldsmiths and watchmakers to be recorded? We are thus thrown back on what is usually termed "family tradition"—consisting sometimes of old letters, diaries, photographs in family albums, pedigrees in the family Bible, etc., but at other times merely of oral tradition handed down from father to son. While such evidence is often reliable, it should be checked wherever possible—for memory plays strange tricks. In the course of my researches, I have received much help from Mrs. Storr, cousin and widow of Vernon Faithfull Storr, Sub-Dean of Westminster. Among papers sent for my inspection was a number of letters written in 1924 to the Sub-Dean by a Mr. Walter William Storr, of Darlington, Durham. The letters dealt with the question of family relationship. The great-grandfather of W. W. Storr was John, a hatter of Westminster,[2] whose brother, Thomas, was the father of Paul Storr. The baptismal certificate, preserved by W. W. Storr, reads as follows:

This is to certify that John Storr son of Edward by Elizabeth was born the 9th and baptized the thirteenth of January One thousand seven hundred and forty one

---

[1] See *History of the Abbey Church of St. Peter, Westminster*, Ackermann, Vol. II, No. 231 and Pl. 54. The inscription reads: "To the memory of John Storr, Esquire, of Hilston, in the county of York, Rear-Admiral of the Red Squadron of His Majesty's Fleet. In his profession a brave and gallant officer; in private life, a tender husband, an honest man and a sincere friend. He was born August 18, 1709; died January 10, 1783, and interred near this place." See also *History and Antiquities of the Abbey Church of St. Peter, Westminster*, illus. by J. P. Neale, text by E. W. Brayley, Vol. II, 1823, Pl. IV, facing p. 30, with a short description on pp. 204–5. The Plates in these works show Storr's bust over that of Sir Gilbert Lort. This memorial has been removed and Storr is now next to John Holles, Duke of Newcastle.

[2] *Bailey's British Directory* of 1784 gives him as of St. Margaret Street, Westminster, and the *Universal British Directory* of 1790 as of 12 Union Street. The house was actually only two doors from where these two streets met.

as appears by the Register of Baptisms belonging to the parish of St. Margaret's Westminster this 4th July 1787.

Signed: Jos. F. Fox

Parish Clerk and
Register Keeper.

After John's death in 1792 his widow, Mrs. Ann Storr, carried on the business with her two sons, William and John William Nicholson. William appears to have died unmarried, while John (1781–1854) had married about 1819 and had a son, John, born in 1821. This John had three sons and a daughter, one of the sons being Walter William, to whom we have already referred. In one of Walter's letters he says that both his father and grandfather always regarded themselves as of the same family as the Admiral, and that this claim appeared to be supported by the fact that his grandmother repeatedly told him that the Admiral often visited John and Ann, not merely to get his hats made in the then latest naval fashion but socially—to chat to them. Furthermore, Walter's father used to visit Joseph Storr of Owstwick, who was descended from Isaac, the brother of Marmaduke (2). Thus a friendship seems definitely to have existed between members of the Yorkshire Storrs and those of London. The reason may well be that they were related. Walter also mentioned a fire which occurred in the hatter's shop in 1804. He was under the impression that it stood on the site of the statue of Canning in Parliament Square. But here he has muddled up two different Storr houses. In 1804 Parliament Square did not exist, and Storr's shop, over which they lived, was in Union Street. It was their subsequent premises that were near the site of Canning's statue—namely in Bridge Street. However, this "family tradition", so largely oral, has proved quite sufficient for the purposes of research, and the results have fully justified the trouble involved.

We will begin with the fire of 1804. Mr. W. W. Storr had preserved a cutting about it from *Bell's Weekly Messenger*,[1] but the account given in the *Times* on the following day—4th October 1804—is very much fuller, and contains details of the house itself which are of importance to our enquiry. No apology, therefore, need be made for the following extract:

> Yesterday morning [Wed. 3rd October], about half past three o'clock, a fire broke out at the house of Mrs. Storr, hatter, in Union-street, Westminster. Mrs. Storr's was next door to the corner of New Palace-Yard. She was a widow, and, with her two sons, William and John, carried on the business. Mrs. Storr slept in the front room, one pair [expression, now obsolete, for "on the first floor"]; her son William in a back room, on the same floor; the front two-pair [i.e. the front room on the second floor] room was used as a dining-room; and, in the back room, on the same floor, an elderly maiden lady, named Ann Freeman, slept, who was a lodger in Mrs. Storr's family. In the back garret Mrs. Storr's

---

[1] There was also an account of the fire in the *Gentleman's Magazine*, Vol. LXXIV, Pt. II, 1804, pp. 971, 2.

35

younger son, John, slept; and in the front garret two young women [an apprentice and a servant girl] slept.

Then follows a detailed account of how the fire started, what great damage it did, what efforts were made to control it, and how Mrs. Freeman was burned to death and the young apprentice dashed to pieces by jumping from the window. John carried his mother on his shoulders across New Palace-Yard to the Coach and Horses, a watering-house for hackney-coaches which kept open all night. Not only was the Storrs' house practically destroyed, but the corner house, belonging to Mr. Godfree, an upholsterer, was burnt out. The house on the other side, belonging to Mr. Windsor, the boot-maker, was only partially damaged, while the premises of Mr. Edgar, the painter, on the opposite side of the road were "much scorched and the windows burst open". Mrs. Storr, who was inadequately insured,[1] lost practically all her possessions, except the books and money which were in an iron chest in the shop.

At first sight it might appear that there is little to be learned from this account of the fire, but actually the contrary is the case, especially in view of subsequent discoveries. But first of all let us deal briefly with the site in question. The best map of London about the time with which we are dealing is undoubtedly that by Richard Horwood published in 1799.[2] Not only is every house shown, but wherever they are numbered those numbers are also given. As we shall see later, this will prove most helpful in tracing the exact position of Paul Storr's changing business premises. From the section of Horwood's map here reproduced, it will be seen that Union Street led from King Street to Margaret Street adjoining [New] Palace Yard, and consisted of only about a dozen houses. All the buildings in the whole of this area have long since been pulled down, and any attempt to identify the actual house of the Storr family would appear impossible. But while inspecting the rate-books at the Westminster Public Library, the Archivist, Mr. Osborn, produced two original drawings of William Capon[3]—one of Union Street and the other of Margaret Street (Pl. III, p. 85). By a strange coincidence the drawing of Union Street was made only a week after the fire, and the wooden hoarding in front of Mr. Godfree's shop

---

1 She was insured with the Westminster Fire Insurance for £200.

2 *Plan of the Cities of London and Westminster, the Borough of Southwark, and Parts adjoining shewing every House. Surveyed by Richard Horwood.* [32 sheets numbered A–H, in fours]. The sheets are issued both plain and coloured. A second edition, increased to forty sheets, was published by Wm. Faden in 1807, a third edition in 1813, and a fourth edition in 1819. The British Museum has editions 1, 2 and 4, while Guildhall has 1, 2 and 3. Owing to the fact that Faden made continual alterations when demolitions or new buildings warranted, it is of importance to trace the history of a street or district through all the editions. Very little is known of Richard Horwood. As his Prospectus Sheet of 1st Dec. 1795 shows (copy at Guildhall), he was a land-surveyor of Hackney and issued his map by subscription for five guineas, or 7s. 6d. for the first sheet, 5s. for each subsequent one, except the last which was to be 2s. 6d. The work was commissioned by the Phoenix Fire Insurance Company.

3 Born at Norwich in 1757, William Capon studied architecture under Novozielski and was later engaged by John Kemble at Drury Lane as scene painter. He gained a great reputation for historical accuracy and correct measurements in all his work. His drawings of the streets and old buildings of Westminster, where he lived, are among his finest work. His plans of the old palace of Westminster, which took thirty years to complete, are at the Society of Antiquaries. Other drawings are in the British Museum. He was a frequent exhibitor at the Royal Academy, the Society of Artists, etc. See further Redgrave's *Dictionary of Artists*, the *Dictionary of National Biography*, and Thieme and Becker, *Allgemeines Lexikon der Bildenden Künstler*, s.v. He died in 1827.

36

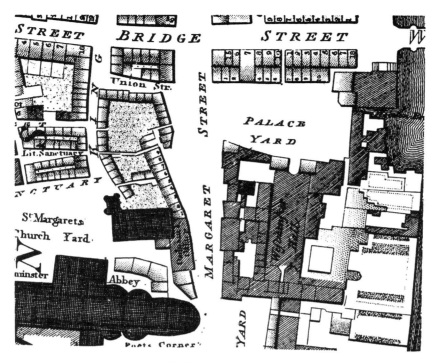

The Union Street District

clearly shows in both drawings, as his premises extended a considerable way into Margaret Street. It will be noticed that all this hoarding is vertical, while that next to it in Union Street is horizontal. This is, with little doubt, Storr's burned-out shop with a partially destroyed upper floor just visible. Whether the marked "shop circular front" was also part of Storr's premises is difficult to determine.

According to the Poor Rate-Book of St. Margaret's, Westminster, for 1802, also at the Westminster Public Library, there were seven houses on Storr's side of the street occupied in order, from the King-Street end, by Sanders, Burton, Bunn, Robinson, Windsor, Storr and Godfree. The rack rents and watch rates show that the premises of Sanders and Robinson were twice as large as any of the others. All this confirms the correct position of Storr's house. On the opposite side of the street the names given are Hodgson, Harris, Wallis and Glasier. Of these, the first two can be clearly seen in the drawing. Turning to the sketch of Margaret Street, we can see the boarded-up corner of Union Street and the Coach and Horses at the corner of [New] Palace Yard opposite to which John Storr carried his mother to safety. Thus, with these two Capon drawings, the whole scene of the fire and Mrs. Storr's rescue become much more real and the actual house identified. In the *Times* account of the fire the houses are described as wooden and very old. We may take it as certain that those destroyed in the fire were never rebuilt, and in a few years the remaining houses were pulled down to make way for the new Parliament Square which was completed in 1814–15.[1] New Palace Yard became the enclosed courtyard to the north of West-minster Hall—in fact the car-park for the Houses of Parliament! Having recovered from their loss during 1805, Mrs. Storr and her two sons continued their business at 6 Bridge Street, just north of Union Street, the following year. At that time Bridge Street continued further west joining Great George Street at the crossing of King Street, which extended as far as Broad Sanctuary and St. Margaret's.[2] In the direc-tories of 1807 onwards they described themselves as "Hat-makers and Furriers". In 1816 they moved south to Little Peter Street. After this we lose sight of them altogether.

PAUL'S FATHER AND GRANDFATHER

As already noted, John Storr, the hatter of Union Street, had a brother named Thomas. As the baptismal certificates printed above shows, their father's name was Edward. If family tradition is to be credited, Edward was an inn-keeper, or victualler, in Tothill Street, Westminster. In view of subsequent events, this would appear to be quite correct.

It is reasonable to assume that at one time the two brothers, John and Thomas, lived at the inn with their father. John, with but little doubt, became apprenticed to a hatter from about 1753–60 and at some unknown date started business at the three-storied old house in Union Street, separated from Tothill Street only by Broad Sanctuary. Thomas, on the other hand, decided to take up silver-chasing,[3] and in 1757 we find him paying £5 as an apprenticeship premium to John Christopher Romer of St. James's, Westminster.[4] Now the records also give an Edward Norton

---

1 This is proved by a study of the different editions of Horwood's maps. In the 2nd edition of 1807 we see that the whole block of buildings between Union Street (including the south side of Union Street itself) and St. Margaret's has gone. By the time the 4th edition appeared (1819) the block consisting of the north side of Union Street, and the south side of Bridge Street has also gone, and the entire space as far south as St. Margaret's has become a grass lawn, as it is (with certain changes of design and the placing of the statues) to-day. The actual plan of improvements and dates of the Government purchases of the land can be seen in the map-room of the British Museum, 1808. *Report from Commissioners under 46 Geo. III (1805–6) for Improvements in Westminster.*

2 King Street will not be found in modern maps. In the days of Whitehall Palace it formed the southern portion of the only thoroughfare from Charing Cross to Westminster. It was a narrow street, starting opposite Downing Street, and ran a little west of the line of the present Parliament Street, which was built parallel to it during the reign of George II. When Parliament Square was made in 1814–15 it was shortened so as not to extend past the line of Bridge Street. By 1900, with the widening of Parliament Street, it entirely disappeared.

3 In Thomas Storr's day the term "silver-chaser" meant only one thing—ornamental work done with hammer and punch. It included chasing, embossing and repoussé on sheet metal. It still means this to-day, but *in addition* the term is used to mean the cleaning up of any roughness on a casting: taking off the seams, sharpening blurred details and giving appropriate surface textures—bright in some cases, matted in others. The silver-chaser is not an engraver. The two processes are entirely different. In engraving the gravers are operated entirely by the right hand, and actual shavings of metal are cut away. In chasing the left hand is the one that guides the tool. Hammer blows given by the right hand need less control. No metal is removed. Chasing involves a knowledge of modelling, and consequently far more aesthetic understanding and skill of hand and eye than any other branch of the craft. Any chaser, worthy of the name, must be a much more highly trained person than the hammer man or mounter. Chasing as a craft is little practised to-day, and hardly survived the end of the nineteenth century. See Ch. 16 of *A Silversmith's Manual*, 2nd edit., 1949, by Bernard Cuzner, to whom I am indebted for much of the above. Herbert Maryon's *Metalwork and Enamelling*, 1912, Chs. XIII and XIV, may also be consulted with advantage.

4 Apprenticeship Records, Great Britain, Inland Revenue Books, 1757, 21/101.

Storr who had been apprenticed to Romer in 1753. The inference is, of course, that Edward Norton was a third son of Edward and Elizabeth, and possibly the elder brother of John and Thomas. The second Christian name, Norton, suggests that this was his mother's maiden name. Of his career as a silver-chaser we know nothing. It may well be that Edward Norton and his younger brother Thomas—both silver-chasers—worked together at their father's house in Tothill Street.[1] The date of the father's death has not been ascertained but it may have been about 1782, because the Westminster rate-books show that from 1783–6 the only Storr in Tothill Street was a Thomas Storr on the north side. Unfortunately no Will has been found. With Thomas, however, we are more lucky, as his Will is at Somerset House and shows him to have been a man of considerable property. We shall return to this shortly. We must now consider the lease, and later the sale, to Thomas in 1788 of a house and some ground in the Horseferry Road. In it he is described as a "Victualler of Union St. in the Parish of St. Margaret's Westminster". Two interesting points at once emerge. Firstly that Thomas had now (1788) abandoned his trade as a silver-chaser and taken on that of his father—an innkeeper or victualler. Secondly that by 1788 (from what date we do not know) he had joined his brother John at his house in Union Street. We can only speculate on the reasons for these happenings. If Thomas had been apprenticed to Romer for the usual term of seven years (i.e. 1757–64) and had lived with him during this period he would not have returned to his father (and brother Edward Norton) until 1764/5. He must have married about 1770 as Paul was born in 1771. Whether this event occurred at Tothill Street or Union Street is hard to determine. Something must have happened prior to 1788 to make Thomas turn victualler, and that "something" was surely a death through which Thomas inherited the inn in Tothill Street. It was almost certainly the death of his father, Edward. The fact, mentioned above, that a Thomas was paying rates for a house in Tothill Street from 1783–6 supports this conjecture. Of Edward Norton, whom we have tentatively called the elder brother, we hear nothing more. Possibly he inherited money and moved away from the district, while the inn fell to Thomas's share. However this may have been, it is clear that by 1788 Thomas had either made or inherited sufficient money to leave Union Street and move to a house of his own on the Horseferry Road, facing the open Tothill fields. We shall return to the lease later.

Up to this time, then, the place in Union Street must be regarded as the Storr family home. The date when Thomas joined John is unknown. The fact that he was paying rates on an inn in Tothill Street for three or four years does not necessarily mean that he was living there. He may well have been married from Union Street in 1770, in which case Paul would have been born there in the following year. If, however, this interesting event occurred at Tothill Street, there is no doubt that he was often at the hat shop with his aunt and cousins. It would have been at this period that

[1] As with engravers and enamellers, silver-chasers were almost always "outworkers", and all they needed was a single room, outhouse or garden shed. Only really large firms, such as Rundell, Bridge & Rundell was to become, employed silver-chasers on the premises as part of the permanent staff.

Paul might have met the Admiral during one of his visits to the shop, and it is not difficult to imagine with what thrilling tales of the fight off Quiberon Bay and the destruction of the French fleet he would have entertained young Paul.

By 1788, the date when Thomas decided to leave Union Street, Paul was already serving his apprenticeship as a plate-worker in Soho, having literally grown up to the sound of the goldsmith's hammer and chasing tools.

The lease of Thomas's new property, dated 18th April 1788, is preserved in the Westminster Abbey Manuscripts (Lease Book 50, f. 401) and, briefly, is as follows:

> Lease from the Dean and Chapter to Thomas Storr of Union Street in the parish of St. Margaret's Westminster Victualler of a piece of Ground being part of Tothill Fields whereon one tenement is now built fronting Eastward on the Horseferry Rd. (containing therein in breadth from N. to S. 85 feet) abutting W. on Sd. Fields (and containing therein in breadth from N. to S. 165 ft.), S. on Sd. Fields (containing therein in depth from E. to W. 305 ft.) & N. on ground and buildings in the tenure of Wm. Gibbard (and containing therein in depth from E. to W. 290 ft. more or less). Premises formerly demised to Thomas Martin. Term 40 years from Feast of Annunciation of B.V.M. just past.
> Rent: £2.13.4.

The site of the property was south of the Grey Coat Hospital at a point where the Horseferry Road turns east and is met by New Street (now Gillingham Row), Carey Street (now Rutherford Street) and the broader Regency Street. In a rating list of 1821 the premises are given as the last house (northwards) in Carey Street. Thus the property must have been at the corner of Carey Street and Horseferry Road. The plan of the property, shown in Lease Book 60, f. 206, supports this by its shape. Soon after he had acquired the lease, Thomas built another house on the property. This led to his surrendering his lease in 1802 and getting a new one, "whereon two tenements are now built", on 7th December of the same year, and at the same rent.[1]

Now the Westminster rate-books show that from 1790 till 1792 a John Storr was at premises in Horseferry Road, so it looks as if Thomas had leased the newly-built house to his brother (perhaps as a warehouse) for this short period. Thomas was the only ratepayer until 1802, after which date various members of the Storr family lived here. But we are anticipating. In 1803, when all the land was beginning to be built over, the Dean and Chapter agreed to sell Thomas the property, the price being fixed at £192 13s. 4d., and prepared the indenture accordingly.[2] It was dated 19th January 1804, but Thomas died on the last day of 1803. The amount due was paid out of Thomas's assets on 22nd January 1804, but, as recorded in Lease Book 60, f. 206, Paul was now required to apply for a new indenture at the cost of 5s. as the original one had become "an inoperative conveyance". By his Will Thomas had made Paul his sole executor and residuary legatee, and left his property to his wife (for

1 Lease Book 55, f. 295.　　　　　　　　2 Lease Book 56, f. 34 (end of Vol.).

life) and then to his three children Paul, Ann (Mrs. Amplelet) and Sarah (Mrs. Bishop). From 1803 until 1822 the ratepayers of the property had been Mrs. Thomas Storr, Sarah Storr and [another unnamed] Storr. In 1823 the house was empty, and we may perhaps conclude that by this time Paul had sold it. At any rate, another indenture between the Dean and Chapter and "Paul Storr of Harrison Street, Grays Inn Lane, Co. Middlesex, Gentleman" was drawn up.[1] It was dated 2nd June 1820, and after reciting the previous indenture of 1804 and quoting from Thomas's Will, transferred the sale of the property legally to Paul.

It remains to add a few more details about Thomas's Will. The witnesses were G. Hamilton of Berwick Street, Soho, Julianna Lewis of Tothill Fields and Thomas Watts of Horseferry Road. His real estate was considerable for apart from the leasehold (as it was when the Will was made) in Westminster, there was also a house in Oxford Street and a freehold in the City of London. Unfortunately there is nothing to identify these properties, and one wonders if they eventually came to Paul. The Will had been made on 5th October 1803 and was proved on 27th January 1804.

PAUL STORR'S FAMILY

As we shall see when discussing his business career in another part of the present work, Paul was apprenticed to a plate-worker[2] in Church Street, Soho, from 1785 to 1792. During this period he doubtless made many friends, and foremost among them were the Beyers, pianoforte and organ builders, in Compton Street,[3] the next street running parallel to Church Street. This family was said to have come from Erfurt in Saxony about 1759, and there is some evidence that other members of it, apart from those who settled in Soho, followed to London at a later date. Adam Beyer, with his brother Lorence, started business in Compton Street, with their sister Catherine to look after them. Adam married Ann Lewis, also of Soho, in January 1760, and by her he had four daughters. Of these the eldest, Catherine, named after her aunt, was born late in 1760, and subsequently married Richard Hunt. It was their son, John Samuel Hunt, who in later years was to save Paul from a business crisis occasioned by his partner John Mortimer.

The next daughter, Sarah, married one John Reid, but they play no part in our history. Mary Ann, the third daughter, was born in 1767 and married James Bird. It is to their great-grandson, Sir Charles (Bird) Locock, 3rd Bt., that I am indebted for his indefatigable work on the Beyer and Storr pedigrees. Lastly, in 1770, was born Elizabeth Susanna, who married Paul in 1801 and was to bear him ten children, their

---

[1] Lease Book 60, f. 206, with a plan of the property.

[2] This term, now obsolete, meant: (a) one who works in gold and silver, also (b) a worker in sheet-metal.

[3] Horwood's map of 1799 shows (Old) Compton Street running from Princes Street to Greek Street; Little Compton Street from Greek Street to Crown Street (later part of Charing Cross Road); and New Compton Street, which had been formed from Steedwell Street and Two Brewers Yard, from Crown Street to Broad Street. Princes Street became part of Wardour Street in 1879, while Shaftesbury Avenue, of which King Street, shown in our map, formed a part, was not built until 1886.

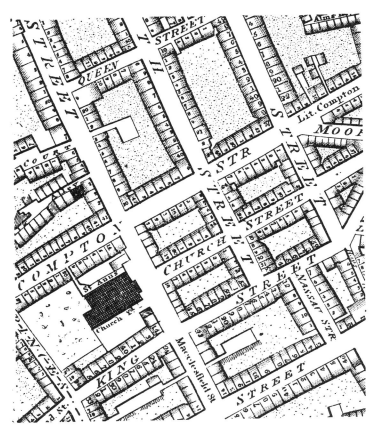

The Soho District

grandchildren numbering no less than fifty-four!

But we are anticipating. When Paul first came to Soho he was fourteen years old, and Elizabeth a year older. This boy and girl friendship gradually ripened into a romance, and Paul must have longed for the day when his apprenticeship would be over, and he could go to Goldsmiths' Hall and register his own mark. It would then be only a matter of a few years before he became established and was in a position to marry Elizabeth.

Meanwhile, the Beyer family had suffered a loss in Adam's brother, Lorence, who died in 1789. He left everything to his niece Mary Ann, with a legacy to her sister Sarah, and his trade tools to Adam. It was just about this time that the pianoforte was taking the place of the spinet,[1] and the change-over from plucked keyboard instruments to those in which the strings were set in vibration by the blows of hammers doubtless called for new tools. However this may be, the firm continued until Adam's death in 1804,[2] after which we hear of it no more.

Having finished his apprenticeship in 1792, Paul worked in the City for a few years with William Frisbee. In 1796 he moved to Air Street, Piccadilly, where he started on his own. He soon began to make a name for himself, and after five years he was in a position to marry Elizabeth. Their first child, named after her mother, was born in 1802 and in due course married one Thomas Shearman, who was an Inspector of Gaugers in H.M. Customs.[3] Two years later another daughter, Harriet, was born. Little appears to be known about her except that she married a certain John Brothers[4]

---

1 Spinets by Beyer appear to be scarce. One, dated 1779, was sold for £52 on 16th Sept. 1952. It was in the collection of Sir John Wood of Hengrave Hall (lot 565).

2 He had retired to Pond Street, Hampstead, and is buried in Hampstead Churchyard. The grave also contains Lorence, and James Beyer Bird (James Bird's son, who died in 1811, aged fifteen).

3 He appears thus in the British Imperial Calendar until 1855, when he retired.

4 He is given in the Navy List as a lieutenant from 14th July 1818 until July 1864, at which date he was placed on the retired list, with the rank of commander.

who was in the Navy. In 1805 Paul was presented with a son and heir whom he named after himself. If Paul wanted his son to follow his own trade as a goldsmith, he was doomed to disappointment, for the young Paul had no wish for a sedentary life and longed for travel and adventure in foreign lands. Accordingly, when he was about fourteen years old he joined the Merchant Service and sailed the seven seas.

Meanwhile, Elizabeth had given birth to another daughter, Emma, in 1806. She married Rev. Robert Chapman Savage[1] in 1837, and bore him eleven children, among whom were Ernest Bickersteth (1849–1915), who became Rural Dean of Douglas and an antiquarian of repute[2]; and Henry Edwin (1854–1939), who became Dean of Lichfield from 1909 until his death.[3]

Then comes Paul's second son, Francis, who was born in 1808. He turned out to have a very different temperament from his elder brother, and in him his father saw a possible future goldsmith. However, like so many fathers, Paul was determined to give Francis what had been denied to himself—the best education money could buy. Accordingly, he was sent to Harrow from 1821–4 where he distinguished himself and made a wide circle of friends.[4] As was only natural, Francis now wanted to go on to Oxford, complete his education, get his degree, and possibly take holy orders. This was in all probability Paul's original idea too, but while Francis was at Harrow business responsibilities had unexpectedly increased. The year previously, in 1823, Paul had joined John Mortimer at 13 New Bond Street and was most anxious to make this new venture a success. With his workshop in Harrison Street to run as well, Paul needed all the help he could get—particularly from someone in whom he could place absolute trust.

Accordingly, he explained the situation to Francis and asked him to forgo Oxford and come into the business. This must have been a sad disappointment to Francis, but out of the great affection he felt for his father he agreed to do what he asked. As time went on and Francis began to show promise as a goldsmith, Paul decided to teach him the craft from the beginning, hoping, doubtless, that he would entirely give up any idea of Oxford and succeed to his business when he retired. It was arranged, then, that Francis should be apprenticed to his father for the usual term of seven years. The indenture, reproduced here from the original in possession of the Storr family (Pl. II), was a civil one made between father and son, and not through one of the City Livery Companies. It is dated 17th April 1828 and is of interest as showing to what extent the moral character of the apprentice is protected—quite apart from considerations of instruction. In less than a year, however, it became obvious that the

---

1 Born 1806 at Hayes, Mddx.; St. John's College, Cambridge, 1830–3 (B.A., 1835; M.A., 1840); Ordained (Lichfield), 1835; Curate of Tamworth, 1835–41, and Vicar, 1842–5; Vicar of Nuneaton, 1845–51; Hon. Canon of Worcester, 1849; Domestic Chaplain to Viscount Lifford. He died in Oct. 1871.

2 *Alumni Cantabrigienses; Who was Who, 1897–1916.*

3 *Alumni Cantabrigienses; Who was Who, 1929–40;* and P. Bury, *College of Corpus Christi,* Cambridge, 1952, pp. 227–8.

4 *Harrow School Register, 1800–1911,* 3rd edit., 1911, p. 102.

experiment was a failure, and Paul bowed to the inevitable. But here we can let Francis speak for himself.[1]

It was for me a memorable day when my father came into the room where luncheon was laid in Bond St., and said "It is open to you now Frank, to go to College, if you will". I had left Harrow five years previous to this time at the earnest desire of my father, who had entered on a business of some magnitude, and at some risk, and wanted such help as he might hope to receive from me— at any rate for a few years—in bearing with him the anxieties necessarily accompanying new and untried experiences. I never regretted the sacrifice which I then made. It cost me something to give up the career which I had pictured to myself and the associations with which I was surrounded at Harrow. But it cemented into an indissoluble friendship the love which my father bore me. . . . For about five years I put energetically my shoulder to the wheel in Bond St, when the announcement which doubtless spoilt my appetite for luncheon, while it filled my heart with joy and thankfullness [sic], set me free to follow the bent of my desires, and brought me, as it were, into a new world.

And so Francis went to Queen's College, Oxford, in 1829, taking his B.A. in 1833 and M.A. three years later.[2] Here we must leave him for the present, and return to Paul and his family.

With the single exception of John Bridge Storr (named after one of Paul's business partners), who was born in 1814 and died in infancy, the remaining four children were girls, and all married clergymen. First came Mary Anne who married W. W. Champneys, then Eleanor who married J. S. Utterton, thirdly Sophia Jessy who married C. F. Champneys, and lastly Anna Maria who married J. R. Quirk.[3] As it was J. S. Utterton's sister, Susan, who married Paul's eldest son, it will be seen that, except for Anna Maria, we are concerned only with two families—the Champneys and the Uttertons. For the better understanding of this part of the history, a brief account of both these families seems necessary. As an Utterton married Paul's son and heir, we shall discuss that family first.

Col. John Utterton (1778–1843) had married in 1807 Frances Anne Robins, who lived with her father, John Robins, a friend of Paul Storr, in a house at Norwood Green, Heston, near Hounslow. After John Robins's death in 1831 he left both the house and furniture to Frances. While Col. Utterton was quartered at Ipswich his wife gave birth to a son—John Sutton Utterton—in 1814. Two years later he was posted to Gibraltar as Barrack Master, retiring in 1825. On returning to Norwood Green he sent his son to Dr. Benson's school at Hounslow. In 1832 he went to

---

[1] Extracted from a MS. book of "Reminiscences of Francis Storr" in possession of members of the family.

[2] *Alumni Oxonienses*, Vol. IV, p. 1361. His father is described as "of St. Anne's, London, gent".

[3] Born in 1819, James Richard Quirk went to St. Edmund Hall, Oxford, in 1837 (B.A., 1841; M.A., 1863). He took holy orders in 1842, and was successively Curate of Clifton Campville, Staffs; Nuneaton, Willoughby, War; Perp. Cur. of Attleborough, War, 1851–63, and Blandford Forum, Dorset, from 1863 till his death in 1876. They had four sons and three daughters.

Oriel College, Oxford,[1] and took his B.A. in 1836 and M.A. in 1839. He remained at Oxford till 1838 as private tutor, but spent his vacations at Norwood Green. It was during these periods that he became engaged to Eleanor, fifth daughter of Paul Storr, who had taken a house on the opposite side of the Green. They were married in July 1839 and went to live at Holmwood, Dorking, where, the previous year, John Sutton had been appointed incumbent. After taking various livings,[2] he became Bishop of Guildford in 1874 and died at Ryde Parish Church in 1879.[3] Meanwhile Francis Storr had left Oxford in 1832 and returned to his father's home at Norwood Green preparatory to taking holy orders. Here he met Susan Utterton and fell in love with her. Unfortunately for him, his elder brother, Paul, returned suddenly from abroad and with his smart appearance and sophisticated manner soon won Susan's heart. Francis stepped aside, and Susan and Paul became engaged. They were not married, however, until 4th August 1836. They had four children[4]—Susan, Fanny, Jessy Maria and Paul. Of these it will suffice to mention Jessy Maria. As we shall see later, Francis was to become Vicar of Brenchley, Kent, in 1854. Ten years later one Charles Slegg Ward,[5] who had just left Cambridge, was appointed curate to Francis and tutor in his boys' school. There he met Jessy Maria, and it was not long before they became engaged. On his being presented with the living at Valley End in 1867 they decided to marry at once, and the wedding took place at Reigate from Jessy's grandmother Utterton's house, Earlswood Lodge. They had nine children, so we are not surprised to hear that when Ward became Vicar of Wootton St. Lawrence it was found necessary to build a larger vicarage. Although he moved to Suffolk in 1907, he is buried at Wootton St. Lawrence next to his first wife Jessy. Among their numerous progeny was Helen (Nelly) who married Henry Whistler in 1898. In their sons,[6] Rex and Laurence, Paul would have seen once again that perfect craftsmanship and artistic excellence (somewhat obscured in his family by surplice and cassock) brought strangely close both to him and his times—for the elegant mantle of Regency days had been caught by the brush of Rex and the graver of Laurence. And Paul's heart would have rejoiced.

[1] Actually, he was first admitted as a pensioner at St. John's College, Cambridge, but he could not have resided for more than half a term as he matriculated at Oriel on 29th Nov. 1832.

[2] Rector of Calbourne, I.O.W., 1851; of Farnham, 1853; Archdeacon of Surrey, 1859; Canon of Winchester, 1860. They had three sons and four daughters. One of the sons, Frank Ernest (1844–1908), became Archdeacon of Surrey and Canon Residentiary of Winchester. For further details see *Who was Who, 1897–1916*.

[3] See *Times*, 22nd Dec. 1879, p. 6e.

[4] Actually there were five children, but the youngest, Frank, only lived twenty-one days—see later.

[5] Born at Battle, Sussex, 29th May 1840; Lewes Grammar School; Emmanuel College, Cambridge, 1860–3 (B.A., 1864; M.A., 1867); Ordained (Canterbury), 1865; Curate of Brenchley, 1865–6, of Chobham, Surrey, 1867; Vicar of St. Saviour's, Valley End, Chobham, 1867–76; of Wootton St. Lawrence, nr. Basingstoke, 1876–1908; Perp. Cur. of Walsham-le-Willows, Bury St. Edmunds, 1908–13. Jessy Maria died in 1889, and Ward married again in 1891, Henrietta Shute, of which marriage there is one surviving son, Alexander. Ward is remembered for the really excellent series of guide-books, known as the "Thorough Guides", which he edited with his friend M. J. B. Baddeley (see *Dictionary of National Biography*, 2nd Supp.). Twenty volumes were published, those by Ward including N. and S. Devon, Eastern Counties, S. Devon and S. Cornwall, Ireland, Surrey and Sussex, and the Isle of Wight. The Welsh guides were edited by them both. Originally published by Dulau & Co., they were later sold to T. Nelson & Sons, and Ward, Lock & Co.

[6] See *Rex Whistler, His Life and His Drawings*, by Laurence Whistler, 1948.

Meanwhile tragedy was to overtake Susan. In the summer of 1845 she left her home in Brixton to stay with her mother, Frances Ann Utterton, who had left Norwood Green and was living at Earlswood Lodge, Reigate. One day she took a carriage to visit her brother and sister-in-law at Holmwood. The bad state of the roads, or other unknown reason, caused her to give birth, apparently prematurely, to another son—Frank—who lived only twenty-one days. Susan never recovered, and died three months later.[1] Francis had been sent for, and saw Susan once again—in death. Eleanor looked after Susan's other children and for a time brought them up with her own.

Of Paul (the younger) we hear but little. In 1848 he married again, one Ann, the daughter of Major-General Miller. They had two sons and two daughters.

We now pass on to a brief account of the Champneys family, two members of which, as with the Uttertons, married children of Paul Storr. The first mention of this family, so far as can be ascertained, is in the Parish of Stansted Mountfitchet from which Thomas Champness (later Champneys) moved to Westminster. In 1731 he married Mary Weldon, daughter of the well-known musician and composer John Weldon (1676–1736), a pupil of Henry Purcell. Among their numerous family[2] was Weldon Champneys, D.D. (1736–1810), who was described as the greatest pluralist of his time. Among many of his preferments he was Vicar of St. Pancras and Sub-Dean of St. Pauls. By his second wife, Frances Portier, he had a son, Rev. William Betton Champneys, B.C.L. (1778–1835), of St. John's College, Oxford, who married Martha, daughter of Samuel Stable of Kentish Town, a member of the Ironmongers Company. They had, among other children, two sons, both of whom married daughters of Paul Storr. The elder, William Weldon Champneys (1807–75),[3] married Mary Anne, Paul's fourth daughter, at Beckenham in 1838. They had six sons and three daughters. The eldest, Weldon,[4] married Frances Sophia Feilden of Witton Park, whose mother was Caroline, daughter of Sir Oswald Mosley, 2nd Bt. Their daughter, Frances Mary, married Edward Parker Stapleton, O.B.E., of Trinity House.[5] The second son, Montague Storr Champneys, entered the Indian Civil Service[6]; while Basil, the third son, distinguished himself as an architect.[7] Of the

1 The Holmwood Church registers read: "Frank Storr of Brixton, buried 5th July. Age 21 days. Minister J. S. Utterton; and Susanna Storr of Brixton, buried 28th Oct. 37 years. Officiating minister Francis Storr 1845."

2 Mention may be made of Samuel Champness [sic] for whose fine voice Handel wrote some tenor parts. His name occurs in concert programmes and operas of the time. See W. C. Smith, Concerning Handel, 1948, pp. 242, 245, 252 and 254.

3 He entered Brasenose, Oxford, 1824, M.A. and Fellow, 1831; Curate of St. Ebbe's, Oxford, 1831; Rector of St. Mary's, Whitechapel, 1837–60; Canon of St. Paul's, 1851; Vicar of St. Pancras, London (like his grandfather), 1860; Dean of Lichfield, 1868 until his death in 1875.

4 Born 1839, Charterhouse and Brasenose, Oxford (B.A., 1861; M.A., 1864); Vicar of Haslingden, Lancaster, 1874–92; Rural Dean and Hon. Canon of Manchester, 1886; d. 1892.

5 Stapleton is an old school friend of mine, and both he and his son, Henry, have gone to endless trouble in searching wills, directories, rates-books, registers, monuments, etc., on my behalf. His wife is my fourth cousin, as we are both descendants of Sir John Parker Mosley, 1st Bt., whose daughter, Frances, was the grandmother of Frances Smith who married Claude Bowes-Lyon, 13th Earl of Strathmore.

6 Born 1840; Charterhouse and Exeter, Oxford; d. unmarried, 1868, and buried at Tooting with Paul and Elizabeth.

7 Born 1842; Charterhouse and Trinity, Cambridge; built or enlarged colleges, schools, libraries, etc., at Cambridge, Oxford, Manchester, Harrow, Winchester, etc.; d. 1935. See Who was Who, 1929–40.

remaining children, mention should be made of Sir Francis Henry Champneys, 1st Bt., the famous gynaecologist and obstetrician.[1] Further details appear in the pedigree. The younger son of William Beeton Champneys was Charles Francies (1817–74), who married Paul's sixth daughter, Sophia Jessy, in 1849. He was Vicar of Wendover, Bucks, and perpetual Curate of St. Mary's, Bishops Hatfield, Herts.

We must now return to Francis Storr, who, as we have seen, had left Oxford in 1832 and returned to Paul's house at Norwood Green where he met Susan Utterton. Having been ordained in 1833, he went as Curate to Up Waltham in Sussex the following year. Here he remained only until the summer of 1835, when Rev. Vernon Harcourt, Rector of Beckenham, offered him the curacy there. Paul now decided to leave Norwood Green in order to join his son and be nearer to his business. Accordingly in 1835 he moved to the Clock House,[2] Beckenham. From here he drove to his business in New Bond Street every day in a carriage and pair. Among the new friends Paul and Francis made at Beckenham were Lancelot Holland and his daughter Caroline, and it was not long before Francis and Caroline became engaged.

In 1836 Francis was offered the living of St. Mary's, Otley, Suffolk—a village in the depth of the country, eight miles north of Ipswich. Francis decided to accept the offer, as he was anxious to get married and have a living of his own. Accordingly the wedding took place at Beckenham Church in 1838 and preparations were made for the long journey to Otley. Paul took great interest in the appointment and accompanied Francis to Otley (apparently he had actually begun his ministry in the early autumn of 1837) in order to see the church and rectory. The journey was no easy one as the train only went as far as Colchester. Here a coach from Ipswich met them, while from Ipswich to Otley horses or a carriage were the only means of transit. The church proved to be Gothic with an embattled western tower and a clerestory to the nave. Paul and Francis were apparently well satisfied, but the rectory was in so neglected a state as to be almost beyond repair.[3] However, Francis and Caroline made the best of it, but decided to apply to the Governors of Queen Anne's Bounty for £1,400 to build a new rectory. The house was completed in 1839. By this time Paul had taken a hand in affairs. His first interest was naturally in the Church plate. This consisted of an old pewter flagon and an unmarked Elizabethan chalice of the mid-sixteenth century.

Paul made an exact copy of the chalice and designed a paten on a $3\frac{3}{8}$-in. foot to match.[4] He then gave a beautiful east window of three lights, surmounted by

---

1 Born 1848; Winchester and Brasenose; d. 1930. See further *Who was Who, 1929–40*; and Burke's *Peerage* for details both of him and other members of the Champneys family.

2 This was a large house, probably built in the early part of the eighteenth century, on Beckenham Road, the site of which is now occupied by the public baths. Its name was so called from a large clock which was fixed over the stables adjoining the house. Clock House station, a little further along the road on the opposite side, perpetuates the memory of the house.

3 Otley was doubtless one of the many parishes held in plurality, and before Francis arrived no rector had been resident for many years.

4 See Pl. LXXX on p. 238 where further details are given.

Gothic tracery. It is partly stained, in light colours, and bears texts, not figures. Francis laid out an avenue leading to the window, thus giving it a fine and dignified setting.

When Paul and Elizabeth died it was in Otley Church that Francis erected a memorial to their memory. The plaque is set up in the Sanctuary on the south wall to the right of the window. During the nine years that Francis remained at Otley his wife presented him with six children, the youngest of whom, Emma, died in infancy in 1854. She is buried in Otley churchyard. Francis's first son, named after himself, was born on 28th February 1839.[1] He became a master at Marlborough College (1864–75) and chief master of modern subjects at Merchant Taylors' School (1875–1901). He married Rose, daughter of Francis Lloyd, by whom he had a son and three daughters, the youngest of whom, Erica, married Sir Alexander Lindsay, Master of Balliol, who was created Lord Lindsay of Birker in 1945, and died in 1952. Francis died in 1919.

The second son, Edward,[2] was born in 1840 and entered the Indian Civil Service (Madras) in 1861, but after serving as Assistant Collector and Magistrate in South Arcot, Coimbatore, Kurnool and Cuddapah, was forced by ill-health to go on furlough in 1873. He married Emily Mary Faithfull, daughter of Rev. James Faithfull, Vicar of Cheshunt, Herts, by whom he had three daughters and one son, Vernon Faithfull, who became Canon and Sub-Dean of Westminster, and married his cousin Katherine Cecilia Storr. The third son, Charles,[3] was born in 1842. He was ordained in 1865, and, after holding several curacies until 1876, became Vicar of Matfield, Kent, from 1876 to 1906. He married Katherine Davies, daughter of Cecilia Grantham Storr by her first husband Rev. R. Davies, Vicar of Brenchley and Francis Storr's predecessor. As we shall see later, Cecilia became Francis's second wife. They had two sons and four daughters. The eldest son, Frank,[4] became a clerk at the Admiralty, married Rebe Phillips and had no issue. Their second son, Charles Lancelot,[5] was born in 1874 and had a distinguished career in the Army, from which he retired in 1921. He became Ecclesiastical Secretary to the Lord Chancellor, 1924–8, and Assistant Secretary to the Cabinet. He had been created a C.B. in 1919. He married Josephine Mary Dickinson, there was no issue, and he died in 1944. Of the daughters, mention has been made of Katherine Cecilia who married her cousin Vernon Faith-

[1] Harrow, 1853–7; Trinity, Cambridge, 1857–60 (Bell Scholar, 1858; B.A. (6th Classic), 1861). After retirement as master in 1901 he acted as Occasional Inspector under the Board of Education in London, Wales and Scotland. He was the author of many school and education books. See further Venn's *Alumni Cantabrigienses*.

[2] Winchester, 1855–9; New College, Oxford, matric. 1859 (Scholar, 1859–64; B.A., 1862; M.A., 1867). See *Indian Army and Civil Service Lists* for the years 1862–76; and *India List*, 1877–8, where he appears among the ''Invalid Annuitants''. He died in 1878.

[3] New College, Oxford (B.A., 1864; M.A., 1866); Curate of Chilham, Kent, 1865–7; Child's Hill, Hendon, Mddx, 1867–9; Brenchley, Kent, 1869–76; and Vicar of Matfield, Kent, 1876–1906. He died in 1922.

[4] Harrow, 1885–90; New College, Oxford, 1890–4. He appears in the *British Imperial Calendar and Civil List* for 1897 as an Assistant Superintending Clerk in the Department of the Accountant-General of the Navy. He became Superintendent Clerk in 1903, Assistant Accountant-General from 1905, and the Deputy Accountant-General in 1932. He died in 1938.

[5] For details see *Who was Who, 1941–50*.

full (1869–1940),[1] the son of Edward Storr, in 1902. They had two sons, Noel and Anthony, both of whom became doctors, and two daughters, Mary and Rachel. The fourth son, John,[2] was born in 1844, and after holding several curacies became Vicar of Little Horkesley from 1897–1916. He married Amy Leycester, by whom he had a son and a daughter. They retired to Bexhill-on-Sea where he died in 1917. The fifth, and last, son, Henry, was born in 1845 and went to Rugby in 1860. Subsequently he became a manufacturer of phosphates at Maidstone. He married Marian Martin by whom he had two boys and two girls. He died in 1936. In 1846 Francis was appointed to St. Mary's, Acton, near Nantwich, Cheshire, where he remained eight years. During this time two more girls were born, Julia and Caroline Minnie, the latter dying in early childhood. Caroline had been ailing for some time and her strength was failing. In 1854 Francis was made Vicar of Brenchley in Kent. Hither he moved with his sick wife, their large family, a number of pupils and an aged church worker who would not be parted! Two years later Caroline died.

Francis had succeeded Rev. Richard Davies at Brenchley, and in December 1857 he married his widow Cecilia. By her he had a son, Gerard, born in July 1859. After going to Marlborough and Shrewsbury he entered Henry Storr's phosphate business at Maidstone. He lived a very uneventful life at Brenchley vicarage until his father's death, and then moved to Matfield, where he is buried, having died in 1930.

Francis remained at Brenchley till his death on 22nd February 1888.

PATRI MATRIQUE DILECTISSIMIS,
HANC TABULAM .
DESIDERII MONUMENTUM, PONI CURAVIT
FILIUS RECTOR A . D . 1845.

MORTALITATEM HAUD VITAM DEPOSUERE

𝕴 . 𝕾 .	𝕰 . 𝕾 . 𝕾 .
DIE MART: XVIII^{M.O}	DIE NOVEMB: IV^{T.O}
1844.	1843.

DEO GRATIA,
QUI PER DOMINUM NOSTRUM IESUM CHRISTUM
NOBIS VICTORIAM DEDIT.
I. EP. CORINTH: CAP. XV.

Stone tablet affixed to the south wall of the Sanctuary in Otley Church, Suffolk,
by Francis Storr in memory of his father and mother

---

[1] For his long and distinguished career see *Who was Who, 1929–40*; and especially G. H. Harris, *Vernon Faithfull Storr*, 1943.

[2] Rugby, 1859–63; Corpus Christi, Cambridge, 1864–7 (B.A., 1868); Ordained Deacon at Ely, 1867; Curate of Silsoe, Beds, 1867–9, of Flitton, 1869–74, of Penge, 1874–5, of Brenchley, Kent, 1875–6; Rector of Great Horkesley, Essex, 1876–1916; and Vicar of Little Horkesley, 1897–1916.

CHAPTER THREE

STORR'S BUSINESS CAREER

HAVING decided that his son should follow the trade of a goldsmith, Thomas sent Paul as an apprentice to a Swede, one Andrew Fogelberg of [30] Church Street, Soho. This would probably be in 1785 when Paul was fourteen years old, because the year 1792 marked the end of his apprenticeship and the period usually lasted seven years, although outside the city boundaries it was sometimes reduced to five years. Nothing whatever seems to be known about Fogelberg—when he came to England, how long he worked here, where he died or if he ever returned to Sweden. Owing, however, to the kind help of Erik Andrén, a curator of the Nordiska Museet in Stockholm, and part author of the great *Svenskt Silversmide*, I have been able to find a Swedish goldsmith of the same name, and one whose dates, so far as they are known, correspond perfectly with our Andrew Fogelberg. The facts are these. No man bearing the name is recorded as an eighteenth-century goldsmith living in Sweden. There was, however, a boy by the name of Anders or Andreas (i.e. Eng. Andrew) Fogelberg born about 1732. He entered service as an apprentice for six years with Berent (Berndt or Bernhard) Halck,[1] a goldsmith of Halmstad, about Christmas-time 1746. In 1752 he became a journeyman, after which his subsequent fortunes are unrecorded. It is probable, says Erik Andrén, that he worked for a few years as a journeyman in Sweden and then undertook the usual "wandering" in the same capacity in different parts of the Continent. He might well have reached England in the 1760s, and by the time Paul Storr went to him in 1785 he would be a man in his early fifties.

Although there is no actual proof that Halck's pupil and Storr's master were one and the same person, the comparative rarity of the name Fogelberg in Sweden during the eighteenth century, the unexplained disappearance of young Anders Fogelberg from Sweden, and the complete agreement of the dates would seem to give ample justification in accepting it as a fact. For some reason or other—possibly connected with his foreign nationality—he was not a member of the Goldsmiths, and his name appears neither in the Apprenticeship nor the Freedom Book. This fact may explain why Paul was not a member either. So, too, when Francis Storr was apprenticed to his father in 1828, he likewise never became a member. According to information received from Goldsmiths' Hall, there is no record as to when Andrew Fogelberg entered his mark. This has caused some confusion as to the dates of his earliest

---

1 For him see Gustaf Upmark, *Guld- och Silversmeder i Sverige*, Stockholm, 1943, p. 341, and for examples of his work see *Svenskt Silversmide*, Vol. II, pl. 613, and Gustaf Munthe, *Falk Simons Silversamling*, Pls. 126 (Nos. 388 and 410—boxes) and 139 (No. 541—spoon).

productions. Jackson (p. 256) gives his "earliest mention" as 1773, and (p. 223) the date when he entered his mark as 1776. One wonders what evidence he had for such statements, for, as already mentioned, there is no record whatever at the Hall of the date of his registration. Both Jackson's dates are incorrect, for among the examples of Fogelberg's work at Buckingham Palace (Royal Inventory, No. 1105) are two shaped hand-candlesticks with extinguishers, weighing 20 oz., and made in 1770. Dating from the same year is the pair of remarkable two-handled vases sold by the notorious Elizabeth Chudleigh to Catherine II of Russia, and given by her to her favourite, and incidentally her husband, Prince Potemkin. These vases, 3 ft. in height, clearly show Fogelberg's predilection for the Adam style—wide bands of oval cartouches between beaded borders, laurel swags hanging from circular rosettes, and high reeded handles terminating in oval ornaments from the centre of which festoons are joined to rosettes on the neck. A calyx of lanceolate leaves and a spreading foot covered with acanthus foliage, changing at the base to anthemion, is a further indica-cation of the neo-classic trend.[1] Furthermore, there is that lovely tea-caddy engraved with *genre* subjects highly reminiscent of Morland—possibly the work of the Alsatian artist then in London, Philippe Jacques de Loutherbourg—which Fogelberg had made in 1772.[2] Thus it is clear that during the years 1770–2, if not earlier, Fogelberg was established as a working goldsmith at some unknown address—possibly in rented rooms in Church Street, Soho. Sir Ambrose Heal finds him first mentioned as living in Church Street in 1773, but he is not entered in the London directories at this time. In fact, his name never appears alone but only in conjunction with that of his partner, Stephen Gilbert, who joined him in 1780. Even so, the name of the firm is not found until 1789, when it is entered in *Andrews's New London Directory*, where the address is given as 30 Church Street, Soho. Neither Kent nor Lowndes gives them for that year. But in 1790 they appear in the *Universal British Directory* as "Fogilberg and Gilbert", and are similarly spelt in *Bailey's London Directory* for the same year. Andrews (1790) spells the name correctly, and so does the *Universal British Directory* in 1791. Kent and Lowndes continue to ignore them. By 1793 Andrews has dropped them, although they appear for that year in the *Universal British Directory*. After this they disappear altogether. Thus it looks as if the firm dissolved immediately after the completion of Storr's apprenticeship.

Whether Fogelberg died or returned to Sweden is not known, while no mention of Stephen Gilbert has been recorded after 1794. Passing on to Paul Storr's apprenticeship, the indenture has, most unfortunately, not been discovered, but evidence from other sources affords sufficient proof of the fact that Fogelberg was indeed his master. In the first place, Storr's name appears for the first time in 1792—and the address given is the same as that of Fogelberg. This fact is significant enough, but the

---

[1] See S. Troinitsky, *Old English Plate*, Petersburg, 1923, Nos. 52, 53, and cf. the Russian text to No. 3. For photographs see E. Alfred Jones, *Old English Plate of the Emperor of Russia*, p. 92, and Pl. XLVI, No. 2. When in Russia these vases were converted into wine fountains, the square hole for the spigot appearing in Jones's illustration, *supra*.

[2] *Connoisseur*, May 1938, pp. 261–2.

PLATE II

CIVIL INDENTURE DATED 17TH APRIL 1828, MADE BETWEEN
PAUL STORR AND HIS SON FRANCIS

date itself is even more so, for it fixes the year in which Storr was made "free". As we shall see shortly, it was in the spring of that same year that he moved to Snow Hill to join William Frisbee. It may be that he still lived with Fogelberg, because although the 1792 joint mark of Storr and Frisbee has the Snow Hill address shown with it at the Hall, we find that when Storr entered his own mark separately on 12th January 1793 his address is still given as 30 Church Street, Soho. In the second place much of Storr's early work shows a close affinity to that of Fogelberg, in fact certain pieces made by both men are so similar as to be practically indistinguishable.[1] Thirdly, and lastly, comes the literary (MS.) evidence. This consists, in the first place, of a letter written by John Samuel Hunt in which he recalls the history of the firm and speaks of Storr's "foreign" master, and in the second place, of papers shown to me by one of the managers of J. W. Benson Ltd., who bought Hunt and Roskell, the successors to Paul Storr & Co., in which the statement is definitely made that Storr was apprenticed to Fogelberg.

Before considering the style of work produced at 30 Church Street, Soho, and the influence it had on Storr, a word should be said about Fogelberg's partner. In May 1752 one Stephen Gilbert was apprenticed to Edward Wakelin of Panton Street (later John Parker and Edward Wakelin, and finally Garrard's) for a term of seven years. He was made Free of the Goldsmiths' Company by Service on 1st February 1764 and returned to Panton Street where he worked as a goldsmith from 1766–71. In 1780 he became the partner of Fogelberg, but whether he was with him first as a shopman from 1771–80 is not recorded. On 17th July 1780 Fogelberg and Gilbert entered their joint mark at the Hall. It is unknown to what degree Gilbert influenced the style of work produced after 1780, so in speaking of the productions of 30 Church Street—whether before or after the partnership—we shall regard Fogelberg as the maker.

It may well be asked whether Fogelberg's work in any way betrays his Swedish origin, and if so whether it is also reflected in the early work of Storr. To both these questions we can answer a very definite "No!" Although it is not too easy to define the characteristics of Swedish silver owing partly to the changing boundaries of the country and partly to the fact that her style was dictated first by German and then by French influence, yet, however elusive the native Swedish style may be, an inspection of Fogelberg's work shows that so far from borrowing from Sweden, it was he who was partly responsible for furthering the acceptance in Sweden of the neo-classic style, of which he was an enthusiastic supporter. This is clearly shown in his love for the oval—the vase and the urn, while his decoration includes the floral swag, the lanceolate leaf, the narrow reeded leg and, above all, the pearled or beaded edging and the oval silver cameo. This last calls for some further comment. Just behind Fogelberg's workshop, at "Compton Street, 2nd door from Greek Street Soho", was the workshop (from 1772 to 1777) of James Tassie, modeller and reproducer of

1 See Pl. IV, p. 86.

antique gems.[1] In these beautiful reproductions Fogelberg saw the possibility of copying them in silver and applying them to some of his neo-classical productions. Tassie had supplied casts to Wedgwood and Bentley for reproduction in their own paste, and most of the cameos and intaglios in Wedgwood's 1773 catalogue were from casts supplied by him.[2] And now Fogelberg's silver cameos were to popularize Tassie's casts still further, for they could be exported in bulk to silversmiths and used as occasion demanded. It will be seen that in this way Fogelberg became an active disseminator of the Adam style, for such cameos at once demanded a neo-classical setting.

As Oman has pointed out,[3] Swedish silver decorated with medallions adapted from Tassie casts is by no means rare, and in that magnificent work *Svenskt Silversmide* fifteen such pieces are illustrated in Vol. III, dating between 1786 and 1801. It is, however, not only the medallions which appear in the productions of such Swedish goldsmiths as Smedberg, Klinck, Gertzen, Holmberg, Vogt, Nyberg and Brandt (as shown in Vol. III, Pls. 16–83), but other characteristics of Fogelberg such as beaded edges, lanceolate leaves and floral swags. Now although Storr's early work clearly displays the Adam style (see e.g. Pls. IVB, VIIB, XV, etc.) he appears never to have used the silver medallion, and once he was on his own the influence of his master, so far as style is concerned, gradually disappears.

The use of the small medallion or cameo as an ornament to Swedish silver, however, had been made in the seventeenth century, as can be seen from the decoration on the tankard made by Johan Nützel (Nijssel)[4] of Stockholm (1676–1715). Here Roman heads, encircled with laurel wreaths, appear on the round ball feet, on the floral scrolled panels by which they are secured to the tankard, and on the round purchase of the lid.[5]

Similar classical medallions also occur on a tankard made in 1727 by Johan Lorenz Starin of Stockholm and on another rather similar one by Lorentz Pihl of Västervik in 1738. In this latter example the cameos are set at intervals on a chased background just below the rim.[6]

It is clear, then, that even if Fogelberg was chiefly responsible for the introduction

---

1 So the address is given on the title-page of his *A Catalogue of Impressions in Sulphur, of Antique and Modern Gems, from which Pastes are Made and Sold* . . . J. Murray No. 32 Fleet Street, 1775. It consisted of 3,106 items. In 1778 Tassie moved to Leicester Fields (Square) where he employed R. E. Raspe (of *Baron Munchausen* fame) as his cataloguer. By now his collection numbered 12,000, and in 1786 Raspe issued his *Account of the present state and arrangement of Mr. James Tassie's Collection*, in which reference is made to the order recently received from Catherine II of Russia for a complete set. In 1791 appeared the important *Descriptive Catalogue of a General Collection of Ancient and Modern Engraved Gems*, 2 vols., but numbered throughout, containing a description of 15,800 items and 57 plates.

2 For details see John M. Gray, *James and William Tassie*, Edinburgh, 1894, pp. 15, 20–2. The work is bibliographical as well as biographical and contains details of the publications both of James and his nephew and successor William, besides a catalogue of their portrait medallions.

3 "Andrew Fogelberg, and the English influence on Swedish silver", *Apollo*, June 1947, pp. 158–60.

4 G. Upmark, *Guld- och Silversmeder i Sverige*, Stockholm, 1943, pp. 66–7.

5 *Svenskt Silversmide*, Vol. I, Pls. 317–20.

6 For these makers see Upmark, *op. cit.*, pp. 108 and 745, and for photographs of the tankards see Gustaf Munthe, *Falk Simons Silversamling*, Stockholm, 1938, Pls. 54, 55, with text on p. 140.

of Tassie's gems at the end of the nineteenth century, we cannot regard it as an innovation to Swedish goldsmiths' art.

Owing to the scarcity of examples of Fogelberg and Gilbert's work (except for the tea-urn which they appear to have made in considerable quantities) it may be of interest to enumerate the piece in the Royal collections. Those by Fogelberg alone include two silver hand-candlesticks (1770), and four silver candlesticks (1777), while those with the joint mark are: two gilt mazarines (1788 and 1791), eight gilt oval dishes, a tea-urn and eighteen soup plates (1792), and a plain oval casserole-dish

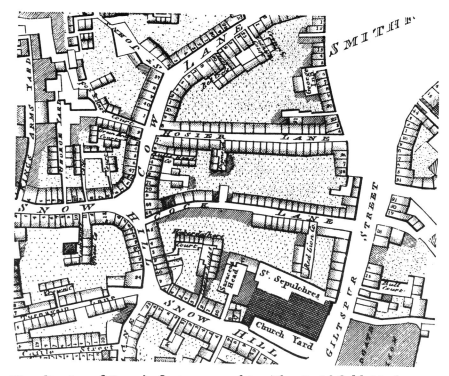

The district of Storr's first partnership. The Smithfield Market area

(1809).[1] If this last date of 1809 is correct (which I rather doubt) it extends Jackson's latest recorded date (1791) by eighteen years!

We can now return to Storr's business career. Having been made free in 1792, Storr joined William Frisbee, a plate-worker of 5 Cock Lane, Snow Hill—just south of Smithfield Market. Frisbee, the son of John Frisbee, Tallow Chandler, was apprenticed to John Crouch of Giltspur Street (out of which Cock Lane leads) in October 1774. He received his freedom by Service on 6th February 1782; became a member of the Livery of the Goldsmiths' Company in October 1806, and died on 9th December 1820. It would appear, then, that Frisbee was about ten years older than Storr.

1 *Descriptive Inventory*, 1914. Nos. 1105, 745 and 1094 (Fogelberg alone), and 151, 150, 87, 898, 192, 859, 116 and 50 (with Gilbert).

Frisbee entered his own mark in 1792, and on May 2nd of the same year the joint mark of Frisbee and Storr was duly recorded in the Assay Office book at Goldsmiths' Hall. As can be seen from the reproduction made from the photograph kindly sent me by Mr. G. R. Hughes, late Clerk of the Goldsmiths, it was in Roman Capitals, WF above

PS, in a square stamp of two sizes.   None of these marks were

recorded on metal plates, as was also the case with all Storr's own marks.[1]

In view of the neo-classical type of work which was to form so much of Storr's

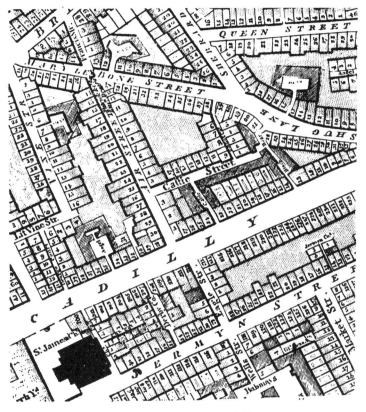

20 Air Street, Piccadilly

output, it is interesting to note that in the first year of their joint mark, Frisbee and Storr produced a two-handled vase of Greek form (see Jackson, p. 222). Storr entered his own mark from 30 Church Street on 12th January 1793. The partnership was of but short endurance. In 1795 Frisbee moved to another turning off Snow Hill, known as Cow Lane, but whether Storr accompanied him here is uncertain. If so, it was a very temporary arrangement, for Storr had determined to move west, and in the autumn of 1796 we find him firmly installed at 20 Air Street, which runs from Piccadilly across Regent Street to Glasshouse Street. Here Storr remained eleven years, and it was here that he made a name for himself as one of London's leading manufacturing goldsmiths, and, as we have already seen, it was from here that he married Elizabeth Beyer in 1801. It would appear from a note by Warren Dawson[2] that Benjamin Smith was one of Storr's silversmiths before he started business on his own account. If this was so, and certainly much of his work closely resembles that of

1 These are discussed later in Chapter V, "Miscellanea—The Registered Marks".
2 *The Nelson Collection at Lloyd's*, 1932, p. 12, note 28.

Storr, he must have left him before 1802, for on 4th October of that year he entered his mark with that of his partner Digby Scott. Dawson adds that there was no date of entry recorded for the combined marks of Benjamin Smith and his later partner James Smith. This is incorrect. Their joint mark was registered on 23rd February 1810, i.e. before the London Goldsmiths' year of 1810 (27th March) had started. This fact explains why several of their pieces at Windsor Castle bear the date-letter of 1809-10. Among them mention may be made of eight silver-gilt two-handled vases with covers, for sugar.[1] They can hardly be distinguished from a set of four made by Storr for Lord Harewood in 1814.[2] In 1797–8 Storr produced the unique gold font for the christening of William Henry, Marquess of Titchfield, eldest son of the fourth Duke of Portland.

Orders came in from the great houses of England for cups, vases, kettles, wine-coolers, dishes and plates. The Goldsmiths' Company possesses 125 plates of 1809–11, while Lord Desborough's dinner service of eighty-two pieces had been made in 1797–8. The two-handled cup and cover, dated 1800–1, and presented to the Hon. Society of the Middle Temple by King Edward VII when Prince of Wales, was made by Storr for George III. Whether such orders were commissioned through Philip Rundell is not proved, but it is certain that at this time he was very anxious to get Storr to work for him exclusively. Already Rundell had engaged William Theed, R.A., the elder, to model for him, and was shortly to take him as a partner in the firm. Rundell now wanted John Flaxman to design for him and Storr to execute the work. In both of these plans he was successful. It would appear that Rundell (whose history we shall consider in detail later) persuaded Storr to leave Air Street and move to larger premises at 53 Dean Street, Soho, quite near his old address in Church Street.

But before he agreed to move Storr made it plain that by so doing he had no intention of losing his identity. He would ensure this by turning himself into a company which he would call "Storr & Co", continue his own work at the new address and execute any orders which Rundell might give him. Matters were satis-factorily settled, the move was made in 1807, and the following year the Directories gave "Storr & Co. Working Silversmiths, 53, Dean St., Soho". If the author of the *Memoirs of . . . Philip Rundell* is to be credited, 53 Dean Street was Rundell's own manufactory and the firm of Messrs. Storr & Co. had simply been put in to manage it. However this may be, Storr had been made a partner by 1811, or earlier, as in replying to the question at the Sessions[3] as to whether he was a partner in the firm at 53 Dean Street, he replied: "I am; the partners are Paul Storr, Philip Rundell, John Bridge, Edmund [or Edmond] Waller Rundell and William Theed." It is obvious that Storr was engaged not so much in his own firm's work, but chiefly in

1 See E. A. Jones, *Gold and Silver of Windsor Castle*, 1911, p. 164, and Pl. LXXXIII, No. 4.
2 For these see Pl. LII of the present work.
3 *The whole Proceedings on the King's Commission of the Peace. Oyer and Terminer . . . held at Justice-Hall in the Old Bailey on Wed. the 5th Dec. 1810*, 3rd Session, 1811, p. 129. The case concerned the theft by two men of 127 oz. of silver cuttings from Dean Street. They were found guilty and sentenced to seven and fourteen years' transportation respectively.

executing the orders that poured into Rundell's shop in Ludgate Hill. In fact, it is clear that as time went on and trade increased past all expectations there was little chance of anything being produced by Storr & Co. Rundell must have known perfectly well that once he got Storr in as a partner he would keep him so busy with the firm's orders that Messrs. Storr & Co. would be but a name in the Directory. Meanwhile the workmen at Dean Street were being fully trained in Storr's methods and perfection of workmanship, and Rundell must have been well satisfied with the way things were going. But Storr soon found himself becoming merely the head of what amounted to a mass-production workshop, and felt his individuality and personal craftsmanship rapidly disappearing. Moreover, so numerous were the orders, and so quickly had they to be executed, that to a great extent Paul's work must have been reduced to that of a supervisor. It soon became obvious that if he was to recapture his own individuality he must leave the firm and once more work on his own. It is here, then, that we get a glimpse of Storr's character.

Let us consider the situation for a moment. The cunning Rundell had now reached the summit of his ambition. In John Bridge he had found the "complete courtier", the "contact man", well fitted to get orders from royalty and the nobility, "beating the bush to drive the game to Ludgate Hill", as one of the firm's employees wrote in after years.[1] Bridge was the one man with whom Rundell could not afford to quarrel, for, as we shall see later, he it was who, with the help of his rich farmer cousin in Dorset, not only brought capital into the firm, but enlisted the personal interest of George III, which led to their obtaining the Royal Warrant and all the prestige that went with it. On one occasion Rundell had visited Buckingham House himself, but his complete ignorance of court etiquette, coupled with his clumsy and uncouth manners, made it clear that in future all such visits must be left to John Bridge. So much, then, for getting the orders. The next triumph of Rundell had been in his persuading Storr to join the firm. The enormous increase of business ensured a long and lucrative position for Storr at the head of the ever-growing workshop staff, and many men would have been content to sacrifice their individuality and personal ideals so long as work and money continued to pour in. As we shall see later, Rundell died a millionaire, his nephew left over half a million, and Bridge also made a fortune and retired to an estate which he had purchased in Dorset. There is little doubt that Storr, too, could have acquired very great wealth had he been prepared to stay in Rundell's workshop as general supervisor. Neither Rundell nor Bridge was married, but Storr had a wife and family of ten to support and educate. Yet in spite of all this his conscience would not permit him to stay in a job—however lucrative and permanent it might be—in which he felt that the opportunity for personal creation was at an end and the hand of the individual craftsman lost in the soulless glitter of the filed and polished surfaces now mechanically produced. In order to appreciate this fact it is only necessary to compare, and if possible to handle, an

1 This was George Fox whose important MS. on the history of the firm will form one of the chief sources for our next chapter.

early piece of Storr, such as the bread-basket of 1794 (Pl. VII), with any of the big centre-pieces or presentation cups of the time of Waterloo and the years immediately following. And so Storr decided to leave the firm and move elsewhere. We can conclude that his severance was absolute, and that he resigned his partnership and any other interests he might have had. This was not such a loss to Rundell as might be imagined, for by this time he had already made his great fortune and was thinking of retiring himself—which he actually did in 1823. Furthermore, the peak years of the firm's prosperity were over and with the fall in the price of gold and silver at the end of the war, the agricultural depression and the decline in landed rents, money had become scarce and a stricter economy was the order of the day. Had Storr left in 1815 or 1816 the result would have been very different, but in 1820 it was not so serious.

There is one point, however, that should be mentioned concerning the stamps used in the marking of the silver. As actual maker, Storr had always stamped it with his own mark. In many cases Rundell, Bridge & Rundell had added their Latin ascription usually somewhere on the base of the particular piece. Rundell was not a working goldsmith but a jeweller, while Bridge, as we have seen, was the "contact" man. Thus neither of them troubled to register their marks. But with the resignation of Storr the situation was different, and it became necessary for one of the directors, at least, to affix his personal mark to the products of the workshop. Accordingly, on 4th March 1819, Rundell entered his mark at the Hall. After his retirement in 1823 John Bridge did likewise on 13th November of the same year.[1]

What then must be made of pieces marked by Philip Rundell in 1819 and the two following years? The largest number of pieces bearing his mark are in the Royal collection and if we examine each one described in E. Alfred Jones's work (*Gold and Silver of Windsor Castle*) we shall find that either an earlier piece was being copied,[2] small stands added to existing pieces,[3] the work designed and modelled by others being cast,[4] or snuff boxes being melted down and remade into trays, etc.[5] In other pieces produced in 1819 we can see Storr's hand clearly,[6] for it is obvious that many of his unfinished pieces as well as his designs, casts, models, etc., remained in the workshop as the property of Rundell, Bridge & Rundell.

With John Bridge the circumstances appear to have been very different, for

---

[1] In his *Gilda Aurifabrorum*, p. 94, Chaffers says that Bridge stamped his name on the plate as actual maker "from about 1780 to 1790". Of course he did nothing of the kind. The mistake was due to Chaffers assigning a small Roman "l" on one of Bridge's pieces to the wrong alphabetical cycle, thus making the date 1786 instead of 1826. Considering Chaffers had access to the books at the Hall there was no excuse for such carelessness, which, unfortunately, was repeated at the great 1862 Exhibition. See *Catalogue of the Special Exhibition of Works of Art . . . on Loan at the South Kensington Museum, June 1862*, London, 1863, p. 497, Nos. 5,969 and 5,970.

[2] Jones, p. 84, where the bread-basket is made to match that by Phillips Garden of 1751–2.

[3] Jones, p. 102, where the Viennese crystal cup and ewer of the later eighteenth century are concerned.

[4] Jones, p. 106—the Flaxman Shield of Achilles.

[5] Jones, p. 188—the gold salver.

[6] E.g. see Jones, p. 144, the set of dessert-stands, or the altar candlesticks on p. 198. Here Jones has given the date incorrectly. It should read 1821–2. Storr's four candelabra of 1804 and 1809 had come in for additional stands to be added. The work was practically finished when Storr left, but Rundell stamped them with his mark. See Jones, *op. cit.*, p. 126.

although he also furnished new parts to older pieces (e.g. the table ornament partly by George Wickes, 1743, Jones, p. 78), added rims to crystal cups, etc. (Jones, p. 80), or copied designs by Flaxman (Jones, p. 108), we must consider his "marine" productions of 1826 to 1829 as well as other pieces to be mentioned shortly.

The first of Bridge's "marine" pieces is rather a puzzle. It is a most elaborate and composite production, as can be seen from Jones, Pl. XXXVI. In the text opposite (p. 72) Jones, strangely enough, attributed it to Augustin Courtauld, with the date 1741–2. But in a letter to me in 1943, only a few months before his death, he asks me to correct the maker's name to Paul Crespin, and adds that he found that portions of it had been made in Turin! The curious point is that Jones appears to have overlooked the mark of John Bridge (1826) on the "marine" part of the pedestal.[1] If any doubt about this exists we can but compare the prancing fish-tailed horses with those definitely by Bridge on his "marine" soup tureens made the same year.[2] The next "marine" piece was the massive pair of ice-pails with tritons blowing conchs, spearing fish, etc.,[3] but the really amazing production was the enormous wine-cooler[4] weighing 8,000 oz. made in 1829–30. Other important works of Bridge were the pair of large 20-in. oviform jars of 1828 and 1829[5] and the sconces of 1829–30.[6] According to the *Gentleman's Magazine*, October 1834, p. 408, Bridge received orders from William IV to make an exact model of the Chapel of Eton College, with the Arms of Henry the Sixth, the founder, and "H.R" on one side, and the contemporary Royal Arms and "W.R" on the other. It was to be about three feet in length and over two feet in width. It is interesting to note that Bridge never attempted it himself, but gave the work to John Thompson (perhaps the elderly silversmith of that name who had entered in 1785) by whom it was duly executed. For details see E. A. Jones, *Plate of Eton College*, Plate XXII and p. 35.

But we must return to Storr's resignation. Once his mind was made up he lost little time in putting his plans into effect. It appears that in 1818 an additional workshop was acquired at 74 and/or 75 Dean Street. Whether this was Rundell's property or a temporary move by Storr is not clear. It is entered in the Directories in Storr's name, but this proves nothing for, as we have seen, No. 53 had been under his name since 1808.[7] However this may be, Storr's search for new premises was successful, and early in 1819 he found just the place he was looking for at 18 Harrison Street, off

[1] In the Royal Inventory of 1914 (No. 163) the piece is attributed solely to Bridge, 1826, but this tells us only part of the story.

[2] See Jones, Pl. LXXXI.

[3] Jones, Pl. LVI and p. 110.

[4] Jones. Pl. LXXXIX and p. 176, where, most unfortunately, he wrongly calls it a punch-bowl—just because it has a huge ladle.

[5] Jones, p. 156 and Pl. LXXIX.

[6] Jones, p. 174 and Pl. LXXXVIII.

[7] The Directories and Poll Book about this time are somewhat contradictory. From 1813–17 some of the Directories, especially Kent's, give the address of the workshops as 53 *and* 54. The London Directory of 1818 gives Storr as still at 53 Dean Street, while the Middlesex Poll Book of the same year gives his address as 75 Dean Street. In 1819 the Directory gives it as 74 Dean Street. If 74/5 Dean Street was not another of Rundell's workshops, it may possibly have been the house at which Storr lived for a time.

Gray's Inn Lane (later "Road"), and in the Directories for 1820 and 1821 this is given as his only address. No plans of the premises seem to have survived, but some years later Storr purchased an adjoining house, together with workshops and a large yard, in Francis Street, which runs from Harrison Street to Sidmouth Street. Now in 1831 Storr leased the place to Messrs. Robert, James & Sebastian Garrard of Panton Street for a period of ten years, and the indenture contains a plan of the premises in which portions of Storr's own adjoining property appears.[1] Harrison Street is not marked on the plan as it is a little too far north to be included. Storr's own "manu-factory", yard and garden all faced on to Harrison Street.

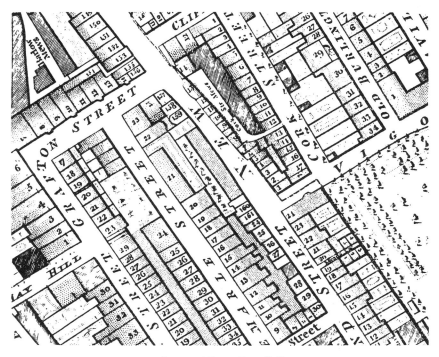

13 and 156 New Bond Street

Having now acquired premises of his own, the next step was to find a "shop-window" in the West End. Now in 1768 one Robert Gray had set up business as a cutler and toyman (one who sells requisites for sports, trinkets and fancy goods) at 13 New Bond Street. As time went on the nature of the business became exclusively that of a goldsmith and jeweller, and in 1789 Robert took his son, William, into partnership, retiring himself three years later. William carried on the business until 1821, when he, in his turn, wished to retire. Hearing that Paul Storr was looking for a retail place in the West End, Gray approached him with a view to amalgamation. He

1 The indenture, a large document of three parchment sheets measuring 2 ft. 3 in. by 3 ft., has been most kindly given me by Mr. H. Sulman, the late Managing Director of the distinguished firm of Messrs. Garrard & Co., Ltd.

63

wanted to provide for his principal assistant, a certain John Mortimer, and suggested that if the two firms combined Mortimer could manage the retail business, while Storr would run the manufacturing side. Matters were agreeably settled, and in 1822 the firm of "Storr and Mortimer, Gold and Silver Smiths, 13, New Bond Street" was formed. In 1824 Storr's son, Francis, had come down from Harrow, and Paul decided to take him on as an apprentice to learn the trade and help in the new venture. All went well until 1826, when it appears that Mortimer had brought the retail business to the verge of ruin by overbuying stock, and neither he nor Storr had any further capital to put in to save the situation. The crisis, however, was averted by an appeal to John Samuel Hunt, son of Richard Hunt and Catherine Beyer, Storr's sister-in-law. Hunt agreed to come in as a third partner, bringing £5,000 as capital. The business was continued successfully by the three partners from 1826 to 1838, although Hunt's name does not appear in the Directories at this time. It was in 1838 that Storr and Mortimer moved to 156 New Bond Street, a better site, being at the corner of Grafton Street almost opposite No. 13 diagonally. In 1834 the address of Storr & Co. had changed from 18 to 26 Harrison Street, and in the Directory of 1838 the two new addresses are combined under a single heading as follows: "Storr & Mortimer, Goldsmiths & Jewellers to Her Majesty, 156 New Bond St., & Silversmiths and Goldsmiths to Her Majesty, 26 Harrison St., Gray's Inn road."

Mortimer seems to have been a very difficult person to deal with, and there were constant disputes between him and Storr. Before the end of 1838 matters came to a head and there was a big Chancery partnership action. Ultimately it was settled (apparently out of court) and Storr, now a man in his sixty-eighth year, decided to retire. Before doing so, however, he arranged for John Samuel Hunt's son, John, to come in as junior partner—the firm being now styled "Mortimer & Hunt". They entered their mark, IM over ISH crowned, in 1839, the year of Paul's retirement. In 1842 John Mortimer retired, whereupon the Hunts took Robert Roskell (of Liverpool) as a new partner, the firm changing its name to Hunt and Roskell, their mark being simply ISH crowned. John Samuel Hunt died in 1865, when the mark was altered to IH over RR crowned. This remained unaltered until 1882. Meanwhile John Hunt had died in 1879. He had a daughter, Kezia, who married Henry Francis Makins, and their grandson, Sir Roger Makins, has recently been appointed British Ambassador to the United States. John also had a son, John Mortimer Hunt, who, by entering the business on his father's death, revived the old name of the firm. Robert Roskell's son, Allen, joined the firm at the same time. From 1882 to 1889 their mark was RR over AR over IMH crowned.

By 1889 the firm had neither a Hunt nor a Roskell left. In that year it was bought by Messrs. J. W. Benson, and from 1889–95 their mark was AB (for Alfred Benson) over HHW (for H. H. Wintle) crowned. For the next two years (1895–7) the mark was changed to AB over AHB (for Arthur Henry Benson) crowned. All this time, i.e. from 1842–97, the name of the firm remained Hunt & Roskell. In 1897, with the creation of a company, the mark was altered once again, this time to "H & R Ltd" crowned. In 1901 the crown, which had surmounted every mark since the days of Mortimer & Hunt, was finally abandoned.

After his retirement Paul and his wife lived at Hill House, Tooting.[1] Elizabeth died on 4th November 1843, while Paul's death occurred on 18th March of the year following. Their simple grave can be seen in Tooting Parish Church yard. In it also rests Montague Storr Champneys, their grandson, who died aged twenty-seven in 1868. The inscription is as follows:

PAUL STORR OF HILL HOUSE TOOTING

DIED MARCH 18 1844

ELIZABETH SUSANNAH STORR

DIED NOV 4 1843

MONTAGUE STORR CHAMPNEYS THEIR GRANDSON

DIED JULY 28 1868 AGED 27

Storr's Will is dated 4th November 1843, the day of his wife's death, and was proved on 3rd April 1844 by "the oaths of Paul Storr Esquire and the Reverend Francis Storr Clerk the sons The Reverend William Weldon Champneys Clerk and the Reverend Robert Chapman Savage Clerk the Executors to whom Admo^n was granted. . . ."

The value of his estate was only £3,000, but Paul was a kind and generous man and would already have provided for his large family before his death. Everything was left to his executors as named above. No silver is mentioned as such, being included under his "personal effects". His trade tools, draw bench, etc., remained in his workshop, but were all destroyed, together with many of his papers, in the last war.

1 It is now a resident house for nurses, in the grounds of St. Benedicts' Hospital, Church Lane, Tooting. It was built in 1767 by a Mr. Morgan Rice on the Order of the Parish Vestry, but plans were altered and Rice enlarged the house into a small mansion. Photographs from every elevation are in the L.C.C. County Hall.

65

CHAPTER FOUR

PHILIP RUNDELL AND HIS FIRM

PHILIP RUNDELL (also spelt Rundal and Rundall) was born in Bath, or more exactly in the Parish of Widcombe outside the city (now a part of it), in 1743.[1] He was the son of Thomas Rundell, a doctor, who apparently practised at Widcombe, as he was not made a Freeman of the City of Bath until 1764.[2] The following entries in the Widcombe Parish Registers support this conjecture:

1755 Jan. 22   Elizth Rundal d. of Thomas
1757 Jan. 23   Mary Rundal d. of Thomas
1759 Jan. 7   Thomas Rundall s. of Thomas

Dr. Rundell's name first appears in the 1778 *Bath Guide* in the list of surgeons, with an asterisk indicating that he practised midwifery. Entries also occur under his name in the *Bath Guide* from 1779 to 1796, while after 1787 his address is given as 4 Bennet Street. He is said to have had a large family, chiefly girls, but, apart from Philip, those mentioned above seem to be the only ones recorded. Philip received but little education, and displayed no interest in the medical profession. It so happened that the leading Bath gem engraver of the day, John Wicksteed, had his workshop at Widcombe, and it would appear that Philip spent most of his time there watching the workmen and learning all he could. His father, anxious to get the boy started in life, had him apprenticed in 1760 to one William Rogers, a jeweller, to whom he paid a premium of £20.[3] No trace of this man can be found in the Lists of Freemen, and as he could not have carried on his craft in the city without this qualification it seems obvious that he was either one of those tradesmen who only visited Bath during the season, or else he was connected with some other firm. In view of the apprenticeship, the latter seems the most probable.[4] John Wicksteed had died in 1754, and Rogers might well have been his leading craftsman. The business was managed at this time by the widow, and later by the son. This would in no way prevent Rogers taking an apprentice. Whatever may have been the facts, Philip learned the trade of the jeweller, and became expert at cutting and setting semi-precious stones, especially garnets, which at the time were much worn in swordhilts

[1] According to the Fox MS. (to be discussed later) Philip Rundell was born in 1747 at Philips Norton, the youngest of sixteen children. He obviously means Norton St. Philip, six miles south-east of Bath.
[2] Chamberlain's Accounts, 1764, "October 8, Recd. of Thomas Rundell his Freedom fee 6.0". Until this had been taken up he could not practise in the city. I have to thank the Director of the Victoria Art Gallery and Municipal Libraries, Bath, for information concerning Dr. Rundell, John Wicksteed, etc.
[3] Apprenticeship Records, Great Britain, Inland Revenue Books, 22/127.
[4] In 1738 the Apprenticeship Records show that Rogers, who is described as "of Walcott" (Bath), was apprenticed to one Peter Goulett of Bath.

and shoe buckles. His apprenticeship finished, Philip was anxious to get to London and start earning his own living. But money was short and his father had little to spare. His sisters, however, came to the rescue and enabled him to start the career which was to be such a success. Whether he had other jobs first we do not know, but in 1767 or 1769—the actual year is uncertain—he went to London and was engaged as a shopman by Messrs. Theed & Pickett, goldsmiths and jewellers of Ludgate Hill, at the sign of the Golden Salmon. Rundell had turned up at a lucky moment —in fact so far as making money was concerned he was destined to be "lucky" throughout his career—for Theed had either just retired or was about to do so.[1] Having now got Rundell firmly established at Ludgate Hill we must trace the history of the firm to this point, for the story is an interesting one.

It starts early in the eighteenth century at a small shop on the north side of St. Paul's Churchyard, the premises of one Henry Hurt, a dealer in toys, to which was added the sale of fishing-tackle. This latter appears to have formed an important part of the business as his shop sign was a Golden Salmon which hung outside the shop. A second one appears to have hung inside the shop for, as will be shown later, there were definitely two Golden Salmon. The expression "dealer in toys" does not imply that he was a "toyman", i.e. a seller of trinkets and fancy goods, although this is what he became after his move to Ludgate Hill. The Fox MS. clearly states that he sold Dutch (? German) and other toys, and if the expression had a wider application it did not include jewellery or plate. Hurt is described as a man of no education who never kept any books for the simple reason that he was unable to write. He sold only for ready money and kept his accounts with the tradespeople in an "alphabetical drawer".[2] As business increased he decided to move to larger premises which he had found in Ludgate Hill, and in 1744 disposed of his lease to a Mr. John Brown whose business was in small silver articles, common jewellery, toys, china, etc. According to Fox, Brown remained there for "a vast number of years",[3] and his business seems to have declined sadly for when he died the sale of his stock and furniture hardly defrayed the expenses of "a plain decent funeral", while his aged housekeeper was removed to the workhouse. The only interesting item in the sale was the two original Golden Salmon, which, being an integral part of the shop before street numbers had become common, had remained as "fixtures". They were knocked down for the sum of three shillings and sixpence!

---

[1] All contemporary directories enter Thead (or Theed) & Pickett, usually as "Goldsmiths and Toymen", from 1759 to 1768. The *London Directory* of 1769 still gives them together, but Kent's Directory for that same year shows that Theed has now retired, for the entry has become, "Pickett, William, goldsmith and toyman . . .". It is thus clear that Theed must have retired in 1768.

[2] Sir Ambrose Heal (*London Goldsmiths*, 1935, p. 115) describes him as a "jeweller & goldsmith" of 76 St. Paul's Churchyard, and his dates as 1768–96. This merely indicates the years in which his name has been found in certain London directories. Two points, however, should be noticed. From the type of his stock in 1744 he would have been described as a toyman, but by the time his name appeared in the Directory he had become a jeweller and goldsmith. The fact that his shop is now numbered suggests that he no longer dealt in fishing-tackle. Perhaps the Golden Salmon had been removed and relegated to a lumber room. It is not stated if 1796 represents the date of his death, but this seems probable.

[3] Directories show that he was still there in 1811.

The premises were subsequently occupied by a series of booksellers—Edward Lacey from 1829–48, Thomas Holmes 1849–63 and D. O. Smith 1864–6. By 1745 Henry Hurt was established on the north side of Ludgate Hill in premises which later were to be numbered 32, but which now were indicated by the sign of a brand new Golden Salmon. He soon increased the scope of his stock by adding cheap light jewellery, box-combs, etc.—in fact he became a toyman. Four years later, in 1749, he was joined by a jeweller named Thomas Chesson,[1] who from 1732 had a business at the Unicorn and Pearl, near Queen Street, Cheapside. Whether Chesson was connected in any way with Hurt in business, or whether he merely rented an upper floor or a number of rooms is not clear, but the latter seems the more probable. In the first place Sir Ambrose Heal tells me that he still kept his sign of the Unicorn and Pearl on his trade-cards, secondly his wife ran a millinery business from the same address until 1754. It is also significant that Fox never mentions Chesson at all. Directories give him as being at Ludgate Hill from 1749 to 1760, which latter date is several years after Hurt's death. Thus there is good reason to believe that Chesson had nothing whatever to do with Hurt in the way of business. As early as 1750 Hurt had an assistant named William Theed,[2] and it would appear that in course of time he was made a partner in the firm, for when Hurt died in (?) 1758 he took over the business.

A certain goldsmith and jeweller named William Pickett had married into the Theed family and was taken on first as a shopman (possibly in Hurt's life-time) and in 1758 as a partner, the firm being known as Theed & Pickett,[3] and appearing thus in directories from 1759–68. It was during this period that the jewellery business was much extended and the sale of plate introduced. Theed seems definitely to have retired in 1768 and to have died in 1772. It was at this juncture that Rundell made his appearance and engaged himself as shopman to Pickett at a salary of £20 a year with a small attic room on the fourth floor of the shop. And here for a moment we must leave him in order to mention the sources of much of the remainder of the story.

By far the most valuable material is to be found in a long manuscript account of the history of the firm written by one of the employees, George Fox, between 1843, the year the firm was finally dissolved, and 1846, the year of the death of the writer. Fox had been a member of the firm from July 1806 to March 1833, so that he participated in most of the events he describes. There appear to have been two men of the same name—perhaps father and son—for in the codicil to Philip Rundell's Will, dated 4th February 1827, he gives and bequeaths to "George Fox, the elder" and others "formerly in my service in business" the sum of £100 each. Thus it is clear that as George Fox the elder had left the firm some time before 1827, the writer of the manuscript, who was with the firm to the very end, can be described as George

---

[1] Both Chesson and Hurt appear in Osborn's *Complete Guide* for 1749.

[2] Heal has in his collection one of Hurt's bills receipted and signed by Theed on 3rd August 1750.

[3] The earliest bill extant is probably that in Heal's collection dated 20th Sept. 1759. It is reproduced on the Plate facing p. 80 of the *London Topographical Record*, Vol. II, 1903. The Golden Salmon occupies a very prominent position on the bill-head.

Fox, junior. He had intended publishing his account, but death intervened and the MS. remained unpublished and unknown. In course of time it became the property of Fox's great-granddaughter, a Mrs. Lydia Burgess Brownson, who presented it to the Baker Library of the Graduate School of Business Administration, Harvard University. An interesting account of it appeared in their *Bulletin*, Vol. XXIII, September 1949, pp. 152–62, by Robert W. Lovett.[1] After corresponding with this gentleman, I had the complete MS. micro-filmed and suggested to the Librarian of the Victoria and Albert Museum that they might like to have it photostated to size. This has now been done so that those interested can consult it in the Library. It proves to be a curious and entertaining document, and, disclaiming all literary merit, the writer has given us an intimate and gossipy account of a fashionable House which he hopes will entertain the "Nobility, Gentry and the Public in general". It is no business history in the modern sense of the word, and it suffers at times from effusion and repetition, but as a first-hand sketch of Philip Rundell and John Bridge and the vicissitudes of the firm it is unique.[2] We are not told exactly what position Fox held in the firm except that it was one of trust. From the fact that he appears to have been at banquets and receptions helping to look after the loaned plate, we may assume that he was one of John Bridge's chief assistants, a position doubtless gained after a long and arduous apprenticeship. Apart from the manuscript are the so-called *Memoirs of Philip Rundell*.[3] They appeared anonymously in 1827, the year of his death, and give a brief account of his life and the history of the firm, interspersed with gossip and anecdotes. A certain amount of information not to be found in the MS. gives them a special value, in particular the Will which is given in full. There was also an undated pirated edition by a Mr. Doran, with a much more racy title and more scurrilous in its contents.[4]

We can now return to Rundell at the commencement of his career. His first task was thoroughly to understand the business, make himself pleasant to the customers and, above all, become more and more indispensable to Pickett. This was not difficult because in the first place he was now quite alone in the business and needed assistance, and secondly he was becoming tired of the work and his only ambition was to attain civic honours. Rundell did all he could to encourage this resolve, assuring Pickett that he was now quite capable of looking after the business himself. This led to Rundell's first important victory—he was taken on as partner and in 1772 the firm

---

[1] I have to thank Mr. G. B. Whitworth, a Director of Hunt & Roskell Ltd. (J. W. Benson Ltd.) for telling me of this.

[2] The MS. consists of fifty sheets, 9½ in. by 15 in., closely written on both sides, two columns to a page. Its number in the Baker Library is MSS.: 597,1843,F792. At the time of writing the number of the photostat copy at the Victoria and Albert Museum has not been fixed.

[3] *Memoirs of the late Philip Rundell, Esq. Goldsmith and Jeweller to His Majesty and the Royal Family, late of The Golden Salmon, Ludgate Hill, who by industry and perseverance accumulated the immense fortune of One Million and a Half. Interspersed with Anecdotes. To which is added, His Will.* By a Gentleman many years connected with the firm. London: Printed and Published by John Fairburn, Broadway, Ludgate-Hill, 1827. Price, one shilling and sixpence. Pp. 42.

[4] "By W. Doran, sixteen years confidentially employed by the Deceased", London: printed by Duncombe, 19, Little Queen St, Holborn. Pp. 18. It was reproduced, enlarged to quarto size, by E. Alfred Jones in "A Royal Goldsmith —Memoir of Philip Rundell, Esqu", *Apollo*, Sept. 1942, pp. 74–6. The Cambridge University Library has copies of both publications bound together (8450.d.129).

became Pickett and Rundell, and thus appears in Kent's *Directory* for that year. Thus released from all business responsibilities Pickett was able to indulge his wishes to the full, which he did with considerable success.[1] Meanwhile Rundell, now left almost entirely to his own devices, sought for means by which he could get the entire business for himself. The first thing necessary was money, and here once again he was lucky for his elder brother Thomas, a doctor, was rich through having married an heiress, one of his patients—a Miss Ketelby. Having thus procured a substantial loan he awaited a suitable opportunity for his next move.

Pickett was a man of moods and liable to fits of deep depression partly occasioned by a domestic tragedy which had occurred at his house in Harpur, Holborn, in 1781, when his favourite daughter, Elizabeth, was burned to death while dressing to accompany her father to an evening party. Finding him in one of these dejected humours Rundell took the opportunity of adding to his misery by telling him that trade was so bad as to be hardly worth the time and trouble of carrying on at all.

What little there was could easily be managed by himself, so if Pickett liked to sell him his share he would take the whole thing over and relieve him of any further trouble and anxiety. "He played his part so well", writes Fox, " that before they parted that evening both of them had signed a Memorandum of Agreement in which they mutually agreed—the one to sell and the other to purchase the share of the business. During the night Mr. Pickett considered what he had done and sincerely repented the bargain he had made, and the next morning wished Mr. Rundell to agree to set the former evening's work aside, but Mr. Rundell with an Oath refused to allow him so to do, and thus placed himself at the head of the House which afterwards was to become the object of envy to all the Trade and the wonder almost of the World." The date of this incident was apparently 1785 for in Lowndes's *London Directory* for 1786, Pickett's name has gone, and "Rundell, Philip, goldsmith, 32 Ludgate Hill" is substituted. So also in 1787. Kent, however, still prints "Pickett and Rundell" for these two years, while in 1788 all directories have "Rundell and Bridge".

But if the *Memoirs* are to be credited, Fox has not told us the whole story. It appears from these that a few years previously Pickett, perhaps with a view to keeping the business in the family, had offered Rundell the hand of his only surviving daughter, Mary. But Rundell had already formed his plans and a wife did not form part of them.

1 He was elected Alderman of Cornhill Ward in 1782, having unsuccessfully contested Cordwainer Ward in the previous year. He served as Sheriff in 1784. At the Common Hall for the election of Lord Mayor in 1788 he proposed the demolition of Temple Bar, but received no support. He was Lord Mayor in 1789. Among his improvements may be mentioned the demolition of the block of houses lying between Butcher's Row and the Strand, the thoroughfare north of St. Clement Danes Church being then known as Pickett Street. It disappeared, however, when the site was cleared for the erection of the Law Courts between 1874 and 1880. Pickett was a Liveryman of the Goldsmiths' Company, and was anxious to be elected to the Court of Assistants, but ordinary courtesy appears to have been sadly lacking in the Company at that time (see *Memorials of the Goldsmiths' Company*, Vol. II, p. 280, for 16th June 1786), and, after ignoring Pickett's letter, no order was made. In 1790 and again in 1796, the year of his death, he unsuccessfully contested London in parliamentary elections as a Whig. See A. Beaven, *Aldermen of the City of London*, 1908, Vol. II, p. 137, and E. Beresford Chancellor, *Annals of the Strand*, 1912, pp. 17, 18, 74 and 75. I am indebted to Mr. Raymond Smith, Librarian and Curator of Guildhall Library, for these references.

In after years he confessed that the only lady to whom he ever gave a thought, as far as marriage was concerned, was Mary Wilkes, the daughter of the celebrated John Wilkes. Mary Pickett had shares in her father's business and after his death in 1796 Rundell bought her out for a yearly sum finally fixed at £1,000. If this is true she must have held a large number of shares, and it is obvious that Rundell did not become sole owner of the firm after the fateful night of 1785.

As we shall shortly see, a new assistant had been taken on by the firm in 1777, one John Bridge, and so hard working, competent and trustworthy did he prove to be that after Pickett's "retirement" Rundell left much of the management of the shop to him.

Just as Pickett had enjoyed the winning of civic honours, so now Rundell showed a very marked *penchant* for the theatre and the company of actors and actresses. He was on intimate terms with such famous actors as Thomas King and Charles Bannister, while one of his own nieces, Elizabeth Harper, was the principal singer at the Haymarket. She subsequently married Charles's son, John Bannister, the well-known comic actor. "He was naturally what the world calls a Gay Fellow", writes Fox, "and he might often be seen at his shop door early of a morning with his jockey cap, scarlet coat, buckskin smalls, booted and spurred waiting the arrival of his groom with the horses that he might go and follow the chase to settle himself down a little after a night spent over the Bottle or the Card Table." So while Rundell was indulging his pleasures, Bridge made himself more and more indispensable. He was fully aware of the fact that he was being underpaid, and that he would never become a partner in the firm unless he paid for it—so that was exactly what he did! In 1788 Bridge became a partner of the firm, and the name was changed to Rundell & Bridge, and, as already noted, appeared thus in the London directories for that year. From this date all the future prosperity of the House took its rise. But we must first learn a little more about John Bridge, how he came to join Pickett & Rundell, and how he got the money to buy the partnership.[1]

John Bridge, the eldest of three sons of Thomas (d. 1792) and Mary (d. 1779), was born at Piddletrenthide,[2] Dorset, on 21st January 1755. In 1769 he was apprenticed, strangely enough, to the same man as Rundell had been—William Rogers of Bath, to whom he paid a premium of £42.[3] His apprenticeship finished, he went to London in 1777, being then twenty-two years old, and (whether by chance or, more probably, at the advice of Rogers) applied for a position with Pickett & Rundell. He was taken on as a shopman and, as has already been mentioned, applied himself so thoroughly to mastering every branch of the business that he became an invaluable

[1] According to W. Doran's edition of the *Memoirs*, p. 6, Bridge left the firm for a short period, having been offered a more lucrative situation in Bond Street, but was induced to return by an offer of a share in the business. If this is true, it was perhaps only a piece of clever bluff on Bridge's part to make Rundell realize how indispensable he was. The "share" in the business became a partnership as soon as the necessary money was forthcoming.

[2] The village lies on the River Piddle, seven miles north of Dorchester. The church is full of the Bridge family memorial tablets. See John Hutchins, *History and Antiquities of Dorset*, 3rd edit., 1870, Vol. IV, pp. 486–8.

[3] Apprenticeship Records, Great Britain, Inland Revenue Books, 26/51.

member of the firm—but just how valuable even Rundell had no suspicion at this time. Bridge had a cousin, two years his junior, also named John, who was a wealthy and highly successful farmer living at Wynford Eagle,[1] seven miles ENE. of Bridport. It was from him that Bridge borrowed the money to buy the partnership. Farmer John Bridge was highly regarded in all agricultural matters and his advice was constantly sought and as often quoted.[2] In June 1789 George III left Windsor after his first serious illness to recuperate at Weymouth, and his interest in agriculture prompted him to call at Wynford Eagle in order to discuss Bridge's mode of farming. A mutual respect and understanding was the outcome of this visit and among other marks of Royal favour the King ordered a flock of fine Merino sheep to be driven over to Dorset from his farm at Windsor.[3]

At one of the many meetings which followed, Farmer Bridge told George III about his cousin's firm at Ludgate Hill and begged of the King his support for him and Royal recommendation. This was promised and as graciously fulfilled. On his return to London John Bridge was sent for and so pleased the King that he was introduced to the Queen, the whole of the Royal family, as well as many members of the Court and nobility. But this was not all, for "whenever he heard of a marriage about to take place in the great world, he would almost command the parties to go to Ludgate Hill for any Plate or Jewels they might want for the occasion, and very many splendid orders were received in consequence".

His Majesty not only gave the firm his private business, but caused the Lord Chamberlain to appoint Messrs. Rundell & Bridge to the office of Jewellers, Gold & Silversmiths to the Crown, and they also obtained a similar warrant from H.R.H. the Prince of Wales, the Duke of York and Princes and Princesses of the Royal family. Thus Rundell had indeed been lucky when he took Bridge as a partner! It will be readily understood that this sudden vast increase of business necessitated the acquiring of a much better stock. The shop had been enlarged after the partnership had been formed, and the stock improved, but now the whole standing of the firm was on a new level and the type of merchandise had to keep pace with the new *clientèle*. Not yet having their own manufactory, the new stock would be obtained from the usual wholesale houses and individual goldsmiths who worked entirely for the "trade". This was satisfactory so far as it went, but any firm could do exactly the same thing and get a very similar stock. What was needed now was something new and "exclusive"—jewellery and plate which by the excellence of its setting, the beauty of its design and high quality of its workmanship would have an instant appeal to the "Nobility and Gentry".

The French Revolution provided just what was wanted. The refugees, whose sole

[1] The house was known as Manor Farm and was rebuilt about 1630. For a good photograph and description see *An Inventory of the Historical Monuments in Dorset*, Vol. I, West. Roy. Comm. Hist. Mon., 1951, Pl. 206 and pp. 269, 270. The present tenant tells me that George III is said to have stayed at Wynford Eagle when discussing agricultural matters with Bridge.

[2] William Stevenson, *General view of the agriculture of the County of Dorset*, 1812, Board of Agriculture, *passim*.

[3] For the results of the experiments which followed see *Annals of Agriculture*, Vol. XL, 1803, p. 350.

wealth consisted in what jewellery and plate they were able to bring with them, on asking where they could best dispose of it were naturally directed to the Royal Gold-smiths. Thus Rundell was able to acquire a large amount of French plate by the leading craftsmen.[1] Apart from jewellery, in which he was particularly interested,[2] he would make his first acquaintance with the rococo work of Meissonier and his school, the fine table services of Thomas Germain and of his son François. Then there would be examples of the beautiful sauce-boats and tureens of Jacques Roettiers and the classic grandeur of Henry Auguste. No wonder Philip Rundell, *the jeweller*, was soon looking for a really first-class craftsman who could use some of this French plate as a pattern-book and produce articles of similar quality and design.

The renewal of the war with France in 1803 and the consequent advance of rents generally, from which the landed gentry profited, produced a fresh outburst of extravagance and orders for large services of plate and costly suites of jewellery poured into Ludgate Hill. By this time Edmond Waller Rundell, the eldest son of Philip's deceased brother Thomas, had joined the firm, bringing with him more capital to increase the stock. His mother (the former Miss Ketelby previously mentioned) became famous as a writer of cookery books and produced the earliest manual of household management (see *Dictionary of National Biography*). One of her daughters, Maria, married Thomas Bigge, who joined the firm in 1807. In 1804 John Bridge had introduced his nephew John Gawler Bridge, who served as an assistant to his uncle for more than seven years without any salary. In 1817 he became a partner. But we are anticipating. The name of the firm had been altered in 1805 to Rundell, Bridge & Rundell, and with the great increase of business a manufactory had been established in Greenwich.[3] Since 1796 Paul Storr had been producing first-class work from his place in Air Street, Piccadilly, and both Rundell and Bridge recognized the hand of the master craftsman. As a goldsmith working on his own, the whole trade could order from him, and Rundell was anxious to persuade him to work for him entirely. What inducements he offered we do not know but it may have included the promise of a partnership, for he only joined the firm in 1807 and was a partner some time before 1811. As was mentioned in the last chapter William Theed, R.A., was another of the partners at this time. Theed (no relation of the man of the same name who figures earlier in the history of the firm) deserves some notice here, if only because Storr worked from many of his designs. He was born in 1764, and became a student in the Royal Academy schools in 1786, turning his attention chiefly to classical subjects. Subsequently he visited Rome where he became friendly with Flaxman (who also worked for Rundell) and largely due to his advice forsook the brush for the chisel. On returning to England he worked for Wedgwood till 1803

[1] It is said also that he secured a considerable amount of cash, jewels and plate deposited with him at an earlier date by members of the French nobility who saw the trouble coming. But neither they nor their heirs lived to claim their property.

[2] According to the *Memoirs*, Rundell had bought up "Mr. Duvall . . . a leading jeweller . . . honoured by the custom of the Royal Family". This was doubtless John and Peter Duval of 5 Warnford Court, Throgmorton Street.

[3] I can find out nothing about this. Fox alone mentions it and adds that the best workmen and artists were employed. It could have been only temporary until the acquiring of the one in Dean Street managed by Storr.

when he was persuaded by Rundell to come and work for him. Joseph Farington in his famous *Diary*[1] gives us a glimpse of Rundell's methods. He records a visit on 4th July 1811 from Theed, who told him of his employment by Rundell. On 20th September of the same year Farington called to see him at Dean Street and writes: "He shewed me several of his models: Candelabriums for the Prince of Wales & other works, and described the great scale on which Rundle & Bridge (silversmiths) carry on their works." Finally, on 2nd February 1813 Theed calls again: " . . . He mentioned some inconvenience which He suffered from their intruding their opinions in matters of taste & design, & sd. he would always go one better if He had access to the Noblemen or Gentlemen who gave them Commissions and were easily led to adopt His opinions."

After some years Theed was made a partner of the firm and remained working there till his death in 1817. Opinions as to his skill as a sculptor differ.[2] Some writers describe his works as "very interesting and creditable", or have no opinion to offer; while others, such as E. B. Chancellor, are scathing: "In his hands the already obviously decadent Georgian school of sculpture appeared always at its worst, his was the last word in effeteness, and he would hardly require mention but that his name has somehow survived as is occasionally the case with mediocrities, in the midst of those of better and more notable men." Luckily for Theed, perhaps, we do not know which of Storr's "presentation" pieces were designed by him, so we can offer no opinion.

And so at last Rundell had got everything his own way. In Bridge he had the ideal partner able to do just those things which he himself was incapable of doing. In Storr he had found the best craftsman of the day. He could afford to hire any artist or sculptor he needed, and business was so great that he could hardly cope with the orders which flowed in from all parts of the world. Agents or correspondents were established not only in Paris, Vienna and St. Petersburg, but also in Constantinople, Smyrna, Baghdad, Calcutta, Bombay and South America. Well-known diplomatists and orientalists, such as Sir Harford Jones Brydges and Sir Gore Ouseley, did not conceive it "derogatory in themselves in many instances to interfere in the arrangement of business for the firm". Doubtless such "arrangement" included the purchase of diamonds and other precious stones, and the obtaining of orders from Oriental potentates. Fox tells us that Rundell sent consignments of jewels annually to the Celestial Empire, via Manilla.

So far we have only looked at Rundell & Bridge as a firm and traced its history to a few years after Storr had joined it. But what of the personal characters of Rundell and Bridge? Their characters are of importance in the present work, because if we know something about them we can the better understand why Storr left the firm and continued work on his own. We can first see what Fox has to say about them, for

---

[1] The *Farington Diary*, Edit. James Greig, Vol. II, 1927, pp. 11, 34 and 147.
[2] W. Sandby, *History of the Royal Academy of Arts*, Vol. I, 1862, pp. 382–3; *Dictionary of National Biography*; and, for the adverse criticism, E. Beresford Chancellor, *Lives of British Sculptors*, 1911, pp. 217–8.

from his MS. he appears to have been a shrewd judge of character, and he was with them daily from 1806 until Rundell died in 1827 and Bridge in 1834.

No two men could have been more opposite in temper and disposition than were Mr. Rundell and Mr. Bridge—indeed so opposite were they that many designated them by the names of Oil and Vinegar. Mr. Rundell was naturally of a violent disposition, very sly and cunning, and suspicious in the extreme. Avarice, covetousness and meanness were so deeply rooted in him that it affected every feature of his face and entered into every action of his life! Not but that he would often perform deeds which would have entitled any other man to the character of a generous person, but when performed by him they seemed to loose all their value in the manner they were performed, seeing that if he benefitted any individual it was with the intent of wounding the feelings of some others or not infrequently with the hope of exalting the person benefitted on a pedestal from which he might in some unexpected moment hurl him down again lower than he was before he raised him up. In his shop he was ever the petty despotic King, not only over his servants, but also over his partners, and all the trades-people he employed, and swearing, scolding and noise were the order of the day, and of every day. . . . Mr. Bridge was quite a different man. He was naturally of a timid quiet disposition, and had philosophically learnt to keep down any Violent temper he might have had, and he would hear any insults or brook any imposition rather than he would contend against his more violent Partner, and this he did not more from the love of peace and quietness than from a strong desire to carry on the business in such a manner as eventually to produce for him the large Fortune which he in the process of time obtained. He could perform well on his own stage or amongst his Customers out of doors, for although he possessed as much Pride as any Person need have yet to any one and to every one by whom he expected to gain any thing he was apparently the most humble and obedient Person that could well be imagined, his back was exceedingly flexible and no man in London could bow lower or oftener than could Mr. Bridge. In fact he was a complete Courtier and was highly respected both in the Palaces of Princes, and the Halls of Servants, for his great humility in the former, and his great conde-scension in the latter. He well knew it was of great importance to him to stand well with all the Servants in a great House and he had learnt (as he often confessed it) that the nearest way to My Lady's Boudoir was down the Area Steps through the Servants Hall and from thence to the Housekeepers Room and so up stairs to My Lady!

The *Memoirs* echo the same sentiments. Rundell was dirty in both his habits and his dress, practically starved himself, never spent a penny if he could avoid it, and even refused to carry out necessary repairs to the shop. His mean and petty mind is shown in countless ways. He pretended to be deaf in order to hear what people said about him, he had the habit of inspecting the workmen's books and private lockers in the middle of the night, in order to trip them up on some trivial point in the morning. Bridge was so accustomed to this sort of thing that he invented a private code for his notes, as even his books were not free from the prying eyes of the "Old Gentleman", as he was called. Rundell never owned a decent house. He lived in Bridge Street, Blackfriars, in order to save a coach ride to business, and stayed for long periods with one or other of his numerous relations, as he was always sure of a warm welcome—by anticipation! Although he never married, he kept a mistress—a Mrs. Wartridge by whom he had two sons; and it was in her house that he died—on 13th February 1827. In his will, printed in full in both editions of the *Memoirs*, he only mentions her in the Codicil, together with various clerks, porters, coachmen, cooks, etc.! Of the million and a half which he left, the bulk—over £900,000—went to his great-nephew Joseph Neeld, who had taken care of him during the last fourteen years of his life.

Fox tells many other tales of this strange man, but sufficient has been said to show the type of man he was, and why Paul Storr finally reached a point when he could stand it no more. Fox places the peak of prosperity of the firm in the year 1816, and Storr left four years later just when the decline started to set in. Philip Rundell retired in 1823 and in accordance with the partnership agreement, his shares were paid for over six years at five per cent. interest. The remaining members of the firm formed a new partnership to last seven years, at the end of which time Edmond Rundell also retired. The firm then started speculating in mining stock in America with disastrous results. Edmond Rundell remarked dryly that "the very best mine he ever knew was the Mine on Ludgate Hill which had been hitherto very productive and would still continue to yield more profit than any South American Mine would ever yield if the parties interested in it would but work it the proper way". He retired in disgust in 1830. A new firm, composed of John Bridge, his nephew and Thomas Bigge, was formed, but with the death of Bridge in 1834 it came to an end. In the spring of 1842 notice was given of sales at reduced prices, and on 13th July (originally advertised for 11th July) began a great ten-day sale of the stock at Messrs. Christie & Manson of King Street, St. James. From the marked auctioneer's catalogue (which Mr. A. G. Grimwade has allowed me to consult) there were 1,671 lots in all, while the final total of the sale was about £20,000. Many of the lots were bought in, and apparently were included in the sale of the business which followed soon afterwards. This will be discussed shortly. There were two bronze copies of the famous shield of Achilles, designed and modelled by Flaxman, which were presented to Oxford and Cambridge respectively. They are now in the Ashmolean and Fitzwilliam museums. The remaining bronze copy of the Warwick Vase was sold to the Duke of Northumberland, who had been elected Chancellor in 1840, for presentation to Cambridge University.

In a final effort to keep the firm going the writer of the MSS., George Fox, and two of his fellow workmen were offered a chance to purchase the property, but all things considered the price seemed high and they knew that trade was moving west. This was the end.

But in order to complete the history of the firm with which Storr spent the twelve best years of his working life, we must glance briefly at events which followed the sale. It concerns the statement that the firm of Rundell, Bridge & Rundell (or rather Rundell, Bridge & Co. as it was from 1833 onwards) was purchased by Francis Lambert and transferred to Coventry Street. This allegation was apparently first made, without comment or reference, by F. J. Britten in his well-known work on *Old Clocks . . . and their makers*. Sir Ambrose Heal copied the statement (from the 5th edition, p. 770) as a note to the Rundell entry in his *London Goldsmiths*, p. 236. In view of the fact that the successors of Messrs. Lambert, Messrs. Harman & Lambert of 177 New Bond Street, have lost their entire archives, it is almost impossible to reconstruct this final chapter of the story. If William Chaffers (*Gilda Aurifabrorum*, 1899, pp. 95–6) is correct, the founder of the business was Francis Lambert, who while employed by a certain Mr. Clark met Thomas Hamlet, the natural son of the notorious Sir Francis Dashwood,[1] who was also an assistant in the same firm. About 1800[2] Hamlet and Lambert took a shop at 2 St. Martin's Court, Leicester Square. Hamlet then moved to the corner of Princes Street (later Wardour Street) and Sidney's Alley, which ran from Princes Street to Leicester Street. He promised to take Lambert on as a partner, but this did not materialize. Lambert became ill and went to Lisbon where he started a kind of bazaar. It was not successful and he returned to England and opened a silversmith's shop at 11 and/or 12 Coventry Street at the corner of Arundel Street, leading to Panton Square.[3] William Rawlings, who had lived with Thomas Hamlet, was taken on as his manager, with a share of the profits, and the firm of Lambert & Rawlings was formed. As the bill-head in my collection proves, this firm was still active in 1826–7. According to Chaffers, Lambert died in 1841 and his son George continued the now successful business after his death. Rawlings died in 1862.

After the shop had been pulled down in 1923, the firm moved to New Bond Street as Harman & Lambert. Meanwhile Hamlet had flourished, and his shop, patronized by Royalty, had become a fashionable meeting-place for the *jeunesse dorée*. But this may have been the beginning of his downfall, for it was said that he was unable to recover certain bonds of the Prince Regent and the Duke of York and became greatly impoverished. Then followed unsuccessful speculation in pearl fisheries, and finally the transforming of the Queen's Bazaar near Oxford Circus, which had been burnt out in 1829, into a theatre to be named

[1] See Ronald Fuller, *Hell-Fire Francis*, 1939. Shorter accounts appear in Lionel Cust, *History of the Society of Dilettanti*, 1914, pp. 9, 28, 43, 46–9 *et passim*; and E. Beresford Chancellor, *The Hell Fire Club*, 1925. For further references see the biography in the *Dictionary of National Biography* (Supplement, Vol. II, 1901).

[2] In the South Kensington Catalogue of the 1862 Exhibition, Chaffers (p. 496) describes plate of 1758 and 1761 as by Thomas Hamlet. This is a mistake for Thomas Heming.

[3] This little square was laid out by its owner, Colonel Thomas Panton, in the seventeenth century, and the narrow street leading to it from Coventry Street was called Panton Passage (later Arundel Street). It is ignored in many maps, and where it does appear the spellings vary: Arrindoun (1803), Arringdoun (1819), Arundal (1827) and Arundel (1836). See further C. L. Kingsford, *Early History of Piccadilly, Leicester Square, Soho & their neighbourhood*, Cambridge, 1925, p. 113. For Sidney or Sidney's Alley, see pp. 55–6.

the Princess,[1] after the future Queen Victoria. So elaborate was the building that it was not opened till 5th October 1840 (three years after the Princess had become Queen!). Hamlet started with promenade concerts, then put on *La Sonnambula* on 26th December 1842, and the next year he went bankrupt. He became a pensioner at the Charterhouse and died about 1849.

And so ends the story of Philip Rundell, his associates, and successors.

[1] For the history of this theatre see H. Barton Baker, *The London Stage*, Vol. II, 1889, pp. 159–86; and especially the detailed account, with photograph, in Erroll Sherson's *London's Lost Theatres of the 19th century*, 1925, pp. 121–84.

CHAPTER FIVE

MISCELLANEA

THE REGISTERED MARKS

*1st M*ark **P·S** **P·S**

PAUL STORR registered his first mark on 12th January 1793 and was entered as a Plate Worker of 30 Chuch [Church] Street, Soho. Two specimens are shown, both being Roman capitals in a plain oblong shield with clipped or shaped corners. The mark to the left clearly shows a dot or pellet between the letters, that to the right being somewhat smaller. The fact that this first mark was registered in January explains why some of his early pieces bear the Roman small ''r'', the letter for 1792, as the goldsmiths' year of 1793 did not take effect until 29th May, the new letter being first struck on the morning of 30th May. It follows that all dates on plate should be given as covering part of two years, thus the Roman small ''r'' is the date-letter for 1792–3 and not 1792.[1]

2nd Mark **P S**

The second mark was registered on 27th April of the same year (1793). The lettering is Roman capitals, without the dot or pellet, the outline of the shield resembling twin circles in contact, with two small concave indents at the bottom producing a point.

3rd Mark **P S**

The third mark was registered on 8th August 1794 and closely resembles the second mark. There are, however, certain differences. It is very much smaller, there is a dot between the letters, and the indents are further apart and so produce a lobe instead of a point. In the next line of the Register is a note stating that on 8th October 1796 Storr ''removed to No. 20 Aire [or Air] S͆ Saint James''.

---

[1] The date-letter, introduced in 1478 during the reign of Edward IV, was formally known as the ''Touch Warden's Mark'', the ''Assayers' Touch'' and the ''Wardens' Mark''. It took the form of a letter of the alphabet which was changed every year on 19th May, the anniversary of the death in A.D. 988 of St. Dunstan, the patron saint of goldsmiths. Consequently, it became more commonly known as the ''Alphabetical mark'', the ''Annual Letter'', and finally the ''Date-letter'', or ''–mark''. After the Restoration the date for the election of the wardens, i.e. the commencement of the goldsmiths' year, was changed to 29th May and has remained so ever since. This, however, applies only to London —other Offices selecting dates in accordance with their own traditions.

4th Mark **PS**

The fourth mark was registered from "No. 20 Are St. Pickadily" on 29th November 1799 and is merely a larger version of the third mark.

5th Mark **PS** **PS** **PS** **PS** **PS**

In the summer of 1807 Storr moved to Rundell's manufactory at 53 Dean Street, Soho, and on 21st August of that year registered his fifth mark. It was similar to the third and fourth but with two differences: (1) the dot or pellet is no longer centred between the two letters, but has been moved to the bottom; (2) the concave indents producing the point resemble those in the second mark, and occur both above and below the letters. Two sizes of this fifth mark are shown, one large and the other (of which four examples are given) about a quarter the size.

6th Mark **PS** **PS**

On 18th February 1808 a further mark was registered very similar to the fifth, but with slightly deeper indents.

7th Mark **PS**

On 15th December 1808 a minute mark was registered, small enough to be used for jewellery. It resembles two tiny circles in contact, and has no dot. So close do the rows of the marks now become in the Register that it is difficult to be sure to which date they all belong.

8th Mark **PS** **PS** **PS** **PS** **PS** **PS**

It seems most probable, however, that to 21st October 1813 belong the group of six, consisting of the same mark in three different sizes, each repeated twice. Although the examples are all very worn, the marks are practically indentical with No. 5, the dot at the base of the letters being just visible in two cases.

9th Mark **PS** **PS** **PS** **PS** **PS** **PS** **PS** **PS**

This mark has no dot between the letters, and the outline of the shield resembles two ovals rather than circles. Two examples each of five different sizes are shown.

The mark was registered on 12th September 1817, and in the next line of the Register is a note saying that on 4th March 1819 Storr moved to Harrison Street, Grays Inn Road.

10th Mark

On 2nd September 1833 a fresh mark was registered, the address being 17 Harrison Street, Grays Inn Road. This may be a mistake for 18, as given in the Directories, or else it may be part of the adjoining house, with its entrance in Francis Street, which Storr also owned and had leased to Messrs. Garrard in 1831. The mark has a double circular outline again. There is no dot, and the points, top and bottom, are longer than in any previous mark.

11th Mark

On 17th December 1834 Storr registered his last mark, or rather, as the Register records: "2 New Marks." To the eye, however, they appear identical, the only difference from the tenth mark being that the points are not so pronounced.

THE PORTRAIT

The portrait reproduced in this book can, I think, be accepted as that of Paul Storr with some confidence. None other is known to exist. I first heard of this painting from Sir C. K. Adams, the Director of the National Portrait Gallery, who said it belonged to a connection of Storr's by marriage, and showed me a photograph. By a coincidence, the owner turned out to be my old friend of boyhood days, Edward Stapleton, who had married Frances Mary Champneys, the granddaughter of Storr's fourth daughter, Mary Anne. The latter died in 1891, and on the death of her last surviving daughter, Mary, there was found among her belongings a box containing a number of family portraits. Two of these portraits formed a pair, painted on wood panels, 10 in. by $7\frac{1}{4}$ in., and depicting a middle-aged man and woman in early-nineteenth-century clothes. To take the woman first: her features are unmistakably Jewish, and to that extent they could very well be those of Elizabeth Susanna, the wife of Paul Storr. It is worth observing that certain of Storr's earlier descendants are known to have been somewhat coy of acknowledging this element in their heredity, and this might account for the obscurity to which the paintings were consigned. For the companion portrait of the man, I sought the help of the experts. James Laver, Keeper of the Prints and Paintings at the Victoria and Albert Museum, and Graham Reynolds, the expert on miniatures, observed that the sitter must have been about fifty, and that the clothes suggest a date between 1820 and 1830. Sir C. K. Adams agreed, adding that the date would appear to be not a great deal later than 1820, because soon after that the shirt collar began to appear above the neck-cloth. The portrait, then, was probably painted soon after 1820, and is of a man about fifty years old. How does this agree with Storr's age? It agrees well enough. He was fifty in 1821.

Let us see, now, what notion we can form of the man portrayed. I asked the opinion of Laurence Whistler, who is the great-great-grandson of Paul Storr, himself a craftsman and artist of no mean order, as well as a writer. He had this to say:

The figure is seated in a chair of contemporary design, and on the table beside him is a book, and a folded paper, which might perhaps be a letter; and in the fingers there is a pair of spectacles. There is nothing to indicate the silver-smith or goldsmith. But that is not significant. A highly successful man, in later years, commissioning twin portraits of himself and his wife, perhaps to celebrate some family event, might not wish to be painted with the emblems of his craft or trade. He might prefer to be portrayed simply as a gentleman. Of the face, one can only say that it is easily acceptable as that of Paul Storr. It seems to be the face of a successful man of middle-class origin, self-reliant, possessed of considerable character, and, one would add, generosity. More than that, it is the face of a craftsman, or at least of a man whose ideas (and one can believe that the ideas behind that forehead are worth while) find ready expression in physical action: the face of a man who knows how to use his hands. Paul Storr, in fact, *ought* to have looked like this. We may conclude, on the evidence as a whole, that he did.

PLATE III

Union Street, Westminster. Drawn by William Capon on 10th October 1804. His notes on the state of the houses, their colours, etc., still remain and can be quite clearly read on the original. The fire actually took place in the early hours of Wednesday, 3rd October, not 2nd October as stated by Capon.

From the original at Westminster Public Library

Looking down St. Margaret's Street towards Old Palace Yard. Drawn by William Capon, 1806. In the right-hand corner we see the "site of Godfree's late house which stood on the spot where now is this Hord". To the left is the Coach and Horses, outside which Capon has drawn an actual coach and horses in faint outline.

From the original at Westminster Public Library

TWO TEA-POTS—SILVER

THE earlier of these two tea-pots is oval and quite plain except for the running wave-and-lotus band on a matted ground between pearl borders. The slightly domed lid has a running floral border. The stand is of classical design, the beaded edge being supported by flat fluted columns on ball feet surmounted by sheep's heads. Laurel swags depend between the heads. Concave beaded stretchers are applied at the juncture of the columns and feet.

Length from handle to spout: $11\frac{1}{2}$ in.   Maker: Fogelberg and Gilbert.
Height to top of knob: $5\frac{1}{2}$ in.   London date-letter for 1786–7.
Weight: 24 oz. 3 dwt.

With the above we can compare the later tea-pot which is the same in every detail, except that at a later date further, and quite unnecessary, chasing has been added on the body, lid and spout.

Length from handle to spout: 11 in.   Maker: Paul Storr
Height to top of knob: $6\frac{1}{2}$ in.   London date-letter for 1799–1800.
Weight: 25 oz. 5 dwt.

It is clear from a comparison of these two tea-pots that Storr had copied a design used when with Fogelberg and Gilbert at 30 Church Street in 1792.

By courtesy of S. J. Shrubsole of London and New York

PLATE IV

CUP AND COVER—SILVER-GILT

VASE-SHAPED, with slender high-shouldered handles divided in the middle by a small water-leaf knop. The lower, and tapering, half is plain and partially wrapped by a long lanceolate leaf. The upper half is reeded, having acanthus leaves on the top of the shoulder as it curves down to terminate in an open acanthus leaf by which it is attached to the broad running border, on matted ground, of vine-stems, grapes, leaves and tendrils, which ornaments the rim of the vase. The body is plain except for the broad border already mentioned, and a calyx of long, pointed lanceolate leaves. A narrow, convex laurel-leaf moulding divides the main body from the shallow, fluted trumpet-shaped foot, the upper part of which is encircled by a narrow wave moulding. The plain round base is surmounted by a band of broad water-leaves. The elegant, concave, shallow fluted cover closely resembles the foot in design, having a narrow running floral band on matted ground, at the top, above which is a convex laurel-leaf border also on matted ground, surmounted by a dome chased with small lanceolate leaves from which springs an acorn-like finial, the lower half of which is fluted, and the upper half of tightly gathered leaves. Around the lower part of the cover is a broad band of roses intertwined with ribbons, between plain fillets. A narrow edging of water-leaf design completes the decoration.

Engraved on one side are the arms, encircled by the Garter (1788), of John Frederick Sackville, 3rd Duke of Dorset (1745–99). "The gay Duke of Dorset", as he has deservedly been called, was a patron of the Arts, purchasing not only pictures and marbles but vast quantities of plate. On his accession to the dukedom he had bought 4,000 ounces of silver, and Miss Sackville-West records (*Knole*, p. 179) that later he bought further enormous quantities of silver—5,920 ounces in one year alone, costing £2,463 17s. 7d., and including 144 silver plates, eight dozen each of forks and spoons, dishes of all kinds, covers and tureens.

On the other side of the cup is an inscription recording the name of the donor, William Gardiner, and the affection felt by him both for the present Duke and also for his grandparents. This William Gardiner was an Irishman who had entered the service of Lionel Cranfield Sackville, 1st Duke of Dorset, in 1735. He served also under the next two Dukes, and was with the family some sixty years, rising to the position of Superintendent. There is a small oval portrait of him in the Black Boys passage at Knole.

Height, without cover: 1 ft.	Circumference at lip: 1 ft. 10½ in.
Height, with cover: 1 ft. 6 in.	London date-letter for 1792–3.
Diameter: 7½ in.	

From the Collection at Knole. By courtesy of Lord Sackville, K.B.E., etc.

An almost exactly similar cup and cover, made by Paul Storr in the same year, was formerly in the possession of Sarah Otway-Cave, Baroness Braye, whose Arms it bears. The only differences are that the position of the lanceolate leaves and the shallow fluting on the lid is reversed. The vine and grape border is replaced by a narrower floral scroll design. Otherwise the two cups are identical. At the time of writing the Braye cup is in the possession of Messrs. Carrington.

PLATE V

ALMSPLATE—SILVER

THIS forms part of the plate at St. Michael, Begbroke, in the Diocese of Oxford. It is quite plain except for a narrow reeded edging to the rim on which is inscribed "The Gift of the Rector". It is not known for certain who the donor was, but in his *Church Plate of Oxfordshire* (p. 18) J. T. Evans has suggested either John Cooke, B.D. (1776–1823), or Ellis Ashton, B.D., who was rector here from 1823–69.

In the centre of the almsplate are the Arms of Brasenose College, Oxford, Patron of Begbroke. There is also a small silver Flagon made by W. R. Smily in 1852–3. This likewise bears the Brasenose Arms.

Diameter: 9 in. London date-letter for 1792–3.
Weight: 8 oz. 10 dwt.

By courtesy of H. A. McCann, Rector of Begbroke

KETTLE AND STAND—SILVER

OF oval shape, quite plain, sloping towards the base, narrow tapering spout with reeding at juncture with body at its broadest point. Flat swing loop-handle attached to upper part of body by applied water-leaves. Plain reeded rim, into which fits a flattened domical lid with a conventional gadrooned finial. The reeding, noticed on the kettle, is repeated on the stand at several places—on the rim of the saucer-shaped holder, on the four flat concave legs with leonine pads, on the lower edge of the plain oblong concave-sided support for the lamp, and on the top edge of the plain spirit lamp itself.

Diameter at broadest point: 9 in. Height of stand: $4\frac{1}{2}$ in.
Height from base to top of handle: $11\frac{1}{4}$ in. London date-letter for 1793–4.

By courtesy of James Robinson Inc. of Fifth Avenue, New York

This fine example of Storr's early work is interesting from several points of view. It clearly shows his appreciation of the beauty of the plain surface and indicates him as a master of line, restraint and balance. The oval design is an early departure from the more usual globular and pyriform types of the period, and it is only the absolute severity insisted upon that has made a kettle of oval shape such a complete success. Finally, satisfaction is afforded to the eye as it travels from the convex sides of the body to the concave sections of the legs and lamp support.

The piece has twice been illustrated in the *Connoisseur*. It first appeared in January 1938, p. 35, with the illustration on p. 36, where it is shown with two charming sweetmeat dishes, also of 1793. They are only an inch or two high, perfectly plain, except for reeded bases, and arranged in clusters of three little containers or baskets with handles held together by bands of ribbon.

A slightly larger illustration of the kettle and stand, with a brief description, was published in the number for March 1944, pp. 42–3.

PLATE VI

SAUCE TUREEN AND COVER—SILVER

ONE of a pair. Of oval shape and plain body chased with a band of running foliage on a matted ground. A beaded edging surrounds a reeded rim. Two arched reeded loop handles with acanthus decoration extend from the base of the body to a point level with the top of the finial. The plain double-ogee-shaped lid has a bud finial rising from pointed-leaf foliage.

A plain reel-shaped stem separates the body from the oval foot relieved by a beaded edging above the plain base.

Height to top of finial (or top of handles):
  $5\frac{1}{2}$ in.
Height to lowest point of rim: $3\frac{5}{8}$ in.
Overall width to extreme of handles: $9\frac{7}{8}$ in.
Internal bowl measurements: 7 in. by $4\frac{1}{2}$ in.

Oval foot: $3\frac{3}{4}$ in. by $2\frac{5}{16}$ in.
Weight: 52 oz. 15 dwt. (the pair).
London date-letter for 1793–4.

By courtesy of Messrs. Christie, Manson & Woods, Ltd. (25th June 1952, lot 66)

BREAD-BASKET—SILVER

OVAL in shape, the sides consist of a series of seven convex bands, with a threaded rim. The handles at each end are also threaded, with leaf terminals at their juncture with the rim.

Length (under handles): $11\frac{1}{4}$ in.
Breadth: $7\frac{5}{8}$ in.
London date-letter for 1794–5.

Height: $2\frac{9}{10}$ in.
Weight: 24 oz. 6 dwt.

From the Author's Collection

PLATE VII

DINNER SERVICE—SILVER

THIS fine service is quite plain except for a narrow reed-and-tie border throughout. The handles are also reeded, and the tureens stand on square plinths. The ladles to the sauce tureens are of the Onslow pattern. Details of the service are as follows:

72 dinner plates, diam. 10 in.

4 circular second-course dishes, diam. 12 in.

9 oval meat-dishes from 19 in. by 3 in. to 22 in. by 6 in.

2 soup tureens, length 15 in., height 11 in.

6 sauce tureens and ladles, length $8\frac{1}{2}$ in., height 11 in.

4 oblong second-course dishes with Victorian covers $10\frac{1}{2}$ in. wide, on Old
Sheffield Plate warmers, $8\frac{1}{2}$ in. and 6 in. high.
Total weight: 2,482 oz. 15 dwt.
London date-letter for 1794–5.

They are engraved with the Arms of the Right Honourable the Earl of Home.

By courtesy of Messrs. Lewis & Kaye Ltd. and Messrs. Garrard & Co. Ltd.

PLATE VIII

CUP AND COVER—SILVER-GILT

OVIFORM, with reeded handles the height of the body of the cup. Swags of laurel depend from the handle ends and are looped each side at the centre by a circular medallion. The calyx is formed of broad lanceolate leaves, possibly intended for laurel, while similar decoration covers the upper part of the lid, which fits flush and is held in place by a slot near one of the handles. The lid is surmounted by a finial of an archbishop's mitre, a reminder that the Presidents of the S.P.G. are always archbishops. A plain trumpet-shaped foot rests on a circular torus moulding of holm-oak leaves. There is a plain square plinth. On one side is the following inscription:

Feby 19th
1796
From the Society
for the propagation of the Gospel
to
John Brathwaite Esqr
as a permanent mark of their Gratitude & Esteem
for his attention in retrieving their Estates in Barbados
£
and for paying to them the Sum of 12769 cleared beyond the Rent
which they consider as a Benefaction.

On the opposite side are the arms of Brathwaite (or Brathwayte): Gu. on a chev. ar. three crosses crosslet fitchée sa; surmounted by the crest: a greyhound couchant ar. collared and lined gu., the collar studded and ringed or.

Height (including finial): 18½ in.	Circumference of base: 13 in.
Circumference (at centre): 20 in.	Weight: 69 oz. 6 dwt.
Diameter of opening: 5 in.	London date-letter for 1795–6.

By courtesy of Lord Fairhaven, 1st Bt., D.L., J.P., F.S.A.

The inscription calls for some explanation. By his will Christopher Codrington (1668–1710), soldier and Governor of the Leeward Islands, left his two plantations in the island of Barbados, as well as part of the island of Barbuda, to the S.P.G., or as he called it in his will "the Society for the Propagation of the Christian Religion in Forraigne Parts". They entered into possession of the estates in February 1712 and started building a college the following year. Owing to lack of funds the work was slow and the building was not finished until 1745. Matters prospered until 1780 when a terrible hurricane caused the college to be closed for nine years. Debts piled up and as help from England proved insufficient it was decided to lease the estates for £500 a year. John Brathwaite, an esteemed member of the English colony, took over the lease and most generously offered to use any surplus profit in discharging their debts. On 2nd May 1783 Sir John Gay Alleyne, The Society's Attorney, handed over the two plantations. So successful was the enterprise that in the next ten years the Society benefited to the amount of £12,769 19s. 8½d. to be exact. "Bound in the strongest sense of gratitude to express their obligations" for this "large sum", which they regarded "in the light of a benefaction", Mr. Brathwaite was "desired to accept a piece of plate of one hundred guineas value, as a more permanent and public mark of the Society's gratitude and esteem".

See C. F. Pascoe, *Two Hundred Years of the S.P.G.,* 1901, pp. 198–9; and T. H. Bindley, *Annals of Codrington College,* Barbados (1910), pp. 24–6.

PLATE IX

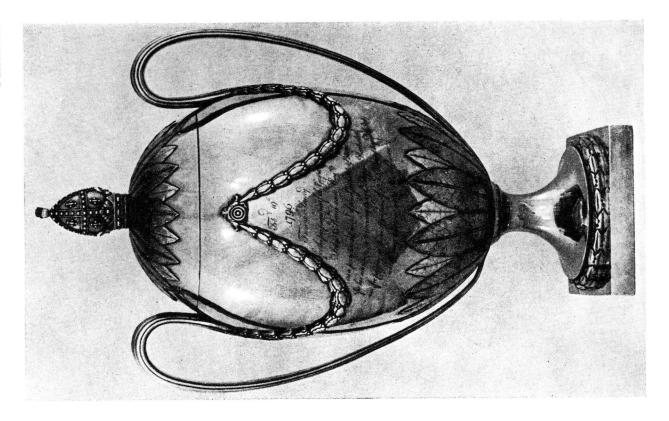

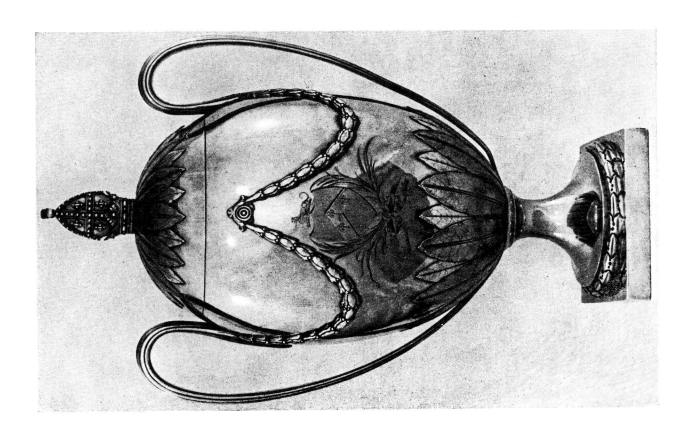

BASKET—SILVER-GILT

THE general effect is that of a basket woven in golden corn. The entwined wire-pattern gallery is turned on the rim in the form of ears of wheat, while the base consists of a band of crossed wire within rope borders.

Height to crest of edge: 5¼ in.
Extreme length: 20½ in.
Extreme breadth: 16 in.
Internal bottom length: 12 in.
Internal bottom breadth: 7¾ in.
London date-letter for 1797–8.

By courtesy of Francis Stonor, Esq.

See the Catalogue of the Sale of the collection of Victor Rothschild, Sotheby & Co., 26th April 1937, lot 20 and Pl. 11.

Storr used very similar baskets to crown centre-pieces or fruit bowls. See Pl. XXXIII of the present work, which shows an example made for the Duke of Wellington in 1810–11.

JUG—SILVER

OF circular shape, completely plain, having three parallel raised bands placed at intervals round the body. The broad flat-sided triangular spout has its lip on the same level as the rim of the jug. In line with the spout on the opposite side is the scrolled ebony handle fitting into two protruding sockets which meet the body at the upper and lower bands respectively. The plain domed un-hinged lift-out lid is surmounted by a mushroom-shaped ebony knop. The finial is a recent repair, being a metal tip to a small wooden bead. The absence of a foot adds to the plain dignity of the jug, almost amounting to severity.

Height: 9 in.
Width (from tip of spout to outer curve
    of handle): 7½ in.
Circumference of body: 13½ in.
Capacity: 2½ pints.
Weight: 16 oz.
London date-letter for 1795–6.

By courtesy of the Misses Storr

With this type of jug it is often difficult to be certain for what purpose it was intended. In the present case, however, an inside strainer points to its use for hot milk. Its shape, capacity and proportions remind us of the coffee-biggin which was soon (c. 1801) to make its appearance. The jug was purchased by Charles Storr, Vicar of Matfield, Kent, and left by him to his son Colonel Lancelot Storr. After the latter's death in 1944 it passed to his four sisters Katherine Cecilia, Margaret Amy, Marion Faithfull and Dorothy Freda.

PLATE X

TRIPOD TAPER-STICK—SILVER

(One of a pair)

THE shafts are of baluster-shape, reeded and enriched at their bases with acanthus leaves. A reel-shaped member surmounting the shafts supports the vase-shaped sockets which have acanthus-leaf calyxes and gadrooned nozzles. The reeded tripod legs project horizontally and bend vertically inwards. They terminate in lions' masks and paws.

Height: $6\frac{3}{4}$ in.   London date-letter for 1797–8.
Weight: 22 oz. 18 dwt. (the pair).

By courtesy of Mrs. Edward Munves of New York City

CHRISTENING FONT—GOLD

FORMED of a circular bowl, plain in the lower part and enriched above by a broad classical border in relief and acanthus foliage at the bottom. The border is surmounted by a plain narrow shelf from the inner edge of which rises the vertical rim with a running floral frieze. The bowl is supported by four winged cherubs' feet. On the square pedestal, with beaded edges, stand figures of Faith, Hope and Charity said to have been made from designs by John Flaxman, R.A.

Made for the christening of William Henry (1796–1824), Marquis of Titchfield, eldest son of William Henry, fourth Duke of Portland. Illustrated in E. A. Jones's *Old English Gold Plate*, 1907, Pl. XXVIII; also his *Catalogue of Plate belonging to the Duke of Portland*, 1935, p. 4, Pl. 1; and the British Red Cross Society Exhibition, June 1915, No. 153.

Height: $4\frac{1}{2}$ in.   The pedestal is $13\frac{3}{4}$ in. square.
Height of the figure Faith $7\frac{1}{4}$ in., and with   Weight: 245 oz.
    cross 9 in.   London date-letter for 1797–8.
Height of Charity $4\frac{1}{2}$ in., and of Hope $4\frac{1}{2}$
    in.

By courtesy of the Duke of Portland, K.G.

PLATE XI

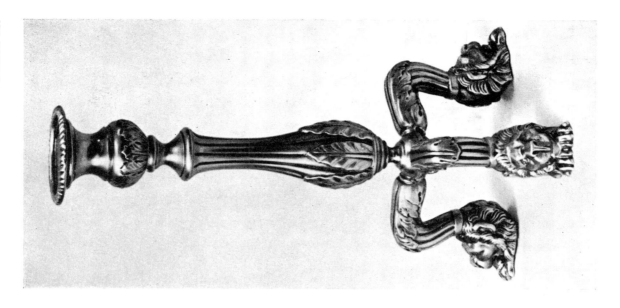

PUNCH BOWL—SILVER

THE oval bowl, quite plain except for a narrow band of laurel leaves which runs through the lion's-head ring handles either side, rests in a calyx of lanceolate leaves. It has a flat gadrooned rim. The high foot is separated from the bowl by a narrow band of laurel and consists of a column decorated with vertical lanceolate leaves and fluting, with a beading separating them. It then splays out with a skirt of applied gadroons on a plain surround. The convex sides of the base display a zig-zag pattern of laurel leaves. The Royal Arms are engraved on the front of the bowl, while in the space above the laurel-leaf band is:

Given by their Majesties
To their God Daughter
Lady Georgina Charlotte Graham
July 1791.

This would appear to be a mistake for Georgiana Charlotte Graham. This lady was the eldest daughter of James, 3rd Duke of Montrose, and his second wife Caroline Maria, daughter of George, 4th Duke of Manchester. Born in 1791 (the bowl was probably presented in 1798), she married George William Finch-Hatten, Earl of Winchilsea and Nottingham (1791–1858), on 26th July 1814. She died 13th February 1835. The Arms of the Graham family are engraved on the opposite side of the bowl.

Her husband will be remembered for his famous duel with the Duke of Wellington in Battersea Fields on 21st March 1829. It was the Catholic Relief Bill of 1829 and in particular a letter from Winchilsea attacking the Duke that brought it about. The first shot fell to the Duke, he fired and missed, whereupon Winchilsea fired in the air and apologized![1]

Length of diameter at rim: 19 in.   London date-letter for 1798–9.
Breadth of diameter at rim: 14 in.

By courtesy of Mr. Ralph Hyman of the Museum Silver Shop, New York City

[1] See *Annual Register*, 1829, pp. 58–63; J. H. Stocqueler, *Life of Wellington*, 1853, Vol. II, pp. 147–8, with portrait of Winchilsea; Andrew Steinmetz, *Romance of Duelling*, 1868, Vol. II, pp. 336–43; and M. Brialmont and G. R. Gleig, *Life of Arthur, Duke of Wellington*, 1860, Vol. III, pp. 351–61.

Plate XII

BEAKER—SILVER

THIS beaker is remarkable in the quiet dignity achieved by its absolute plainness, its gently tapering sides, its absence of foot, and plain banded rim. The interior is gilded. Unfortunately, nothing is known of its history, whether it was one of a set or "nest" of beakers of different sizes, or merely an odd piece made by Storr to emphasize the beauty of silver unadorned.

Height: $3\frac{5}{8}$ in.   Diameter of base: $2\frac{1}{4}$ in.
Diameter of mouth: $3\frac{1}{8}$ in.   Weight: 5 oz.
Circumference of mouth: $9\frac{7}{8}$ in.   London date-letter for 1802–3.

By courtesy of Dr. Anthony Storr

HONEY-POT—SILVER-GILT

MADE in the form of a dome-shaped skep, or beehive, with the separate straw coils bound with strips of briar or wild rose. An enormous bee covers the apex and can be used as a knob for lifting the lid, which is held in place by a pin. The flat-slotted base is detachable. The dish is plain with a border representing a straw coil bound with fillets matching the design of the skep.

Height: 4 in.   Circumference of dish: $17\frac{1}{4}$ in.
Circumference at base: 12 in.   Weight: 14 oz. 10 dwt.
Diameter of dish: $5\frac{1}{2}$ in.   London date-letter for 1799–1800.

From the Collection at Knole. By courtesy of Lord Sackville, K.B.E., etc.

Paul Storr began producing these honey-pots at the beginning of his working life —1792/3—the records of Christie's showing examples from 1793 to 1803 (see Appendix A). They are all very similar except for the handle or knob at the apex. In the example, also of 1799, at the Victoria and Albert Museum there is a looped handle representing plaited straw, with a small bee either side where the handle meets the hive. In other examples there is a vertical ring handle of bound swathes, matching the border of the dish. In some cases it is filled by a disk engraved with a crest or coat of arms. Occasionally there is a hole for a spoon, but this is a later addition.

Josiah Wedgwood made skeps, very like the silver ones of Storr, in cane-coloured stoneware with a glazed interior. See *Catalogue of the Schreiber Collection*, Victoria and Albert Museum, Vol. II, 1930, p. 107, No. 551. It is dated "early 19th century".

PLATE XIII

THE BATTLE OF THE NILE CUP—SILVER

URN-SHAPED, two-handled cup with elaborate Neptune finial. The lower part of the body is decorated with large, broad water-leaves intersected by acanthus foliage on rope stems. The greater portion is plain with an inscription on one side and the Arms of Nelson, surmounted by the Chelengk crest, on the other. Running round the top, like a frieze, above a narrow oak-leaf border, are ten laurel wreaths circling the names of the defeated French ships. The handles, which extend to the full height of the main body of the cup, consist of winged sphinxes issuant from narrow cornucopia. The gently sloping lid is surmounted by a large central pedestal consisting in its lower part of inverted lotus leaves between beaded borders, and in its upper part of a slightly overhanging plinth with a gadrooned base on the sides of which are two rectangular panels depicting a Nile crocodile, separated by garlands of oak and laurel leaves. Above this, resting on the topmost of three circular steps, is a finial of Neptune enthroned, trident in hand, with two dolphins in attendance. The plain spreading foot, separated from the body of the urn by a gadrooned collar, is ringed with a band of oak leaves, while the base is enriched above by a band of water-leaves, and below by a cable. The inscription, surmounted by the Arms of the Levant Company, reads as follows:

> Presented to the / "Right Honble Rear Admiral / Horatio Baron Nelson of the Nile / by the Governor and Company of Merchants / of England trading into the Levant Seas in commemoration / of the Glorious Victory obtained by his Lordship at the Mouth of the Nile on / the first of August 1798 on which ever Memorial day, by the defeat and / capture of a French Squadron superior to his own, he restored to His / Majesty's Arms the Dominion of the Mediterranean and to the / British Merchants the free enjoyment of their ancient and valuable trade to Turkey.

The ten laurel wreaths contain the following account of the captured French ships:

1. Le Guerrier. 74 guns. 600 men. Taken.
2. Le Spartiate. 74 guns. 700 men. Taken.
3. Le Franklin. 80 guns. 800 men.
       Adm l Lanquet. Taken.
4. Le Tonant. 80 guns. 800 men. Taken.
5. L'Aquilon. 74 guns. 700 men. Taken.

       and on the opposite side

6. Le Conquerant. 74 guns. 700 men. Taken.
7. Le Mercure. 74 guns. 700 men. Taken.
8. L'Orient. 120 guns. 1010 men.
       Adm^l Brueys Comm^r in Chief & Le Timoleon.
       74 guns. 700 men. Burnt.
9. L'Heureux. 74 guns. 700 men. Taken.
10. Le Souverain Peuple. 74 guns. 700 men. Taken.

Height: 2 ft. to point of trident.   Weight: 238 oz.
Greatest breadth, with handles: 1 ft. 2½ in.   London date-letter for 1799–1800.
Diameter of opening: 9 in.

By courtesy of the Trustees of the National Maritime Museum, Greenwich

PLATE XIV

SOY FRAME—SILVER

OVAL, or boat-shape, consisting of six reeded rings soldered together and supported on a raised base, with slightly concave sides, by four fluted pilaster legs with leonine pads.[1] These are joined to the base by nut and bolt. Attached to the rings at four points, a central shaft, enriched with matted decoration of square and crescent design, spreads out to receive an oblong open handle with concave corners. The oval sub-base has a reeded edge, acanthus scroll terminals curling downwards, and four small legs in the form of bell-shaped Egyptian lotus capitals. The six rings enclose the same number of contemporary flint cut-glass bottles which taper from the centre in both directions—below into rounded plinths, and above into necks mounted with deep-spreading silver bands at the rims, terminating in twin-lipped spouts. There is, however, one exception—the bottle intended for cayenne pepper has a mount with a rounded rim with a long pepper-spoon fixed to the stopper. The stoppers are spherical and deeply cut to match the central part of the bottles. The arms of Trinity College, Cambridge, are engraved in the centre of the base of the frame together with the words "Trin. Coll. Cant", which also occur on the under rim of the base. As explained in the note below, the term "soy-frame" for this article is a generic one, being used to embrace a number of different sauces, flavourings or essences. It soon became a necessity to label the contents of so many bottles, and the idea of hanging silver labels round the necks of decanters was transferred to the cruets—on a much smaller scale. The date-letter is seldom found on sauce-labels, but with few exceptions they belong to the end of the eighteenth and beginning of the nineteenth centuries. According to the Trinity College Inventory prepared by G. F. Cobb in 1878–9 there was originally a set of sauce-labels for use with this soy-frame, but they have been lost since 1898. The College, however, has been pleased to accept a set from my own collection, which is the work of the well-known label makers Thomas Phipps and Edward Robinson. Heal gives their dates as 1784–96. The names on the labels are as follows: Soy, chili, cayenne, anchovy, lemon and ketchup. These are considered to be the most representative, although in my *Book of the Wine-Label*, pp. 96–7, I have listed sixty different names, apart from variant spellings.

Length: 10½ in.	Weight (of frame): 15 oz. 10 dwt.
Breadth: 4⅞ in.	London date-letter for 1800–1.
Height to top of handle: 9 3/16 in.	The mounts on the bottles have no
Height of pilasters from base: 2¼ in.	maker's mark.

Trinity College, Cambridge. By courtesy of the Master and Fellows

There is a similar soy-frame by Paul Storr among the Mansion House plate, dated 1801–2. Two later ones, of 1816, complete with the six labels, are in the Royal Collection. See *Descriptive Inventory of the various services of Plate, &c. at Windsor Castle & Buckingham Palace . . .*, 1914, Nos. 765 and 1113.

[1] This exact design is to be found at Pompeii in the four legs supporting a marble table in the tetrastyle atrium of the House of Obellius Firmus, often referred to as the Casa del Conte di Torino who was present at the completion of its excavation in 1911. For an excellent photograph see Amedeo Maiuri, *Pompeii*, Istituto Geog. de Agostini, Roma, Parigi [1929], p. 63.

PLATE XV

VASE AND COVER—SILVER-GILT

THIS is converted from the lower part of a tea-urn. It rests in a frame of tripod form on hoof feet surmounted by sphinxes whose wings rest on a broad band, between beaded borders, enriched with alternate anthemions and water-leaves. The horizontal part of the frame supports three grotesque masks and is decorated with a pattern of overlapping quatrefoils, and pendant beads hang like necklaces from the sections which pass over the upper part of the legs. A flat ring similarly decorated passes round and supports the legs below the joints. The flat domed lid of water-leaves is surmounted by a nude water-nymph reclining on a rock round which is a beaded edging.

The whole rests on a triangular plinth, which in turn rests on a stand with water-leaf border. It is supported by leonine pads encircled by beading.

Height: 19½ in.   London date-letter for 1800–1.

The vase was No. 111 at the Woburn Abbey Exhibition held at the Royal Academy in 1950.

By courtesy of the late Duke of Bedford

PLATE XVI

WATER JUG—SILVER

OF helmet shape, with spreading foot and circular base with gadrooned edge. The rim is also gadrooned. A high ebony handle is attached to the jug by silver sockets. Except for the armorial, the surface is absolutely plain.

Height to rim: 10½ in.   Weight: 51 oz.
Height to top of handle: 13 in.   London date-letter for 1801–2.

By courtesy of the Cleveland Museum of Art, John L. Severance Collection

The interest of this jug lies in the fact that it shows the influence of Storr's master, Fogelberg. It is, in fact, based on a cream jug made by Fogelberg and Gilbert about 1780 now in the Victoria and Albert Museum and reproduced here for comparison. It will be noticed, however, that the typical Fogelberg (and Swedish) use of beading and the applied cameo has not been retained by Storr. He has changed the beading for gadrooned edges, while the cameo, which Storr never used so far as I am aware, has not been copied, thus allowing room for a coat of arms on a plain surface. The silver handle of the cream jug has naturally been replaced by an ebony handle in the larger hot-water or hot-milk jug.

TEA-CADDY—SILVER

THIS 1781–2 work of Andrew Fogelberg shows the early use of the pearled border and applied cameo copied later by several Swedish silversmiths.

PLATE XVII

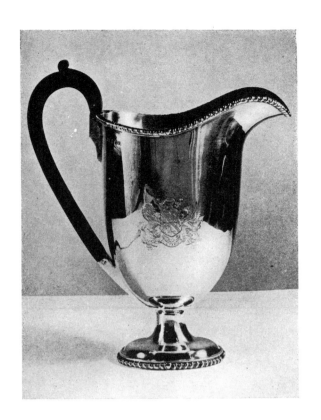

TEA-KETTLE, STAND AND LAMP—SILVER

A LARGE circular tea-kettle, stand and lamp. The kettle has a chased palm-leaf calyx and a broad upper band of diagonal narrow fluting between feathered borders. From the calyx a scaly spigot or vent-peg projects horizontally, terminating in a dolphin's head. The tap, fitted into a square member with floral medallion sides, is operated by a separately attached knob in the shape of an ivory acorn. A double-serpent handle with ivory central grip passes over a low domical lid of palm leaves with an ivory-and-silver finial. A convex ovolo moulding joins the plain edge of the lid. The kettle is engraved on its plain concave shoulder with the Montagu crest and Ducal coronet. The circular stand has a concave upper band of diagonal fluted piercing, matching the band on the kettle, with a narrow guilloche border below. A plain slightly concave moulding, surmounting a vertical border chased with threaded quatrefoils, forms the base. A concave-sided sub-base with guilloche moulding, supporting the concealed cylindrical lamp, is separated from the base by lateral wings attached to a chased acanthus leaf at each corner. Leonine pads below the sub-base, and immediately under the acanthus leaves, form the feet.

Height: 15 in.   London date-letter for 1802–3.
Gross weight: 190 oz.

.Collection of the Duke of Manchester. By courtesy of Messrs. Christie, Manson & Woods, Ltd.
(16th March 1949, lot 38)

PLATE XVIII

ICE-PAIL—SILVER

(Two of a set of four)

THE pails are nearly cylindrical, their rounded bases resting in a calyx of acanthus leaves. Except for the applied Bedford Arms, the lower part is plain. Above is a broad frieze, between plaited borders, with applied Bacchanalian masks, torches, vines, etc. The handles each side consist of two serpents whose heads rest on the broad rims of the pails. The liners and collars are plain. The feet are round and enriched with a border of water-leaves.

Height : 11¼ in.   London date-letter for 1803–4.

By courtesy of the late Duke of Bedford

CRUET—SILVER

OVAL or boat-shaped, consisting of eight reeded rings soldered together and supported on a raised base, etc., exactly like the soy-frame of 1800–1 already described. The only difference here is that the sub-base is edged with gadrooning instead of being reeded. The number of sauce bottles is reduced to four, but the following are added :

1. Two tall ewers (8 in.) for oil and vinegar, with long reeded handles, having concave corners to match the central handle.

2. Two mustard pots of egg-cup shape, with domed lids and ball finials.

Length : 16 in.   Weight : 39 oz. 13 dwt.
Width : 8½ in.   London date-letter for 1803–4.
Height : 11½ in.

By courtesy of Messrs. Christie, Manson & Woods, Ltd. (18th February 1953, lot 94)

PLATE XIX

JUG AND STAND—SILVER

OF classical design, based on the work of the Adam brothers. The jug has a pyriform body with a plain broad band between fillets encircling it at its broadest part. The lower of the two fillets acts as a projecting ledge to support the jug in its stand. A border of elongated gadrooning divides the lower and broader part of the jug from the upper and tapering section, where a plain convex band encircles the neck about an inch from the top. The rim is high and everted in front to form a spout, the small flat lid having a fruit-and-leaf finial. The high curving ebony handle, which meets the body with its voluted socket, is based on that found in the Greek oinochoe wine jug.

The tripod stand is formed of a plain band, with its upper rim gadrooned, to which are attached three square blocks with heavy rings hanging free. From the under surface of these blocks extend three concave ribbed legs with leonine pads resting on the corners of a triangular base in the centre of which is a demi-urn-shaped spirit-lamp gadrooned at the top and base.

As there is no strainer in the jug we may conclude that it was intended for hot water.

Height of jug: 8 in.	Circumference: 1 ft. 8 in.
Circumference at broadest part: 1 ft. 7 in.	Weight of jug: 27 oz.
Height of stand: 5 in.	Weight of stand: 24½ oz.
Diameter: 6 in.	London date-letter for 1805–6.

By courtesy of Lord Fairhaven, 1st Bt., D.L., J.P., F.S.A.

PLATE XX

DINNER SERVICE—SILVER

(Three out of a total of nine)

Large oval tureen on plain oval foot with gadrooned band. The lower part is gadrooned, the centre plain to receive the inscription while above is a reeded frieze surmounted by a gadrooned rim. The handles are reeded and rise from twin lions' heads. The flat plain lid is domed at the centre to receive as finial the Hood crest—a Cornish chough proper, resting the dexter claw on the fluke of an anchor placed in bend sinister or. The base on which the crest stands is oval with a gadrooned border and another outer one of large beading. The inscription reads:

> Presented / by the Merchants of Barbadoes, / to Rear Admiral Sir Samuel Hood, K.B. / In Grateful Acknowledgement of the Protection Afforded / to their Trade, during his Command on that Station / from 1803 to 1825.

The identity of Rear-Admiral Sir Samuel Hood (1762–1814) is not to be confused with that of his cousin Admiral Lord Samuel H. Hood (1724–1816), Nelson's famous older contemporary. The younger Hood was one of Nelson's Senior Captains at the Battle of the Nile.

One (of a total of four) rectangular entrée-dish, to match the tureen, with reeded and gadrooned mouldings, acanthus-leaf and shell *motifs* at corners. Finials on the high-domed lids as on the tureen.

The inscription reads:

> Presented to / Rear Admiral Sir Samuel Hood K.B. / By the Generals, / The Field Officers and the Staff Officers of the Army, / who served in the Expedition against / St LUCIA, TOBAGO, DEMERARY and SURINAM, / in the Years 1803 and 1804. / To make known their grateful Sense / OF THE GENEROUS AND HOSPITABLE CONDUCT / of the Rear Admiral to the Officers of the Army / on board His Majesty's SHIP CENTAUR: / by which the hardships of War were alleviated, / AND THE BONDS OF UNION STRENGTHENED, BETWEEN THE TWO SERVICES.

On the front of the dish is Hood's crest encircled by the motto of the Most Honourable Order of the Bath (TRIA JUNCTA IN UNO), which he received early in 1805 for services in the West Indies—some of the places being named in the above inscription. Pendant from the encircling motto is the badge for the Military Classes of the Order—a rose, thistle and shamrock issuant from a sceptre between three imperial crowns.

Four sauce-boats similar to the tureen in every respect.
The measurements are as follows:

Tureen: Height 12½ in. Width 16¾ in. Depth 10⅛ in.
Entrée-dishes: Height 8¾ in. Width 11¼ in. Depth 9½ in.
Sauce-boats: Height 7 in. Width 9 in. Depth 5⅛ in.

London date-letters for 1806–7 on the tureen and entrée-dishes; and for 1807–8 on the sauce-boats.

By courtesy of Mrs. A. Watson Armour III and Dr. John Shedd Schweppe, in conjunction with the Art Institute of Chicago

PLATE XXI

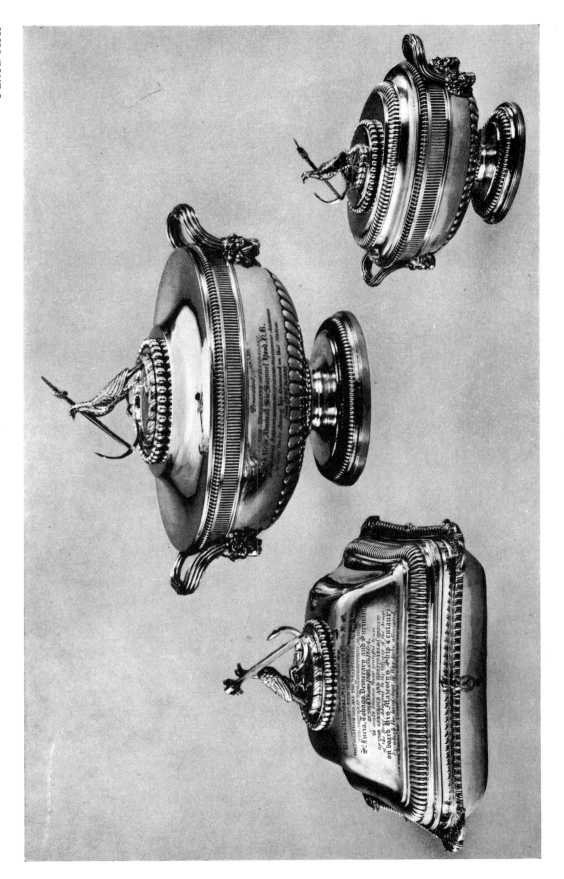

TWO-HANDLED CUP AND COVER—SILVER

THE body of this straight-sided cup is engraved with a design of oak foliage and acorns. A sexfoil central panel bears the Temple crest: on a ducal coronet a martlet or. (Cf also the crest of Dufferin and Ava.) Above is a broad band of anthemion and lotus design between plain fillets. This is repeated on the upper part of the lid, which is surmounted by a large bead edging and acorn finial. The lower part of the lid, which is sloping, is enriched with a running design of oak foliage and acorns. An ovolo moulding surrounds the edge of the lid, while round the rim of the cup itself runs a chaste little floral border. Reeded handles, with acanthus foliage, spring from lions' masks and after sweeping upwards above the edge of the bowl curve down to join the lower part of the body of the cup. A calyx of elongated gadrooning rests in a ring of ovolos, below which is the plain spreading foot. The moulded base consists of a convex band of ovolos, surmounting a slightly concave floral band between beaded borders.

Height (total): 18 in.
Height (without cover): $13\frac{3}{8}$ in.
Diameter: $8\frac{7}{8}$ in.

Weight: 173 oz. 3 dwt.
London date-letter for 1806–7.

By courtesy of the Cleveland Museum of Art. John L. Severance Collection No. 42.816

PLATE XXII

VASE AND COVER—SILVER GILT

OF calyx-krater type with a short plain body, the lower part of which has a bold gadroon moulding. From the base of this spring two reeded loop-handles with broad horizontal grips. On the overlapping edge of the body is an ovolo and fruit moulding, below which is a border of laurel leaves on a matted ground. The plain cover has a guilloche edge, and from a low dome of water-leaves rises a finial in the shape of a spiral fruit resting in a floral calyx and surmounted by a small quatrafoil.

The plain circular foot, with its short stem relieved by a narrow convex moulding, is enriched by a torus of laurels, rosettes and straps in relief. It rests on a plain square pedestal with four fluted feet.

Inscription:

ADDED
TO THE MANSION HOUSE PLATE
IN THE MAYORALTY OF
THE RT HON. SIR JOHN WHITTAKER ELLIS BART
1881–1882

Height: 17 in.   London date-letter for 1807–8.
Weight: 160 oz.

The Mansion House. By courtesy of the Corporation of London

For the exact type of late archaic red-figure calyx-krater on which the present one is modelled see that in the Berlin State Museum, *c.* 500 B.C., painted by Euphronios. A good photograph of it forms No. 68a in Arthur Lane's *Greek Pottery*, 1948. Cf. also No. 87, which shows the effect of a lengthened body. There is, however, one great difference between the antique and the modern. In the case of the pottery the handles appear an inseparable organic part of the whole form and thereby add to the beauty of the pot. But in metal this is impossible, and although Storr has cleverly hidden the join under the base of the vase the handles still look ''applied'' and not an integral part of the whole. The gadrooning has possibly provided some compensation, but the aesthetic value of the Greek is sadly lacking.

In 1798 Storr had made a somewhat similar cup, but with considerably more ornamentation, and a longer body of the campana or bell form. It was presented by William Robinson White (Master) to the Merchant Taylors. See Fry and Tewson's *Illustrated Catalogue of silver plate of the Worshipful Company of Merchant Taylors*, 1929, pp. 54–5 and Pl. 20. Sir John Whittaker Ellis presented a fine vase-shaped cup by Storr to the Company in 1884–5. See *op. cit.*, pp. 56–7 and Pl. 21.

Sir John Whittaker Ellis (1829–1912) was Alderman, Broad Street Ward (1872–1909); Sheriff of London and Middlesex (1874–5); Lord Mayor of London (1881–2); Governor of the Irish Society (1882–94); Master of the Merchant Taylors' Company (1884–5); M.P. Mid-Surrey (1884–5); and Surrey, Kingston Division (1885–92); First Mayor of Richmond (1890–1); Sheriff of Surrey (1899–1900).

He was partner with his predecessor in the Aldermanry, Sir John Musgrove (Lord Mayor, 1880–1), as an auctioneer and estate agent, and was afterwards head of Farebrother, Ellis and Co., having acquired the business formerly carried on by Charles Farebrother (Lord Mayor, 1833–4).

(Adapted from A. B. Beaven, *Aldermen of the City of London*, Vol. II, 1913, p. 206; and *Who Was Who*, 1897–1916.)

PLATE XXIII

CANDELABRA—SILVER

A PAIR of two-light candelabra, with square tapering pedestal stems chased with panels of overlapping pendant husks, or scalework, surmounted by shells, and acanthus leaf on the shoulders. Between the stems and nozzles is a knop consisting of an acanthus calyx separated from a guilloche border by a projecting plain fillet. The vase-shaped fluted nozzles rest on cup-shaped members enriched with alternate trellis-work and conventional voluted anthemions. The two reeded branches, with applied acanthus foliage, are entwined with the tails of twin serpents, their heads forming large looped-handles, while they hold balanced in their mouths a small egg or oval bead. This exact design appears in Pl. XLVII, ''Group of utensils'', in Thomas Hope's *Household Furniture and Interior Decoration*, 1807. The nozzles have a lotus design with gadrooned calyx and upper rim. The gadrooned drip-trays rest on small floral calyxes which act as terminals to the reeded branches.

Below the stems a reeded and cross-banded knop surmounts a campana or bell-shaped foot of which the upper section is formed of over-lapping water-leaves and the lower section of long, narrow leaves heavily ribbed which turn up at the ends as they reach the base. This base consists of a convex ovolo border surmounting a plain vertical basic rim.

Height: 24¾ in.
Weight: 318 oz. 11 dwt.

London date-letter for 1807–8.

From the late Duke of Bedford's Collection. By courtesy of Messrs. Christie, Manson and Woods, Ltd. (14th June 1950, lot 117)

PLATE XXIV

SALVER—SILVER-GILT

OF oval shape, with a broad border of oak-leaves, acorns and husks between plain fillets. Outside this is a narrow band of mistletoe and pearl edging. Broad lateral handles with concave sides bordered by plain fillets, terminate in Ionic volutes with water-leaf decoration. On the matted surface between the fillets are superimposed hooded masks with beards[1] which flow over the broad oak-leaf border. There are four legs formed of lions' masks and pads resting on plain octagonal bases and surmounted by palmettes with lateral volutes. The centre is plain except for the coat of arms and crest of Lord Monson which is as follows:

> Or, two chevronels, gu. Crest—a lion, rampant ppr., supporting a column, or. Supporters—Dexter, a lion, or, gorged with a collar, chained, az., the collar charged with three crescents, of the first; Sinister, a griffin, wings elevated, arg., beaked and membered, az., collared and chained as the dexter. Motto—PREST POUR MON PAIS

Length: 37 in.   Weight: 360 oz. approx.
Width: 24½ in.   London date-letter for 1808–9.

By courtesy of Francis Stonor, Esq. From the Lord Monson Collection

The present Lord Monson writes that to the best of his knowledge this piece was made for and acquired by the 4th Lord Monson (1785–1809), who died at the early age of twenty-five. Entertaining on a much larger scale had probably been planned both in their country house in Lincolnshire as well as in London. Another large piece by Storr which had been acquired by Lord Monson was a very ornate two-tiered centre-piece.

[1] For these see the "Comic and tragic masks of Silenus . . . " in Pl. XXXVII of T. Hope's *Household Furniture and Interior Decoration*, 1807.

PLATE XXV

CENTRE-PIECE—SILVER

THE whole conception of this piece—so full of life and movement—may be described as a marine fantasy. From the centre of a highly rococo base resting on feet of shells and curving acanthus, suggesting eddying water, rises a column formed chiefly of two figures, one of a mermaid lifting a veil to display her beauty, the other of a Triton blowing a blast on his conch shell, or murex. Below, a child emerges from a large head of Poseidon holding a trident in his right hand. Each side of this central column is an oval basket or fruit-dish designed as a large clam shell. At the outer extremity of each basket a prancing winged and web-footed Pegasus, the son of Poseidon, appears about to crest the oncoming waves. Wing-like projections rising from the sides of the basket and spiral volutes meeting the central column suggest some fantastic sea chariot. The baskets rest on twin dolphins, and have marine medallions inserted at the sides, while small shells lie between them on the edge of the base. The clever use of arched acanthus leaves at the base of the column to represent the crest of waves should be noted.

Height: 26 in.
Diameter: 21 in.
Greatest length: 38½ in.

Weight: 672 oz. 13 dwt.
London date-letter for 1808–9.

From the Earl of Abercorn's Collection. Now part of the Thomas S. Grasselli Memorial Collection at the Cleveland Museum of Art. No. 43.189

Plate XXVI

ICE-PAIL—SILVER-GILT

(One of a set of four)

ALTHOUGH described as ice-pails because they are fitted with bottle liners, these objects present an unusual appearance by their dome-shaped lids. The explanation is that the lids do not form part of the ice-pails but cover fruit bowls which are removable. These can then be used quite separately or, if wanted for iced dishes, caviare, etc., can be kept cool by being replaced after the liners have been packed with ice.

Of vase-shape with broad handles ornamented with acanthus and bifurcating as they reach the shoulder of the vase, these vessels have a calyx of lanceolate leaves, with acanthus foliage extending each side to meet the handles. Swags of banded laurel, looped each side by a central boss, surround the body. The foot has an upper band of alternating leaves and rosettes, and a lower torus of banded laurel which matches a similar one forming the rim of the vessel. It is at this point that the ice-pail portion finishes. The fruit-dish consists of a plain domed cover with a circular cornice of acanthus foliage surmounted by a knop or handle of clustered grapes and vine leaves. The lower part of the fruit-dish is not seen as it drops down below the surface of the rim of the ice-pail. The Harewood crest is engraved on the lid, while the full armorial bearings appear on the body of the vessel.

London date-letter (of one pair) for 1809–10. The other pair is dated 1813–14. Number at the 1951 Regency Exhibition: 56.

By courtesy of H.R.H. The Princess Royal and the Earl of Harewood

TWO-HANDLED BOWL—SILVER

THE bowl is quite plain, the only form of decoration being a double beading at the centre which passes directly over the points of juncture of the handles with the body of the bowl. These handles are in the form of snakes which hold an egg (or similar small oval object) between them in their open mouths. This design can be seen as the central handle to a dish in Pl. 47 of Thomas Hope's *Household Furniture and Interior Decoration*, 1807. *Cf.* also Storr's large silver-gilt soup-tureen handle (1803–5) shown in Jones's *Gold and Silver of Windsor Castle*, Pl. LXXXIV, facing p. 166. The plain round foot has a slightly convex band of elongated gadrooning.

Height: 2½ in.
Diameter: 6 in.
Circumference: 18¾ in.

Weight: 12 oz. 15 dwt.
London date-letter for 1808–9.

By courtesy of Dr. Anthony Storr

PLATE XXVII

CANDELABRUM—SILVER-GILT

THIS is one of a pair of massive candelabra designed by John Flaxman, R.A., to illustrate familiar tales in classic mythology. In the present case the subject treated is that of the golden apples of the Hesperides being guarded by Laden, the ever-watchful serpent, and the three daughters of Erebus and Night, Aegele, Erytheia and Hesperethusa. The fetching of apples from the tree was one of the last labours imposed on Heracles. For a useful note on the variants of the tale see Appolodorus (II, V, 11), trans. J. G. Frazer, Vol. 1, pp. 220, 221; and H. J. Rose, *Handbook of Greek Mythology*, 5th edit., 1953, pp. 23, 216.

The candelabrum has three double and six single branches for lights, and it is between these two tiers that the subject described above is shown. The single branches, forming the lower tier, are of scrolled acanthus with anthemion spandrels, and terminate in gadrooned grease-pans and candle sockets. The upper tier of double branches, springing as it does from an apple cluster, is less formal, having ribbed stems decorated with feathery acanthus foliage terminating in floral candle-sockets with drooping calyxes.

The elaborate pedestal consists of a truncated Corinthian fluted column on the projecting base of which sit three piping fauns with the same number of reclining lions between them, and of bearded masks on the sides of the base. The whole rests on a triangular base with plain sides surmounted by an ogee border of acanthus, supported by double lion's paws joined by scrolled foliage and voluted medallions.

In later years (1821) Philip Rundell used the "Apples of the Hesperides" stem for a seven-light candelabrum acquired in 1881 by the Worshipful Company of Goldsmiths. See Carrington and Hughes, p. 102.

Height: 60 in.
Weight: 1,386 oz.
No. in the Royal Inventory: 10.

London date-letter for 1809–10 and 1810–11.

In Her Majesty's interleaved copy of the Royal inventory is a note stating that the candelabrum was bought by George, Prince Regent, in June 1811 for a total cost of £2,017 16s. 0d. The companion piece, purchased at the same time—"Mercury presenting the infant Bacchus to the attendant nymphs"—cost £1,985 19s. 0d. In E. A. Jones's work on the Windsor Plate, the binders have inadvertently put the two plates (LIX and LX) opposite the wrong text (at least in the copies which I have seen).

From the Collection at Windsor Castle. By Gracious Permission of H.M. The Queen

PLATE XXVIII

ICE-PAIL AND STAND—SILVER

(One of a pair)

ON circular fluted feet with lower convex border of water-leaves. Above is a short neck with plain torus moulding, surmounted by a gadrooned collar, on which rest the decorated bodies. The lower part of each body is decorated with acanthus foliage, cup-like flowers filled with fruit, and bunches of grapes. This exact design occurs on Lord Sackville's set of eight ice-pails of 1812 and 1813, see p. 160. At the sides are thick reeded handles, with acanthus leaves on their flat upper surfaces, rising from satyrs' masks. Above, on the main portion of the bodies, are applied groups of Bacchanalian chariots with leopards, horses and attendant figures with satyrs supporting Silenus and carrying amphorae. The whole is on a matted ground with a frieze of grapes, vine leaves and tendrils above. There is an everted ovolo rim, detachable liner, plain collar and guilloche rim. The stands have double borders, an inner one of running anthemion design, and an outer one of gadroons. They rest on four paw feet surmounted by fluted anthemions flanked by palm foliage spandrels.

Height: 14 in.   London date-letter for 1809–10.
Weight: 476 oz. 18 dwt.

From the Collection of the Rt. Hon. the Earl Howe, P.C., C.B.E.
By courtesy of Messrs. Christie, Manson and Woods, Ltd. (Wednesday, 1st July 1953, lot 108)

The *Illustrated Catalogue* of this sale is important to collectors of Paul Storr from many points of view. Attention should first be drawn to the last lot of the sale, No. 139, with folding plate as frontispiece to the catalogue. This is a double breakfast service consisting of the following:

Pair of two-handled oval trays, with entwined serpent and Medusa mask handles, gadrooned rims and palm foliage feet—24 in. wide. 254 oz. 9 dwt.
Two circular teapots—one by Philip Rundell, 1823. Gross weight: 76 oz. 8 dwt.
Vase-shaped hot-water jug, with stand and lamp on three paw feet. Gross weight: 47 oz. 12 dwt.
Circular milk jug and two cream-jugs. 53 oz. 15 dwt.
Two circular sugar-basins, one of different form without the shell and anthemion decoration. 38 oz.
Vase-shaped tea-urn, on square plinth with ball feet, dolphin tap, scroll handles rising from serpents and chased with laurel, and cone finial to cover. 15¾ in. high. Gross weight: 128 oz. 9 dwt.
Pair of triangular egg-stands, each in three wire-work baskets holding cups and central handles, with foliage finials, with shell and hour-glass patten spoons. 67 oz. 8 dwt.
Oval butter-dish, cover and stand, on paw feet, with lotus finial to the cover and glass liner. 36 oz. 13 dwt.
Circular muffin-dish, stand and cover. 42 oz. 8 dwt.
Oval seven-bar toast rack, with Caduceus handle. 25 oz. 5 dwt.
    Total gross weight of service: 769 oz. 15 dwt.

The Arms are those of Richard William Penn, 1st Earl Howe. The service was purchased by N. Bloom & Son of London and New York. See their double-page illustration in the *Connoisseur*, August 1953 (pp. viii, ix).

The Howe sale catalogue had several other Storr pieces: see lots 30, 34 (with illustrations), 95, 96, 107, 110 (illustrated) and 118. Many other items, such as lots 93, 111, 112, 113, 114, 115 and 117 by Digby Scott and the two Smiths, reflect Storr's work to a marked degree. Of interest is lot 29, a pair of circular seal boxes by John Bridge, 1829 and 1830; and lots 99 and 100, altar dishes made in 1819 and 1820 and bearing the mark of Philip Rundell. On Storr's decision to leave the firm, Rundell had registered his mark on 4th March 1819.

PLATE XXIX

TEA-URN—SILVER

OF hemispherical rather than "urn" shape, with gadrooned edge and calyx. The body is plain except for a broad band of alternating palmette (anthemion or honeysuckle) and lotus pattern on a matted ground. It occupies the upper portion of the bowl, passing above the twin-maned lions' masks from which spring each side heavily reeded handles with acanthus decoration. From the calyx gadrooning a scaly spigot, or vent-peg, projects horizontally, terminating in a dolphin's head. The tap, fitted into a square member with scrolled sides, is an ivory palmette. The plain spreading foot has a gadrooned and plain moulding near its juncture with the bowl, and is enriched at the base by a torus, ornamented with a twisted rope pattern of antique guilloche design. A vertical collar with gadrooned edge encloses the lid in the form of a floriated low boss from the centre of which rises a twisted oval finial. The whole stands on a plain square base supported at the corners by lion's pads surmounted by formal palm-leaves with lateral volutes and demi-palmettes.

Height: 14¾ in.
Weight: 226 oz. 6 dwt.

Width, including handles: 16 in.
London date-letter for 1809–10.

By courtesy of the Victoria and Albert Museum, London

138

PLATE XXX

THE ANGLESEY VICTORY TROPHY—
SILVER-GILT

THIS trophy takes the form of a short, thick, stocky column embossed with Roman military scenes, accoutrements, armour and symbolic winged figures. It is surmounted by four rearing horses held by winged female figures of Victory. The capital has a guilloche border with two rows of water-leaves in concave section below. The column rests on a square base with inset panels of battle-scenes and coats of arms. The whole stands on a plain square base on which are four lions. The inscription on the front side of the base reads:

This Piece of Plate is Presented / To Lieutenant General Lord Paget / BY THE PRINCE REGENT / BY H.R.H. THE DUKE OF CUMBERLAND / and the Inscribed Officers of the Hussar Brigade / who have served under His Lordship's Command, in token of their Admiration of / His high military Acquirements and of the Courage and Talent / constantly displayed by him in leading the Hussars to Victory against the French Cavalry / during the Campaign on the Peninsula in 1808.

Height: 2 ft. 10 in.   London date-letter for 1809–10.

By courtesy of the Marquess of Anglesey

The trophy was exhibited at the 1951 Regency Festival held in the Royal Pavilion, Brighton. At the same exhibition was the Waterloo Sword, presented by H.R.H. The Prince Regent to the 1st Marquess of Anglesey to commemorate the Battle of Waterloo, also the trouser-leg removed when he lost his leg on the Field, and the artificial leg subsequently worn by the Marquess.

See *Souvenir Programme*, 1951, Nos. 199, 253, 254 and 255; also Clifford Musgrave "The Regency Exhibition at Brighton", *Connoisseur*, October 1951, p. 94, with illustration on p. 91.

PLATE XXXI

TEA SERVICE—SILVER

THE tea service comprises a circular tea-pot, sugar basin and cream jug, with gadrooned feet and rims and serpent handles—the grip of the tea-pot being ivory. The spouts are formed as Roman lamps chased with anthemion ornament, while the somewhat squat design accords well with that of the antique lamp. The vase-shaped hot-water jug with similar ornamentation, and an upturned spout, rests in a circular frame with gadrooned edge supported by three concave reeded legs, with pendant rings and leonine pads, attached to the corners of a triangular base. A circular lamp, with similar gadrooning, stands in the centre of the base.

Gross weight: 121 oz.   London date-letter for 1810–11.

Collection of Colonel R. J. L. Ogilby. By courtesy of Messrs. Christie, Manson & Woods, Ltd. (3rd December 1947, lot 124)

PAIR OF JUGS—SILVER

BASED on Roman originals, to which spouts and lids have been added, these semi-globular jugs are quite plain except for the masks affixed below the handles and spouts. The plain flattened handles, with high everted thumb-pieces, bifurcate at both points of contact with the body of the jugs. Convex gadrooning surrounds the under-lips of both jugs and spouts. The base is formed of a narrow beading. These jugs were exhibited by J. Anderson Rose (solicitor of Whistler, Rosetti, and many other notable artists of the period, great-uncle of the present owner) at "The Fine Art Exhibition of the Worshipful Company of Cordwainers . . . 21st April–17th May, 1890." They were described in the Catalogue, p. 168, thus:

> Coffee-pots, A pair. Etruscan shape. Head of Jupiter on handles, designed by John Flaxman, R.A. for the Prince Regent and formerly in his possession.
> English Hall-mark 1810. 6½ in.

Height: 7 in.   Order Numbers: 394 and 395.
Greatest Circumference: 16½ in.   London date-letters for 1810–11.
Weight: 31½ oz. and 30½ oz.

By courtesy of C. C. Oman, Esq.

The type of Roman jug (*urceus* or *lagona*) on which the above were based has been found in places as far apart as Kent and Pompeii. For the former see *Guide to the Antiquities of Roman Britain*, 1922, p. 98, fig. 119 (Bayford, Kent), and *ibid.,* 1951 edit., p. 38 and Pl. VI (3)—(Faversham, Kent) and cf. the jug from the Chaource Treasure, *Catalogue of Silver Plate in the British Museum*, 1921, No. 147, p. 39 and Pl. XXIV. For the latter see G. Consoli Fiego, *Museo Nazionale di Napoli* [1937], p. 35 and Fig. 124.

PLATE XXXII

FRUIT BOWL WITH STAND—SILVER-GILT

ONE of a pair, with double bases. Both sub-base and base are of triangular form with concave sides and chamfered corners. The sub-base, perfectly plain, is supported on three feet in the form of voluted capitals cast and chased with acanthus foliage and floral helices. The base is of similar shape to the sub-base, but smaller, with a guilloche moulding on the lower edge and a leaf-and-dart moulding on the upper chamfered edge. It stands on three broad volute feet, resting on the sub-base, each of which is cast and chased with the mask of a bearded man with ram's horns, surmounted by a shell. Between the feet depend heavy swags of fruit and flowers. On each angle of the base stands a female figure, of caryatid type, sculptured in the round, clad in semi-transparent classical draperies and shod in sandals. In each hand the figures hold a thyrsus, the wand or sceptre of Dionysus (Bacchus) and his votaries— one surmounted by a pine-cone (cf. *Anth. Pal.*, VI, 165, i.e. W. R. Paton, *Greek Anthology*, Vol. I, p. 383), the other by ivy leaves and berries (cf. Propertius, Bk. III, 3.35). The figures face outwards, their downward-stretched arms forming a criss-cross pattern with the thyrsi which are crossed and tied near the top with bows of ribbon. At a point on the base equidistant from the heels of the three figures is a large round floral boss, cast and chased. Resting lightly on the heads of the figures is a circular stand decorated with a *rinceau* frieze of foliage and flowers. Fitting into this is a large concave-sided bowl of open basket-work, the grouped and crossing osiers of which rise from a closely woven base to a double plaited edge, resembling gadrooning.[1] From this edge an inner border of grape-vine foliage and fruit clusters is attached. Glass liners fit into the basket-work bowls.

This fine pair of fruit bowls formed part of the first Duke of Wellington's Ambassador Service. They are engraved with the Royal Crest, and the crest of Wellesley within the garter surmounted by a ducal coronet.

Signed on the sub-base: RUNDELL BRIDGE ET RUNDELL AURIFICES REGIS ET PRINCIPIS WALLIÆ LONDINI. Maker's mark of Paul Storr.

Height: 13¾ in.   London date-letter for 1810–11.
Diameter of bowl: 9½ in.   Registered Museum numbers:
Weight: (the pair) 272 oz.   W.M. 325A, 326A—1948.

The Wellington Museum, Apsley House, London

1 For this design see Thomas Hope, *Household Furniture and Interior Decoration*, 1807, Pl. 52.

PLATE XXXIII

CENTRE-PIECE—SILVER AND PARCEL-GILT

FROM the centre of a triangular base with concave sides and chamfered ends, enriched with alternating palmette and lotus decoration, rises a palm-tree the upper branches of which shade three winged Victories. They are clad in diaphanous robes and stand with their backs to the palm tree, holding three laurel wreaths between them. Their eyes are downcast, and the toes of their sandalled feet rest lightly on three globes. On the top of the palm-tree rests a two-handled vase of semi-globular form with a spreading foot separated from the bowl by a gadrooned collar, and terminating in a torus moulding with a guilloche pattern. The foot conceals a bayonet joint holding the vase and stand together. The vase has a calyx of oak leaves and acorns, and a band of laurel leaves forming a broad border around the upper rim. Two reeded handles divide into spiral branches with oak-leaf sprays. The slightly domed lid has a guilloche border, surmounting which is a round loop handle in the form of a laurel wreath with pendent ribbons.

The whole stands on a round plinth surrounded by three recumbent free-standing lions on a projecting sub-base with ornamented bracket feet. Between the lions the Royal Arms are applied to the plinth.

Inscribed on the sub-base: RUNDELL BRIDGE ET RUNDELL AURIFICES REGIS ET PRINCIPIS WALLIÆ LONDINI FECERUNT. Maker's mark of Paul Storr.

The centre-piece was presented to Lieutenant-General Wellesley by the General Officers of the Peninsular Army.

Height: 2 ft. 9 in.	Weight: 955 oz.
Width of top: 1 ft. 4½ in.	London date-letter for 1810–11.
Width of base: 1 ft. 7 in.	Registered Museum number:
	W.M. 799—1948.

The Wellington Museum, Apsley House, London

With this object can be compared the two large dessert stands by Storr in the Royal Collection (see E. A. Jones, *Gold and Silver of Windsor Castle*, Pl. LXXV, p. 148; and the *Connoisseur*, September 1942, p. 19, Fig. IX). Here the place of the palm-tree is taken by a twisted stem, while the three figures support the dish above by their uplifted hands. Bold acanthus scrolls on a triangular base occupy the position of the lions in the Wellington piece.

146

PLATE XXXIV

TWO PAIRS OF EGG-STANDS AND TOAST-RACKS—SILVER

A PAIR of oval, or boat-shaped, egg-stands with reed-and-tie rims, acanthus-leaf terminals and lotus-capital feet. A rope-wire surround encloses four wire-work baskets holding cups with gadroon rims. A reeded central handle enriched with acanthus surmounts a shaft formed of spreading acanthus foliage and water-leaves. The spoons have been added, and are not by Storr.

Length: 11 in.   The weight of one is 55.05 oz. and
Width: 7 in.   of the other 56.10 oz.
Height: 8¾ in.   London date-letter for 1810–11.

A pair of oval seven-bar toast-racks with handles of long pointed water-leaves and truncated tops surmounted by roses (cf. the finial to the bowl and cover of 1813, on Pl. XLII). The bases have reed-and-tie rims, acanthus-leaf terminals, gadrooned sloping sides, with criss-cross moulding above, to the base where the wires are secured.

Length: 10½ in.   Weight: 50.18 oz.
Width: 6½ in.   London date-letter for 1810–11.
Height: 6¾ in.

By courtesy of D. & J. Wellby Ltd.

PLATE XXXV

BON-BON DISH—SILVER

(One of a set of four)

IN the form of a broad-ribbed upturned shell, doubtless based on the *Cardium pseudolima* of West Africa. It rests on the back of a dolphin whose exaggerated upper jaw holds the shell in position. The matted surface of the animal's skin is not true to nature and must be regarded as artistic licence. The base is made to represent water in which the dolphin is floundering.

Height: $2\frac{1}{4}$ in.
Length (from head to tail): $4\frac{1}{2}$ in.
Breadth: $4\frac{1}{2}$ in.

Weight: 15 oz.
London date-letter for 1810–11.
Order No. 527 of Paul Storr.

By courtesy of Lord Fairhaven, 1st Bt., D.L., J.P., F.S.A.

WINE-LABELS—SILVER-GILT

(From a set of fourteen)

OF broad oval shape forming a hollow ring of vine-leaves and tendrils. Across the entire base and over half-way up either side recline two well-developed *amorini*, their feet entwined at the centre. The one to the left of the illustration presents a back view, and that to the right a front view, both showing a three-quarter face. Below them bunches of grapes, finely modelled, depend from the encircling vine. With their right hands they support the name plate, of rectangular shape, with deep concave upper corners and a plain surrounding frame with applied ornamentation. The name of the wine is in plain roman capitals on a matted ground. The enormous size of the labels relegates their use to a bottle or decanter of Jeroboam or Rehoboam size.

The collector of wine-labels will recognize a combination of two distinct types (according to the type-classification in my *Book of the Wine-Label*), that of "Cupids, grapes and satyrs" (No. 10) and "Architectural" (No. 17).

Size: $2\frac{9}{10}$ in. high; $3\frac{1}{10}$ in. broad.
Weight: 36 oz.

London date-letter for 1810–11.

From the Belmore Collection. By courtesy of Francis Stonor, Esq.

PLATE XXXVI

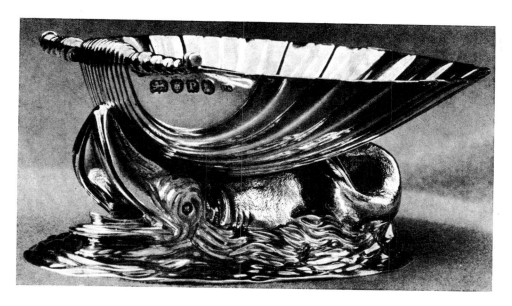

TWO-HANDLED ICE-PAIL—SILVER-GILT
(One of a pair)

OF Greek calyx-krater type, from a design by John Flaxman. The lower part of the body is enriched by a broad band of alternating palmette (anthemion or honeysuckle) and lotus pattern. Below the band four lions' masks support two reeded handles, surmounted by acanthus foliage, which bend outwards and upwards in concave section. A gadrooned collar separates the bowl from the circular foot, which has a gadrooned border and plain sub-base. The rim is gadrooned with a palmette to mark the central point. Applied decoration, consisting of the Royal Arms on one side, and the Coronation medal of William IV and Queen Adelaide enclosed in an oak-wreath on the other, has been added subsequently.

Height: $9\frac{1}{2}$ in.

Greatest width: $10\frac{3}{4}$ in.

Weight: 85 oz. 6 dwt., and 87 oz. 6 dwt.

London date-letter for 1810–11.

By courtesy of the Victoria and Albert Museum, London.
Bond Collection

PLATE XXXVII

CANDELABRUM AND CENTRE-PIECE ON STAND—SILVER-GILT

THIS composite piece is the product of Paul de Lamerie and Paul Storr and has been repaired and regilt many times. It has been fully described by E. A. Jones for a catalogue of the Mansion House plate which still remains in manuscript. With the kind permission of the Chamberlain's Court, Guildhall House, I here reproduce Mr. Jones's description in full.

GREAT CANDELABRUM AND EPERGNE AND STAND

OVAL; applied on the reeded edge are shell, foliage and scroll ornaments; on the sides are medallions of Socrates and Cicero in scrolled frames in high relief, and at the ends are large female heads and scrolls, also in high relief, separated by foliated scrolls, scales and foliage on a matted ground; the lower part is plain; on the base are large shells, ovolo work, foliage and scrolls in relief; it stands on four large scrolled feet with females' heads on the shoulders and with decoration of foliage and rocaille; it is fitted with four foliated and scrolled branches, numbered 1 to 4, and four smaller with female busts.

With it are four circular baskets, decorated on the edges with shells, scrolls and foliated scrolls, and on the borders with shells, scrolls and scale work, separated by fluting; the jointed handles are pierced and decorated with scrolls and foliage, on four scrolled feet.

Height, 8¾ in.; length, 10¾ in.; width, 8 in.

The large pierced basket is later.

Inside is a large plain dish, decorated on the edge with four human masks, scrolls, shells and flowers in relief, and on the border with panels of chased shells, alternating with scale work and shells divided by fluting; it is engraved with the City Arms.

The body is London, 1738–9. Maker, Paul de Lamerie.

The four baskets are not marked, but are of the third quarter of the eighteenth century. Diameter, 6¼ in.; 2⅛ in. high.

The interior dish is not marked, but is probably by Paul de Lamerie. Size, 13½ by 11½ in.; height, 5¼ in.

The six candle-sockets, with fluted edges and with a decoration of foliage in relief, are by Paul Storr, 1811–12.

The whole stands on a great octagonal stand with the City Arms in relief on each side and with four dragons (from the City Arms) supporting the corners; on the top are cornucopias and caduceus in relief; on the edge are laurel leaves in relief; it rests on four large claw feet with scrolls, foliage and rosettes.

Inscriptions:

This PLINTH was made during the MAYORALTY of the Rt. Honble. Sir Charles Flower Bart, by RUNDELL BRIDGE & RUNDELL Goldsmiths & Jewellers To their Majesties, H.R.H. the Prince of Wales and Royal Family.

REPAIRED AND REGILT ANNO DOMINI 1843. Rt. Honble. John Humphery, M.P. Lord Mayor. Repaired & Regilt, Anno Domini 1767 The Right Honble. Thomas Gabriel Lord Mayor.

Size, 18½ by 16 in.; height, 9 in.

The plinth is London, 1811–12. Maker, Paul Storr.

Inscriptions on parts of the centre-piece:

Repaired Anno Domini 1789 William Pickett Esqr. Lord Mayor.

Repaired & part new made Anno Domini 1802, Rt. Honble. Sir John Eamer, Kt. Lord Mayor.

Repaired & regilt Anno Domini 1843 Rt. Honble. John Humphery, MP, Lord Mayor.

Repaired & Regilt Anno Domini 1886. The Rt. Hon: John Staples Lord Mayor.

Total weight, 360 oz. 16 dwt., and of the plinth, 418 oz. 15 dwt.

The mention of William Pickett, as Lord Mayor in 1789, is interesting, for it was doubtless to the firm of Pickett & Rundell (which at this date was almost entirely in Rundell's hands) that the centre-piece was first sent for repairs.

It was exhibited at the Royal Pavilion, Brighton, at the 1952 Regency Exhibition, where it occupied the centre of the great table in the Banqueting Room. See the *Catalogue*, No. 31, and Clifford Musgrave, "Masterpieces of Regency Taste", *Country Life*, 8th August 1952, p. 404. I am indebted to Mr. Musgrave, Director of the Royal Pavilion, for the photograph and to the Right Honourable the Lord Mayor and Corporation of London for permission to reproduce it.

PLATE XXXVIII

CENTRE-PIECE—SILVER AND PARCEL-GILT

A TWO-HANDLED vase standing on a square plinth. The vase, of semi-globular form, has a spreading foot chased with elongated water-leaves resting on a torus moulding enriched with a design of oak-leaves. A gilt laurel-wreath border passes through the two broadly sweeping reeded handles, which divide on the upper rim of the vase into two spiral scrolls terminating in oak-leaf sprays. The low domed cover presents an overhanging border of egg-and-tongue moulding, with a circle of gadrooning at the top. From this springs the finial in the form of a gilt figure of Victory bearing a laurel wreath in her right hand and pointing with her left to the globe, engraved with the continents, on which she lightly balances with her right foot. The vase rests on a plain abacus with chamfered corners, surmounting a square plinth, also with chamfered corners, having at the sides free-standing trophies of flint-lock fire-arms and flags. On each side of the plinth is a gilt panel—one displaying the Royal Arms, the other recording the presentation of the piece to Lieutenant-General Sir Arthur Wellesley after the battles of Roleia and Vimiera in 1808.

Height: 1 ft. 9¾ in.
Width of base: 8½ in.
Weight: [not recorded].

London date-letter for 1811–12.
Registered Museum number:
    W.M. 798–1948.

The Wellington Museum. Apsley House, London

156

PLATE XXXIX

THE THEOCRITUS CUP

THIS famous cup was designed by John Flaxman, R.A., from the description of a cup in the First Idyll of Theocritus (c. 300 B.C.–c. 260 B.C.). Its form is based on that of the krater, a wide-mouthed Greek vessel used for mixing wine and water, although, as we shall see later, Theocritus' description is of a kylix and not a krater. The subjects represented each side of the cup are framed above and laterally by vine branches and grapes. The torus-shaped base is decorated with acanthus and water-leaves in relief. There are two handles of twisted vine stems, placed low down each side of the cup. The circular foot is plain. The cipher of Queen Charlotte and the badge of George IV as Prince of Wales are engraved on the cup.

Height: 9¼ in.   London date-letter for 1812–13.
Weight: 90 oz. 15 dwt.   No. in the Royal Inventory: 526.

From the Collection at Windsor Castle. By Gracious Permission of H.M. The Queen

In order fully to appreciate Flaxman's strict adherence to the text (if only by the side presented in the Plate) of Theocritus the following translation, as given by A. S. F. Gow (*Theocritus,* Vol. I, Cambridge, 1950, pp. 7, 8), will be of interest:

> In the First Idyll the scene is laid by a spring near a pine tree. Thyrsis, a shepherd, is chatting to a goatherd. Compliments are exchanged and Thyrsis asks the goatherd to play on his pipes, but he refuses and says that if Thyrsis will sing the famous song about Daphnis he will give him a beautifully decorated cup. He then proceeds to describe it in detail.
> And I will give thee a deep cup, washed over with sweet wax, two-handled, and newly fashioned, still fragrant from the knife. Along the lips above trails ivy, ivy dotted with its golden clusters, and along it winds the tendril glorying in its yellow fruit. And within is wrought a woman, such a thing as the gods might fashion, bedecked with cloak and circlet. And by her two men with long fair locks contend from either side in alternate speech. Yet these things touch not her heart, but now she looks on one and smiles, and now to the other she shifts her thought, while they, long hollow-eyed from love, labour to no purpose. By these is carved an old fisherman, and a rugged rock whereon the old man eagerly gathers up a great net for a cast as one that labours mightily. Thou wouldst say that he was fishing with all the strength of his limbs, so do the sinews stand out all about his neck, grey-haired though he is; yet his strength is as a youth's. And a little way from the sea-worn old man there is a vineyard with a fair load of reddening clusters, guarded by a little boy who sits upon its dry-stone wall. About him hang two foxes, and one goes to and fro among the vine-rows plundering the ripe grapes, while the other brings all her wit to bear upon his wallet, and vows she will not let the lad be until [she has raided his breakfast-bread]. But the boy is plaiting a pretty cricket-cage of bonded rush and asphodel, and has more joy in his plaiting than care for wallet or for vines. And every way about the cup is spread the pliant acanthus.

The word used for "cup", κισσύβιον, gives no clue as to its shape, and even the classic writers were in considerable doubt on the matter (see Athenaeus, XI, 476 f., 477). That it was a rustic bowl of ivy-wood, from κισσός, ivy, seems probable. The adjective "deep", βάθος, must be understood in a comparative sense—deep as a saucer may be said to be deep, not as a tumbler. (A. S. F. Gow, *op. cit.,* Vol. II, p. 6.) Moreover, the text clearly states that the paintings are "within", ἔντοσθεν, the bowl—not only the one of the maiden and her admirers, but the others also, for Theocritus says: "By these is . . .", τοῖς δὲ μέτα, and when speaking of the boy and the foxes, says: "And a little way from . . .", τυτθὸν δ' ὅσσον ἄπωθεν. . . . Thus it is obviously not a krater type of vessel, but a rustic bowl of kylix shape. In his reconstruction of the arrangement of the scenes, Gow (*op. cit.,* Vol. II, p. 14) places the fisherman in the middle at the bottom of the bowl, with the two other scenes on the sloping sides. The acanthus foliage is almost certainly intended to be on the outside of the bowl, while the position of the trailing ivy is not so clear, although it must have run along the lip one side or the other—or possibly both. It will thus be seen that in Storr's cup, John Flaxman has changed the simple rustic bowl into a far more sophisticated krater, and substituted vines and grapes for ivy. The scenes of the fisherman and boy are put together so as to have one subject each side. The vine-stem handles are a Storr-Flaxman invention.

PLATE XL

ICE-PAIL—SILVER-GILT

(One of a set of eight)

OF campana—or thistle-shape, with rams'-head handles, the horns curving over the rim. The upper part is plain with two applied grape and vine-leaf swags each side, depending laterally from the rams' heads and centrally from a broad ribbon bow partly hidden by the conventional egg-and-tongue rim. The lowest points of the swags touch a guilloche moulding between plain narrow fillets. Below this the convex lower part is ornamented with swirling acanthus leaves separated alternately by a floral cornucopia and vine-stems with pendent grapes. The whole rests in a narrow calyx of water-leaves. Below this is a gadrooned collar surmounting a plain spreading foot with a convex base-moulding of laurel leaves and berries and a four-petalled rose at each central point. The circular base is plain. There is a detachable rim chased with a running frieze of vine leaves and grapes on matted ground. The liners are of plain silver. In the catalogue at Knole these eight ice-pails are entered in two lots of four each, as four have no engraved arms while the other four bear those of Lord Whitworth on the foot, encircled with the motto of the Order of the Bath, and surmounted by an earl's coronet.

Height: 10½ in.
Outside diameter: 9⅜ in.
Inside diameter: 8⅜ in.
Circumference of rim: 2 ft. 5 in.
Weight of the armorial set (4 pieces): 660 oz.

Weight of the plain set (4 pieces): 696 oz.
Date of the armorial set: 1813–14.
Date of the plain set: 1812–13 (2) and 1813–14 (2).

From the Collection at Knole. By courtesy of Lord Sackville, K.B.E., etc.

Charles Whitworth (1752–1825), Envoy Extraordinary and Minister Plenipotentiary to Poland and Russia, K.B. in 1793, had married the widow of John Frederick Sackville, 3rd Duke of Dorset in 1801. For details see V. Sackville-West, *Knole and the Sackvilles*, 1922, Ch. IX, pp. 201–20; Chas. J. Phillips, *History of the Sackville Family*, Vol. II [1930], Ch. XVIII, pp. 277–302, with his pedigree on p. 277 and photograph from a painting by Hoppner facing p. 278.

VEGETABLE-DISH—SILVER

SHAPED dish with gadrooned rim, divided internally into four equal divisions by the insertion of a movable frame. This frame is surmounted by a gadrooned crown at the central inter-section of the divisions. At the points where the divisions meet the sides of the dish lateral anthemion decorations protrude horizontally.

Height: 6½ in.
Diameter: 13 in.

London date-letter for 1812–13.

By courtesy of Mr. Ralph Hyman, of the Museum Silver Shop, New York City

Plate XLI

BOWL AND COVER—SILVER

THE circular bowl and cover on a plain vertical base is entirely without any decoration except for the plain moulded rim and the striking finial on the cover to which the eye is at once directed. From a gadrooned central boss with pearled edging rises the truncated finial of long pointed water-leaves tapering slightly from the calyx upwards. The truncated top is surmounted by a fully opened flower resembling the Alexandra rose. Both bowl and cover are fully hall-marked, and Storr's mark is also stamped on the finial.

The type of finial recalls similar ones used by Scandinavian silversmiths. Compare e.g. that on the coffee-pot by Adolf Zethelius made at Stockholm in 1817 and now in the Royal Swedish collection (*Svenskt Silversmide,* Del. III, No. 313). These truncated finials have become popular with modern silversmiths.

Diameter of bowl: 10 in.	Weight: 46 oz.
Height to top of finial: $5\frac{1}{4}$ in.	London date-letter for 1813–14.

By courtesy of Messrs. S. J. Shrubsole, London and New York

PLATEAU—SILVER

CIRCULAR plateau resting on the backs of four crouching lions. The side is decorated with alternate twin floral cornucopias and anthemions on a matted surface, with a guilloche border below and a narrow astragal moulding above. The lining is of mirrored glass.

Width: $15\frac{1}{2}$ in.	London date-letter for 1813–14.
Height: $4\frac{3}{4}$ in.	

By courtesy of Mr. Ralph Hyman, of the Museum Silver Shop, New York City

PLATE XLII

CANDELABRUM—SILVER-GILT

(One of a set of three)

THIS is one of a seven-branch pair, the third being the central one of greater size and importance and having eight branches. The elaborate rococo decoration is the same on all three pieces. The only difference is that the base of the central candelabrum is square and of much greater size than those of the two side ones, which are round and distinctly too small for the height of their shafts.

From a base formed of a mingled mass of scroll work, shells, flowers and foliage rises the shaft like a striated tree-trunk, decorated near the bottom with a knop of owls' heads, above which there are two dolphins, separated by shells, their bodies twisted and their tails standing erect and free from the shaft. Above is a vase-shaped candle-socket with a circular dish-shaped wax-pan ornamented on the under side with bulrushes and on the upper side with foliated scrolls, foliage, etc. At this level emerge the first three branches formed of double scrolls with vase-shaped candle-sockets, etc., as before. The shaft continues upwards ornamented now with eagles' folded wings, alternating with roses. Above is another candle-socket from which the second tier of three branches emerges resembling the first in all points of ornamentation. Above this the eagles' folded wings and alternating roses are repeated, while the shaft ends in still another candle-socket surmounted by a wicker-work basket filled with flowers and foliage. This can be removed if an extra candle is preferred.

Height: 2 ft. 4½ in.   London date-letter for 1813–14.
Weight: 386 oz.

The large central candelabrum, engraved in several places with Lord Whitworth's Arms and crest, is 3 ft. high and weighs 583 oz.

From the Collection at Knole. By courtesy of Lord Sackville, K.B.E., etc.

In his *History of English Plate*, p. 868, Fig. 1131, Jackson gives an illustration of what appears to be the candelabrum described above. Strangely enough, he says it is in the Collection of the Duke of Portland and that the date is ''about 1740''. No such piece figures in Jones's complete catalogue of the Portland Plate. In the text Jackson says it is ''in the rococo style of about 1740'', but it is clear that either he had never inspected it or, if so, had failed to find any stamped date-letter. It seems, however, as if his notes had got muddled, for it is in actual fact the Knole Candelabrum of 1813 which he describes and illustrates.

Plate XLIII

SIX-LIGHT CANDELABRUM—SILVER-GILT

(One of a pair)

THE dominant *motif* represented here is that of Greek pastoral life. On a plain base, supported by double-lions'-paw and acanthus legs separated by a pendent shell and floral scroll decoration, rests a guilloche torus moulding surmounted by a ribbed concave border with a pearl edge above.

From the centre rises a tree trunk covered with acanthus foliage at the foot of which sit three figures on rocks covered with a lion's skin. To the right we see a shepherd, clad in his *nebris*, or fawn's skin, his hair encircled with ivy, his cheeks puffed out as he plays on the double flute, and his *pedum*, or crooked stick, on the ground beside him. On the opposite side of the tree a Bacchante, nude to the waist, her hair encircled with grapes and vine leaves, raises the cymbals above her head as she regards the child at her knees who clutches a syrinx in its right hand. Above, the tree trunk becomes a fluted column, resting on a round cushion of water-leaves and set in a deep calyx of tall acanthus foliage. From a cornice of leaves encircling the top of the column issue six branches in the form of acanthus scrolls with honeysuckle cusps, gadrooned grease-pans with pendent acanthus rims, and gadrooned-edged sockets.

For an alternative fitting (dated 1812–13) in place of the fluted column see Pl. LXII facing p. 122 of E. A. Jones's *Gold and Silver of Windsor Castle*.

Height: 2 ft. 8½ in.

Weight: 513 oz., the other being 524 oz.

London date-letter for 1813–14.

Number at the 1951 Regency Exhibition: 54.

By courtesy of H.R.H. The Princess Royal and the Earl of Harewood

166

PLATE XLIV

DESSERT-STAND—SILVER-GILT

(One of a set of four)

THE stem is in the form of a tall, narrow vase engraved with winged figures against a background of floral arabesque work. Its pointed base is gadrooned, while at the top narrow arches, bent at right angles, are secured under an ovolo collar, above which is standing a circle of acanthus foliage. From the centre of this foliage depend six ribbed branches of ogee section, ornamented at a central point with acanthus leaves. They support baskets, or bon-bon dishes, formed of vine leaves. Above this are broad pineapple leaves which support a plain circular bowl with pierced foliated borders. There are plain extra linings to the bowl. The vase stem rests on a drum-shaped pedestal with long spiral gadrooning, on the upper edges of which are placed such Bacchic paraphernalia as a *pedum*, syrinx, cymbals, mask, etc. Round it, on a circular base decorated with vine leaves and grapes, stands the large figure of a faun with the thyrsus across his right shoulder accompanied by two dancing bacchantes. The base has a plain raised border, below which is a torus moulding decorated with alternate quatrafoils and bound acanthus leaves. The whole rests on four scrolled acanthus feet, separated by pendent shell and leaf ornaments.

Height: $21\frac{1}{4}$ in.

Weight: 1,697 oz.

Number in the Royal Inventory: 156.

London date-letters (on stands) for 1816–17, and (on the centre dishes) 1813–14.

According to a note in Her Majesty's copy of the Royal inventory this piece was purchased by George, Prince Regent, in 1817 for £1,538 11s. 8d.

From the Collection at Windsor Castle. By Gracious Permission of H.M. The Queen

PLATE XLV

DINNER PLATES AND MEAT-DISHES— SILVER

A SET of twenty-four plain dinner plates with shaped and reeded edges, decorated at short intervals with small medallions of leaves, shells, etc. Although they are stamped with Storr's own registered number of 802 for this particular pattern, it should be realized that it was not an original pattern, as it was ordered to match that previously used by Paul de Lamerie on the plates and dishes made by him for the Mansion House many years earlier. Engraved with the City Arms, supporters, crest and motto.

Diameter: 9½ in. London date-letter for 1814–15.

A set of thirty-six plain meat-dishes of three different sizes made, from a previous design of Paul de Lamerie, to match the dinner plates. Several of them are stamped with Storr's own registered number of 610. Engraved with the City Arms, supporters, crest and motto. Diameters: 22½ by 15¾ in.; 18¼ by 13½ in.; 13¾ by 10¼ in. London date-letter: for the larger sizes, 1815–16; for the smaller size, 1808–9 (twenty) and 1815–16 (twelve).

Only a selection of the meat-dishes is shown in the photograph. The set of six dishes (third size from the bottom) is by Paul de Lamerie, included to show the perfect match of those by Storr.

By courtesy of the Chamberlain's Court, Guildhall House, E.C.2

A MS. catalogue of the Mansion House plate was prepared by the late E. A. Jones in 1939 for the Court of Aldermen. It is kept at Chamberlain's Court, Guildhall House, and has not yet been published.

I am indebted to the Chamberlain for permission to consult the MS. and use the information contained therein. My thanks are also due to the General Purposes Committee of Aldermen for allowing me to inspect and photograph the plate, and to Vice-Admiral T. B. Drew, C.B., O.B.E., the Lord Mayor's Private Secretary, for receiving me at the Mansion House and making all arrangements for the photographs.

A short article on the Mansion House plate by G. C. Maclean appeared in the *Connoisseur*, November 1912, pp. 139–45, with seventeen illustrations in the text.

The usual pattern preferred by Storr for plates and dishes, of which he was an extensive maker, was perfectly plain with a simple shell and gadroon border. The Worshipful Company of Goldsmiths possesses 107 dinner plates of 1809–11 and eighteen soup plates of 1810 of this type. At Lord Desborough's sale at Christie's in 1943 was a dinner service of eighty-two pieces, dated 1797–8 and weighing over 1,825 oz.

The silver-gilt dessert service made by Storr for Edward Lascelles, Earl of Harewood, includes twenty-four plates with shaped gadrooned shell and foliage rims (1814).[1]

The largest number of Storr plates with gadroon and shell borders, however, is that in the Royal Collection. It totals 409, and it is probable that many others bearing the marks both of Rundell and Bridge were also made by Storr. They are divided up as follows:

Grand Service	36	Crown Service	134
Coronation Service (only soup)	6	Lion Service (39 soup)	137
Yacht Service	96		
Dates: 1794–1818.			

The matching dishes (of varying sizes) number 84, as follows:

Grand Service	14	Crown Service	27
Yacht Service	18	Lion Service	25
Dates: 1794–1818.			

[1] They were lent by H.R.H. The Princess Royal for the Regency Exhibition at Brighton in 1951. See the *Souvenir Programme*, No. 63; and Clifford Musgrave's article in the *Connoisseur*, Oct. 1951, where the plates appear, with other Storr plate in the picture of the banqueting table on p. 90.

PLATE XLVI

SEVEN-LIGHT CANDELABRUM—SILVER-GILT

THE tapering shaft, encircled at each end with gadroon and zig-zag bands with lotus decoration, gives the illusion of a hollow tube or sheath encasing three Greek[1] maidens whose heads appear above as capitals and whose bare feet, together with the edges of their pleated garments, project below to rest on a plain circular base. This in turn rests on a corded and ribbed collar surmounting a reel-shaped gadrooned pedestal. The whole is supported by a tripod formed of three lion's feet with gadrooned knee-caps and acanthus decoration. Between the legs are Bacchic masks crowned with grapes and vine leaves, while the pads rest on a triangular concave base in the centre of which is a large boss or rosette of acanthus foliage. Above the capital is a vase, with acanthus and palmette decoration applied alternately, from which springs the first tier of three scrolled acanthus branches with lion-headed rosettes and palm spandrels. They terminate in birds' heads (?)[2] below gadrooned grease-pans and candle sockets. The shaft continues in the form of closely joined narrow serrated leaves from the pendent top of which issues the second tier of branches similar to the first, and also a central socket for the seventh light. This socket, however, is rarely used and is surmounted by a flat fluted boss separated by a small decorated collar from a bowl chased with alternate palmettes and anthemion (honeysuckle). The rims of this bowl afford a foothold for one of the Londonderry crests, the winged dragon *statant* for Stewart. The base in engraved with the Royal Arms and the Londonderry coat of arms.

This candelabrum was made for Lord Stewart, afterwards 3rd Marquess of Londonderry, when British Ambassador in Vienna.

Height: 34½ in.
Weight: 358 oz.
London date-mark for 1814–15.

Number in the 1951 Regency Exhibition: 70, and in that of 1952: 34.

By courtesy of the Marquess of Londonderry

For similar candelabra in the Royal Collection (four of seven lights and twenty-four for four lights) see E. A. Jones's *Gold and Silver of Windsor Castle*, Pl. LXIV, p. 126, and Pl. LXXX, p. 158 (here the weight should read 4,879 oz. 15 dwt.).

---

[1] Previously described as "Egyptian", these heads, with their curled hair and long tresses falling over their bosoms, seem with little doubt to be taken from the well-known archaic Greek *Korai* of about 530–500 B.C., chiefly found on the Acropolis. See Humfry Payne and G. Mackworth Young, *Archaic marble sculpture from the Acropolis* (1936), 2nd edit., 1950, Pls. 40–2, and cf. 50–8, 62–9 and 74–91; also Guy Dickins, *Catalogue of the Acropolis Museum*, Vol. 1, Cambridge, 1912, pp. 202–40, Nos. 666–85.

[2] Jones (*Gold and Silver of Windsor Castle*, p. 158) calls them dolphins.

PLATE XLVII

PAIR OF CANDLESTICKS—SILVER-GILT

THE slightly tapering shaft is octagonal, with pendent husks and overlapping quatre-foils ornamenting alternate facets. The shoulder surmounting the shaft is chased with oak foliage, above which a similar member, in inverted position, supports a ribbed candle-socket into which fits a movable nozzle decorated on the underside with oak foliage. At the lower end of the shaft a band of water-leaves surmounts a knot of floral design with interlacing ribbons, separated by a plain spool-shaped member from a high domical foot of bell shape and ogee section.

The upper part has a band of overlapping broad water-leaves on a matted ground, below which long narrow leaves, heavily ribbed, turn up at the ends as they reach the base. This base is broad, of irregular shape and enriched with shells, human masks, leaves and fruit.

It will be realized that such a rococo base, recalling de Lamerie's work of *c.* 1736, is quite out of keeping with the shaft of Adam design which might date from 1770–90, while the shoulder and knot, so far as their position and relation to the shaft is concerned, were established on candlesticks dating from the end of the seventeenth century. It is only the correct proportions and placing of the separate members that save such an anachronistic creation from complete banality. Made by Paul Storr for Rundell, Bridge & Rundell.

Height: $8\frac{9}{10}$ in.

Base: $5\frac{1}{2}$ in. square.

Weight: 28 oz. 6 dwt.; and 28 oz. 10 dwt.

London date-letter for 1814–15.

By courtesy of the Victoria and Albert Museum, London
From the Duke of Cumberland's Collection. Given by Mr. L. A. Crichton

PLATE XLVIII

STANDING FRUIT-DISH—SILVER-GILT

(One of a pair)

OF circular shape. The slightly sloping sides have a reeded rim and are covered with a broad band of bunches of grapes, vine leaves and tendrils cast in a most realistic manner. The flat bottom of the dish is encircled with a beautifully-engraved band of running acanthus leaves relieved at four equidistant points by baskets of fruit. Its narrow outer border is formed of alternate small leaves and double circles, while the inner border is of gadroon form. The plain centre is engraved with the Royal Hanoverian Arms of George III. A short stem separates the dish from a circular base of concave section enriched with an alternate pattern of water leaves and (possibly) honeysuckle umbels.

Height: 3½ in.

Diameter: 12 in.

Circumference: 38 in.

Weight: 61 oz. 1 dwt.

London date-letter for 1814–15.

By courtesy of Lord Fairhaven, 1st Bt., D.I., J.P., F.S.A.

PLATE XLIX

CIRCULAR DISH—SILVER-GILT

THE subject represented in this dish is the Triumph of Dionysus (Bacchus) and Ariadne. They stand side by side in an ornamented chariot drawn by four prancing centaurs who respectively play the double pipe, the harp, the tambourine or wield the cone-tipped thyrsus. In her right hand Ariadne holds a two handled vase and in her left, which rests lightly on her husband's right shoulder, a long shafted be-ribboned thyrsus. Dionysus embraces his wife's waist with his right arm, and with his left, in which is a thyrsus, presses a young faun (their son?) to his side. Above hover two winged *putti*—one holding a torch, the other a *pedum*. The whole scene is surrounded by a circle of vine leaves and grapes. The broad flat rim has a reeded edge enriched also with vine leaves and grapes, while the wide surface is covered with Bacchic emblems of every description—the syrinx, thyrsus, *pedum*, tambourine and various kinds of masks, many of which remind us of those on the Warwick Vase. They all rest on a ground of trellis-work. The Royal Arms of George IV are engraved below the main subject represented.

The design for the dish was made by Thomas Stothard, R.A. According to Rundell, Bridge & Rundell's bill of 1815 the main cost was £497 7s. 7d., to which was added 18s. for engraving the Royal Arms and £118 for the gilding. See E. A. Jones, *Connoisseur*, March 1947, p. 58.

Diameter: 31 in.   London date-letter for 1814–15.
Weight: 374 oz. 15 dwt.

From the Collection at Windsor Castle. By Gracious Permission of H.M. The Queen

PLATE L

DESSERT-STAND—SILVER-GILT
(One of a pair)

ON a plain concave triangular base with a sloping acanthus upper border, supported by semi-block feet enriched with floral sprays and quatrefoil and honeysuckle spandrels, stands a shallow circular bowl decorated externally with a border of grapes and vines. The plain interior is engraved with the Harewood Arms, while the crest appears in the centre of the plain concave base. The bowl is supported on a tripod formed of a short shaft encircled with a plain central band which divides the water-leaf decoration above from that of the acanthus below. The legs are cast in the shape of muscular feet and pads of the lion, the knees being capped with gadrooning. A large pendent anthemion, or honeysuckle, is placed on the shaft centrally between each pair of legs. In the centre of the base is a large rosette of acanthus leaves with an inner pearl border.

Diameter: 14 in.
London date-letter for 1814–15, the second
piece being dated 1816–17.

Number at the 1951 Regency
Exhibition: 58.

By courtesy of H.R.H. The Princess Royal and the Earl of Harewood

DECANTER STAND—SILVER-GILT

THIS is one of a set of twelve. The sides are cast, pierced and boldly embossed with recumbent figures of the young Dionysus (Bacchus) holding his thyrsus, or sceptre, surmounted by a pine-cone. Between the figures are sleeping lions, the entire background being vine-leaf foliage and pendent bunches of grapes. The rim is in the form of a bundle of reeds spirally bound with ribbon-like lengths of the split vine stem. Above the plain base is a projecting rim, on the sloping upper side of which is a chased border of acanthus leaves. Glass liners enable the decanter stands to be used for other purposes, e.g. as small fruit-dishes, or receptacles for sweets, fondants, salted almonds, olives, etc.

This set formed part of the first Duke of Wellington's Ambassador Service. Each piece bears the English Royal Arms in the centre of the base.

Signed on the plain base: RUNDELL BRIDGE ET RUNDELL AURIFICES REGIS ET PRIN-CIPIS WALLIÆ REGENTIS BRITANNIAS [sic.] Maker's mark of Paul Storr.

Height: 3¼ in.
Diameter: 5¾ in.
Weight: 240 oz.

London date-letter for 1814–15.
Registered Museum Numbers: W.M. 441A–
452A–1948.

The Wellington Museum, Apsley House, London

A set of eight similar decanter-stands, or wine-coasters, formed part of the silver-gilt dessert service made by Storr for Edward Lascelles, Earl of Harewood. They are dated 1815, and were on view at the Regency Festival at the Royal Pavilion, Brighton, in 1951. (See *Souvenir Programme*, No. 57.)

Oriel College, Oxford, possesses a set of four exactly similar to the above, made by Storr in 1818–19. See E. A. Jones, *Catalogue of the Plate of Oriel College, Oxford*, 1944, pp. 78, 79 and Pl. 12.

PLATE LI

PAIR OF SUGAR-VASES AND COVERS— SILVER-GILT

THESE two-handled richly chased vases, suitable for sugar or cream, have a broad central band of acanthus scrolls on a granulated ground between narrow water-leaf borders. From the uppermost of these borders reeded loop-handles with snake heads project at an angle of 40 degrees. The concave neck above the handles is embossed with acanthus foliage separated by a running wavy fillet. A gadrooned edge is met by a similar one encircling the floriated lid, which has a gadrooned dome surmounted by an acorn-shaped finial within a calyx of water-leaves. The lower parts of the vases are embossed with elongated gadrooning. The short fluted stems have a beaded collar with a lower foliage border, leading to a round concave base ornamented with alternate lanceolate flutings and foliage. The four supporting legs are embossed with shells and acanthus leaves.

Height: 7 in.
London date-letter for 1814–15.

Number at the 1951 Regency Exhibition: 61.

By courtesy of H.R.H. The Princess Royal and the Earl of Harewood

With the above we can compare the set of eight two-handled sugar-vases in the Royal Collection (E. A. Jones, *Gold and Silver of Windsor Castle*, p. 164). One was made by Benjamin Smith in 1808, and the other seven by Benjamin and James Smith in 1809. Four ladles, to match, were added by Paul Storr in 1810, while a further four were made in 1829 by William Bateman. (See *Descriptive Inventory* . . . Garrard & Co., 1914, p. 19, No. 121.) In the Earl Howe sale at Christie's on 1st July 1953, lot 111 was a set of four by D. Scott and B. Smith, 1805.

Plate LII

PUNCH BOWL AND LADLE—SILVER

(One of a pair)

THE body, of ogee section, is surrounded at its broadest point by a frieze of repeated roses, thistles and shamrocks within plain fillet borders. The remainder of the body is plain except for two shields applied to one side below the frieze. These shields are placed in a sloping position, leaning towards each other and separated only by a double acanthus ornament. One bears in relief a representation of the corporate seal of Dover—a single-masted vessel with furled sails—and the other the town arms—St. Martin, the patron saint of Dover, dividing his cloak with a beggar. There is a long inscription concerning "Peter Fector Esqu. born 26 May 1723, died 30th January 1814", with his crest and motto. It tells of past hospitality accorded to Fector's father and maternal great-grandfather, Mr. Isaac Minet, a Huguenot who found asylum at Dover in 1686. It also records hospitality meted out to Fector himself.

An ovolo border surrounds the upper edge of the base, and applied acanthus and shell foliage decorates the top of the rim of the bowl. The ladle is in the form of one valve of a clam shell (*Hippopus hippopus*) with a curved reeded handle, acanthus leaf grip and water-leaf finial.

For fuller details of the inscription, seals, etc., see L. Jewitt and W. H. St. John Hope, *Corporation Plate and Insignia of Office*, Vol. I, 1895, pp. 327, 328, with the illustration in the text of p. 325, E. Wollaston Knocker, *An Account of the Corporation Insignia, Seals and Plate . . . Dover*, 1898, pp. 23, 24, with the same illustration as above facing p. 23. One of the bowls, with its ladle, was shown at the Exhibition of Corporation Plate at Goldsmith's Hall, 1952 (No. 157 and Pl. XXXVIII).

Diameter: 12¼ in.	Weight (each ladle): 16 oz.
Height: 8 in.	London date-letter for 1814–15.
Weight (each bowl): 80 oz.	

By courtesy of the Corporation of Dover. Photograph kindly supplied by the Worshipful Company of Goldsmiths

PLATE LIII

EIGHT-LIGHT CANDELABRUM—SILVER-GILT

ON a thick triangular base, decorated below the concave sides with shells and floral scrolls and having three broad voluted acanthus legs, are three bears sejant erm., muzzled and collared, buckled and chained, an escutcheon charged with a cross patonce pendant from the collars. They are adapted from the heraldic supporters of the Harewood Arms. On their backs, helped by a thick fluted central column, they support a triangular pedestal, the concave sides of which carry applied coats of the Harewood Arms and have a floral lower border below which is a pendent shell and acanthus-foliage decoration. The truncated corners are ornamented with applied acanthus plants. On the centre of the pedestal stands a tall slender vase with splayed foot decorated with gadrooning and lanceolate foliage. Around this vase, with their backs to it, stand three Greek maidens clad in the chiton (Χιτών, or *tunica*), holding between them three laurel wreaths. Their eyes are cast down, and they stand on tiptoe as if looking at the armorial supporters below. From the top of the vase rises a pineapple with its foliage—an allusion to the association of the family with the Barbados—from which springs the first tier of four branches of the candelabrum. A central ribbed shaft carries a cornice of conventional water-leaves from which issues the second tier of four branches. Those eight branches take the form of acanthus scrolls with fan-like (honeysuckle?) cusps, gadrooned grease-pans with pendent acanthus rims and gadroon-edged sockets. The ribbed central shaft continues upwards to terminate in a circle of overhanging leaves. This portion may be removed to allow the insertion of a fruit-bowl.

Height: 3 ft. 4 in.	London date-letter for 1815–16.
Weight: 1,010 oz.	Number at the 1951 Regency Exhibition: 53.

By courtesy of H.R.H. The Princess Royal and the Earl of Harewood

PLATE LIV

CHEESE-DISH—SILVER

A FLAT oblong dish, of cushion-shape, with an applied gadroon border including anthemions at the corners, which are rounded. Into the dish fit twelve small movable trays (the corner ones rounded) to receive the toasted cheese. They each carry the College Arms. The dish rests on four ball feet. Into a protruding socket at the back fits a shaped pear-wood handle with an eyelet for a chain by which the lid can be held half-open for convenience in serving. A small hook at the other end of the chain connects with the handle in its half-open position. The slightly domed lid has a border of long gadroons, with a central oval handle reeded above and arboreal below. It is held in place by a screw and pin. The Arms of Brasenose College are engraved in the front of the lid, while behind the handle is the following inscription in roman letter:

D.D. in Us. Principal. Gul. Ellis Gosling Arm: S.O.C. 1814.

William Ellis Gosling of St. George's, London, banker, was matriculated in July 1812 at the age of seventeen and entered the College as a "Gentleman Commoner" from Eton in that year. He removed his name from the College books in 1814, when he presented the cheese-dish. He died in 1834. As the inscription indicates, the gift was intended for the use of the Principal.

Length: $11\frac{1}{2}$ in.

Height with cover: $4\frac{1}{8}$ in.

Height without cover: $2\frac{5}{8}$ in.

London date-letter for 1815–16.

Brasenose College, Oxford. By courtesy of the Principal and Fellows

A short description, with illustration, was published in H. C. Moffat, *Old Oxford Plate*, 1906, p. 126 and Pl. LXI. See also A. J. Butler, *The College Plate*, Brasenose College Monographs V, Oxford, 1909, Pl. XVI. It was last shown at the "Treasures of Oxford" exhibition at Goldsmiths' Hall, 1953. Cat. No. 165.

PLATE LV

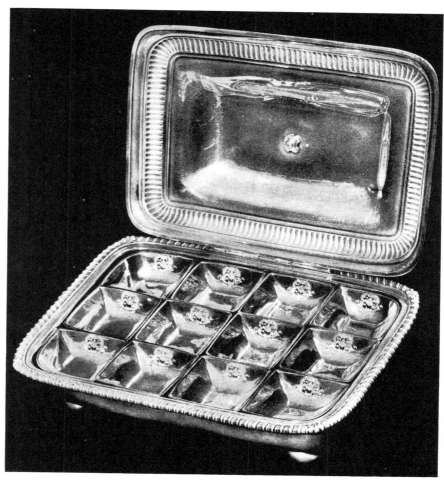

WINE-COOLER—SILVER

THIS is probably Storr's largest work, being over three feet in diameter and two feet in height. It takes the form of a large oval bowl resting on a thick truncated stem which splays out as it reaches the slightly concave base. The bowl is divided midway by a running scroll-fret band between plain fillets. Above this band the plain surface bears inscriptions in English, Latin and Welsh praising the patriotism and military prowess of the recipient, Sir Watkin Williams-Wynn, 5th Bt. (1772–1840). The side shown in the Plate opposite gives the englyn, or Welsh stanzas, composed by the Denbigh bard Nantglyn (i.e. Robert Davies, 1759 (?)–1835). They are separated by the device of the seal of the county town of Denbigh[1] arranged in a shield. On the opposite sides the English and Latin translations are separated by the Arms[2] of Sir Watkin Williams-Wynn supported by his crest, an eagle displayed or.

Below the running scroll-fret a design of elongated egg-and-tongue forms a calyx. The thick stem, or foot, divided from the bowl by a plain collar, resembling an inverted saucer, has elongated fluting widening on reaching the base. The round vertical sub-base is plain. The overhanging rim of the bowl has an egg-and-tongue border surmounted by a plain pearl beading.

It appears that the patriotic Baronet was so immersed in military affairs after the suppression of the Irish rebellion in 1798, in which he took a distinguished part as leader of the ''Ancient British Fencibles'' raised in North Wales, and in forming his militia for service in France in 1814 that the presentation of the wine-cooler by the citizens of Denbigh was deferred until Sir Watkin had returned safely to his fatherland. (See E. A. Jones, *Connoisseur,* July 1935, p. 17.) In 1947 the wine-cooler was sold, and subsequently presented to the National Coal Board by Mr. F. A. Mitchell-Hedges, the well-known explorer and entomologist. It was first awarded to the winning Division in a production competition, and since 1948 has been the main trophy for the Miners' National First-Aid Competition.

Height: 2 ft. 1½ in. (2 ft. 7½ in. with stand).   Weight: 1,707 oz. 4 dwt.
Length (i.e. greatest diameter): 3 ft. 1½ in.   London date-letter for 1815–16.
Breadth (i.e. narrowest diameter): 2 ft. 2 in.

By courtesy of the National Coal Board

[1] Denbigh has no Arms, those on the cup being taken from the seal: On a mound, in front of which is a greyhound couchant, a triple-staged tower or castle with capped turrets, and inside the doorway a leopard's head *jessant-de-lis*. In the field are, on the dexter, a shield of France modern and England quarterly, and on the sinister a shield charged with a lion rampant, each shield being surmounted by a coronet from which rises three ostrich feathers.

[2] Quarterly, 1st and 4th, those of Owen Gwynedd, Prince of North Wales, Vert three eagles displ. in fess or, for Wynn; 2nd and 3rd those of Cadrod Hardd, Ar. two foxes counter-salient in saltire, the dexter surmounted of the sinister gu. for Williams.—*General Armory*.

Plate LVI

DESSERT-BASKET—SILVER-GILT
(One of a set of four)

OF oval shape, the body of wirework decorated on the outside with bunches of grapes, vine leaves and tendrils, with an overhanging egg-and-dart rim. The legs are in the form of the Greek sphinx, i.e. a female head and torso with wig lappets hanging to the breasts, expanded wings and lion's feet.

Width: 12 in.

London date-letter for 1815–16.

Number at the 1951 Regency Exhibition: 60.

By courtesy of H.R.H. The Princess Royal and the Earl of Harewood

Plate LVII

SALTS—SILVER-GILT

(A set of four)

THESE are round in shape and quite plain except for a gadrooning round the base. The chief feature, however, is the somewhat excessive use of four serpents, so arranged that their heads, crossing each other at the bottom of the outside of the bowl, form a flat base. Their coils, arched up over the rim, form handles either side, while the tips of their tails extend a short way each side of the handle in sinuous folds.

Height: $1\frac{1}{2}$ in. ($2\frac{1}{4}$ in. to top of handle).   Weight: 49 oz. 14 dwt.
Diameter: $3\frac{5}{8}$ in. ($4\frac{1}{4}$ in. with handles).   London date-letter for 1815–16.

By courtesy of Francis Stonor, Esq.

A very similar pair can be seen at the Victoria and Albert Museum. In this case, however, the surface is entirely plain, without any gadrooning.

WINE-LABELS—SILVER

(A set of three)

OVAL, with a plain matted surface to which is applied, near the lower edge, the name of the wine in bold roman capitals. These letters form an oval segment following the line of the oval gadrooning which, with a simple anthemion centred at the base, surrounds most of the label. Covering the top part of the border, and spreading over the upper portion of the matted surface, is an applied palmette flanked by trailing acanthus leaves which terminate in central volutes and enclose chain eyelets at their curling lateral extremities.

Height: 2 in.   Weight of all three: 3 oz.
Width: $2\frac{1}{2}$ in.   London date-letter for 1815–16.

By courtesy of Mrs. Jean Rhodes, Editor of the "Wine Label Circle"

PLATE LVIII

CLASSICAL-SHAPED CUP—SILVER

OF Greek krater shape to which non-classical handles have been added.
The base of the cup is a torus moulding decorated with alternate acanthus and water-leaves in relief, the circular foot being plain. The two handles, attached to the lower sides of the cup, are formed of the stem of the vine twisted in the middle. Immediately below the rim, and drooping down at the sides, are branches of vine and bunches of grapes forming a kind of frieze to the subjects represented each side. Although the cup has always been known in the Wellington family as the "Flaxman Cup", and is so called in several of their nineteenth-century wills, there is no actual written record of its having been designed by Flaxman.

It is clearly copied from his famous Theocritus cup made by Storr in 1812–13 for Queen Charlotte (see E. A. Jones, *Gold and Silver of Windsor Castle*, p. 120, Pl. LXI). In the present case, however, the scenes, although classical in design, are not taken from Greek mythology. The subject represented on one side is that of two women pouring libations on an altar, the lower part of which is hung with floral swags. The figure on the left is pouring wine or water from a single-handled vase of oinochoe shape, while the one on the right is emptying a bowl of oil or milk on the dancing flames. On the other side the scene depicts a semi-nude figure —whether male or female is hard to determine as only the back is visible—reclining on a flat rock, represented by a matted ground, leaning with the bent right arm on an inverted torch. A butterfly, with large wings, occupies a central position near some tall plants or reeds. Each side is a cypress tree, that to the right half concealing a flat pillar with an Ionic capital. The scene may be purely fanciful, and if we look at some of the pottery formerly designed by Flaxman and others for Wedgwood we shall find both the butterfly and dragon-fly depicted on tea-pots, etc.

On the other hand, however, the possibility of the scene representing an escape into the world of dreams, if not an actual glimpse of Hades, must not be overlooked. If this be so, then many points, hitherto meaningless, at once become clear. In the first place the somewhat misty background with its curious reed-like plants may be intended to convey the asphodel meadow of the Lower World. In the second place the recumbent figure has closed eyes and is resting on an inverted torch, the *fax*, symbol of sleep and death. The butterfly, the Greek symbol of Psyche, or the soul, is represented as flying away from the figure. Finally we have the cypress trees, which were characteristic of the infernal regions. If this interpretation is correct, it surely follows that the other scene probably represents an offering to the departed.

Inscription on foot in mixed gothic, roman and italic lettering: Bequeathed to Elizth. Saltren, / by Charles Earl Manvers, / her Brother-in-Law and cherished by her / in Grateful and Affectionate Remembrance / of His Kindness and Excellence 1816.

Enclosed in original oak case, with engraved circular label of Rundell, Bridge & Rundell under lid. Inscription in roman capitals on outer rim of base:

RUNDELL BRIDGE ET RUNDELL AURIFICES REGIS ET PRINCIPIS WALLIÆ REGENTIS BRITANNIAS [sic] FECERUNT LONDINI.

Major-General Lord Charles Wellesley (1808–58), second son of the Great Duke, married (in 1844) Augusta Sophia Anne, only child and heiress of Henry Pierrepont, third son of Charles, 1st Earl of Manvers. Mrs. Saltren was sister of Lady Manvers.[1]
Designed by John Flaxman, R.A.

Height: $9\frac{5}{16}$ in.   Width: $9\frac{7}{8}$ in.
Weight: 82 oz. 9 dwt.   London date-letter for 1817–18.

By courtesy of His Grace the Duke of Wellington, K.G.

[1] In a letter to me on the cup, His Grace explains that he has always understood that Lord Manvers left Mrs. Saltren £100 by will, and that she bought the cup with this money as a memorial of him. This would explain the date-letter being a year later than the "1816" of the inscription. It would also agree with my interpretation of the symbolism, with which His Grace wholly concurs.

PLATE LIX

KETTLE AND STAND—SILVER

OF flattened pear-shape, the upper, and broader, part of the body being embossed and chased with sprays of roses, diaper panels in rococo frames, and the Arms of Lord Whitworth in scroll shields forming central cartouches each side. The entire ground is matted. The low domed lid is chased with similar sprigs of roses, the knob, rising from a circle of acanthus leaves, having water-leaves drooping over the rim. A broad double-scroll handle, with acanthus decoration, and having a straw-plaited grip, straddles the lid. The lower part of the kettle has long plain gadroons. From one side a long horizontal spigot protrudes. It is chased with acanthus leaves, and beyond the tap, with its double curved rope handle and petal-shaped ivory knob, has a dolphin mouth with a fish-scale neck. The stand, resting on a triangular base with shell and scroll borders and feet, is a mass of pierced work—acanthus leaves, shells and fruit, with three scrolled flat-sided feet supported on floral bases. The spirit-lamp is fixed to the centre of the plain triangular base, being largely hidden by the deep fringe of the pierced ornamentation. Engraved on the base is the crest of Lord Whitworth.

Height with stand to top of handle: 1 ft. 6¼ in.	Greatest circumference: 2 ft. 9 in.
Height of triangular stand: 6 in.	Weight: 181 oz.
	London date-letter for 1817–18.

From the Collection at Knole. By courtesy of Lord Sackville, K.B.E., etc.

INKSTAND—SILVER

OF rectangular shape with applied rococo border heavily engraved with foliage, fruit and flowers. Large shell-shaped leaves protrude as handles either side. The four legs are of scrolled acanthus leaves with fruit or berry ornamentation. In the centre of the stand on a long oval platform, two round and one square sockets, decorated with overlapping water-leaves, hold three cut-glass containers. The two round ones are ink-pots—that with three holes in the silver cap being for spare steel pens or quills, while that with a single hole contained the ink. The central container is a wafer-box, the lid being surmounted by a taper holder of vase-shaped design with gadrooning immediately above the foot. It has a nozzle with ovolo border, while attached to a chain is a narrow conical extinguisher. All three fittings have a border of ovolo design. Each side of the platform, and extending nearly the entire length of the inkstand, is a concave depression for pens and sealing wax.

On the tray are the Arms of Pierrepont, a crescent for difference, for the Hon. Henry Manvers Pierrepont of Conholt, Hants, 1780–1851, 3rd (2nd surviving) son of Charles, 1st Earl Manvers. On accessories, Pierrepont crest only.

Length: 12⅜ in.	All-in weight: 41 oz.
Breadth: 7⅞ in.	London date-letter for 1817–18.
Height over-all: 5¼ in.	

By courtesy of His Grace the Duke of Wellington, K.G.

PLATE LX

CENTRE-PIECE—SILVER

THE stem has the semblance of a palm-tree, being formed of lanceolate leaves rising erect from a calyx of acanthus leaves, which in turn rests on a base also of acanthus. It is surmounted by an overhanging circle of foliage from which emerge three branches enriched with acanthus decoration, each of which bifurcates into two reeded arms, thus providing six lights in all. The sockets, with gadrooned bases and overhanging rims of egg-and-tongue and acanthus decoration, support gadroon-rimmed nozzles which can be replaced with small cut-glass dishes. The central stem continues in a plain member which supports a large bowl enriched with a broad laurel border, a gadrooned base and overhanging rim matching those of the sockets. The whole rests on a triangular concave plinth, to the chamfered corners of which acanthus foliage is applied. The sides display respectively the seal of the City of Kilkenny, the Arms of the Order of the Bath, General Pack, and a long inscription which reads as follows:

To Major General Sir DENIS PACK

Knight Commander of the Most Honorable Order of the Bath.
Knight of the Royal Portuguese Order of the Tower & Sword.
Knight of the Russian Imperial Order of St. Waladomir.
Knight of the Imperial Austrian Order of Maria Theresa.
&c., &c., &c.

This Piece of Plate is Presented

as a testimonial of the Pride & Gratification so justly & naturally felt By His Friends & Fellow Citizens of the County and City of Kilkenny, at his uniformly intrepid & most distinguished Conduct, during the late protracted warfare, and particularly in the following Actions:—

VIMEIRA	CIUDAD RODRIGO	NIVELLE
ROLEIA	SALAMANCA	NIVE
CORUNNA	VITTORIA	ORTHES
BUSACO	PYRENEES	TOULOUSE
	& WATERLOO	

The base of the plinth has a shamrock border, with an overhang of acanthus scrolls bounded by plain fillets and a palmette centre. It is supported on three broad shell and palmette feet with lateral pendent grapes and vine leaves.

Height: 20½ in.　　　　　　　　　　　　London date-letter for 1817–18.
Weight: 274 oz.

By courtesy of Messrs. Corbell & Co., Ltd., of London, W.8

ICE-PAIL—SILVER

(One of a set of four)

OF krater shape, with low lateral handles of vine branches twisted at the centre, terminating above in formal anthemions, and meeting a narrow calyx of acanthus below a projecting "shelf" from which lions' skins depend as on the Warwick Vase. The entire body is covered with a meandering design of vines on a plain surface, the serrated vine leaves and bunches of grapes standing out in high relief. From the reeded rim bunches of grapes hang free. The lining is of plain silver, the collar being embossed with ivy leaves and berries. The plain spreading foot is separated from the body of the vase by a reeded band similar to the rim.

Affixed to the front of the base of the foot are the Arms of George John, 2nd Earl Spencer, K.G.; impaling those of Bingham; his wife, Lavinia, being the eldest daughter of Charles Bingham, 1st Earl of Lucan.

Height: 11 in.　　　　　　　　　Weight (of the set): 620 oz. 5 dwt.
Greatest diameter: 20 in.　　　　London date-letter for 1817–18.

By courtesy of the Earl Spencer

PLATE LXI

TRAY—SILVER-GILT

OVAL, with a broad cast border of grapes, vine leaves and tendrils. The outer rim is formed of alternate floral quatrefoils and overlapped acanthus leaves. The handles are of entwined snakes, and the short feet of volute form. The otherwise plain centre is engraved with the Arms of the 1st Marquess of Ailesbury, K.T. (1773–1856): Quarterly, 1st and 4th, or, a saltire and chief gu., on a canton arg., a lion rampant az. for Bruce; 2nd and 3rd arg., a chevron gu. between three chapeaux to the sinister az. for Brundenell,—impaling those of his first wife Henrietta Maria, dau. of Noel, 1st Lord Berwick:—erm., on a fesse, sa., a castle with two towers, arg.; on a canton, gu., a martlet, or, for Hill.

Length (including handles): 2 ft. 5¼ in. Weight: 306 oz.
Width (at centre): 1 ft. 8 in. London date-letter for 1818–19.
Height of feet: 3 in. Order No. 452 of Paul Storr.

By courtesy of Lord Fairhaven, 1st Bt., D.L., J.P., F.S.A.

PLATE LXII

TUREEN—SILVER

O F oval shape, with a plain low body relieved by a plain beading passing above the four rococo legs and cast loop handles of equally rococo form. The rim is gadrooned in sections of alternating slope. The high domed cover is quite plain except for a gadrooned border, matching that round the rim, dividing it nearly in half. The tall looped handle to the cover is of rococo design and with its central shell terminal matches the lateral handles of the body.

The Trinity College Arms with a mantling and "Trin. Coll. Cant" are engraved on one side in the centre and below the beading. The same inscription is engraved inside the cover.

Length (including handles): $17\frac{1}{8}$ in.   Inside length: 12 in.
Breadth: $8\frac{1}{4}$ in.   Height to top of cover handle: $10\frac{1}{4}$ in.

Weight: 118 oz. 10 dwt.; originally 110 oz. 10 dwt., but four plates of metal were added inside to support the legs.
London date-letter for 1819–20.

By courtesy of the Master and Fellows of Trinity College, Cambridge

SAUCE TUREEN AND COVER—SILVER

O F oval shape, with broadly fluted body ornamented with applied oak and acanthus foliage, richly cast and chased, terminating in four foliated and scrolled feet. Two upward-curving horizontal looped handles are formed of acanthus stems, by the leaves of which they are attached to the fluted body. Above a projection gadrooned gallery is a slightly domed cover of elongated gadroons crowned with a cluster of applied oak foliage from which springs an oval handle of similar foliage.

Height: $7\frac{3}{8}$ in.   Weight: 74 oz. 6 dwt.
Width: $10\frac{1}{4}$ in.   London date-letter for 1819–20.

By courtesy of the Victoria and Albert Museum, London

PLATE LXIII

PAIR OF SAUCE-BOATS—SILVER

(Two of a set of four)

Of oval shape, formed like a shell, with the ribs inside instead of outside. This effect is produced by a series of channels or grooves on the outside of the body, lengthening as they approach the lip. Conventional acanthus foliage is engraved above and between the grooves and mingles with the uneven rococo rims of the vessels, which are also partly formed of acanthus foliage. The curved voluted handles are entwined by sea-serpents whose wide mouths join the hinge of the shells as they bend inwards between concentric rococo rosettes. The bodies of the sauce-boats are divided from the shell and foliage bases by entwining serpents.

Length of body: 6 in. approx.   London date-letter for 1819–20.
Weight (of the set of four): 130 oz.

By courtesy of James Robinson, Inc., of Fifth Avenue, New York

PART OF FITTED TRAVELLING SET— SILVER-GILT

One round and two rectangular toilet boxes with milled tops and sides within borders of oak leaves. Crests applied to the centre of each lid.

Largest box: 7 in. by 2½ in.   Circular box: 3¾ in. diameter.
Small rectangular box: 4 in. by 2½ in.   London date-letter for 1819–20.

By courtesy of Mr. Ralph Hyman, of the Museum Silver Shop, New York City

PLATE LXIV

GRAPE-SCISSORS—SILVER GILT

(Two of a set of three)

THE ring handles are reeded, the shafts being chased both sides with grapes and vine leaves. A small bunch of grapes projects at the widest part of the under-shafts, thus acting as feet when correctly placed; this position shows the central boss chased with vine leaves, which is absent on the reverse side.

Length: 6 in.; 6⅛ in.
Weight: 4 oz.
London date-letter for 1820–1.

Number in 1951 Regency Catalogue: 48, and in that of 1952: 54.

By courtesy of the Marquess of Londonderry

VISCOUNT'S CORONET—SILVER AND SILVER-GILT

THIS coronet has twelve silver balls, or "pearls" (two, being broken, are not shown in the photograph), fixed to the gilt circlet. Medallions and other ornaments decorate the circlet, which has a matted ground with gadrooned or corded bands, that at the top being fringed with a narrow scalloping. Below are the small holes by which the ermine is attached.

Diameter: 8½ in.
Weight: 24 oz. 6 dwt.

London date-letter for 1820–1.

It is of interest to recall that in 1828 Messrs. Rundell, Bridge & Rundell made the Imperial State Crown used at the Coronation of Queen Victoria and that of Edward VII. It was worn by successive sovereigns on state occasions. See Sir G. Younghusband and C. Davenport, *Crown Jewels of England*, 1919, pp. 19–21, and H. D. W. Sitwell, *Crown Jewels*, 1953, pp. 56, 68.

By courtesy of Christie, Manson & Woods, Ltd.

PLATE LXV

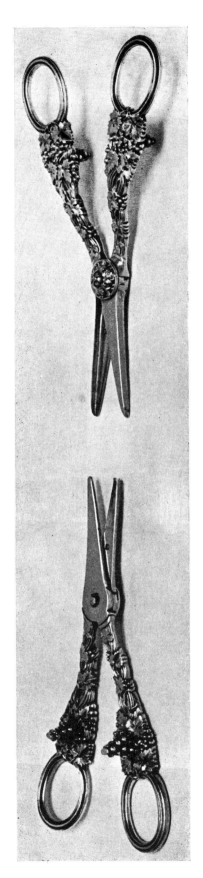

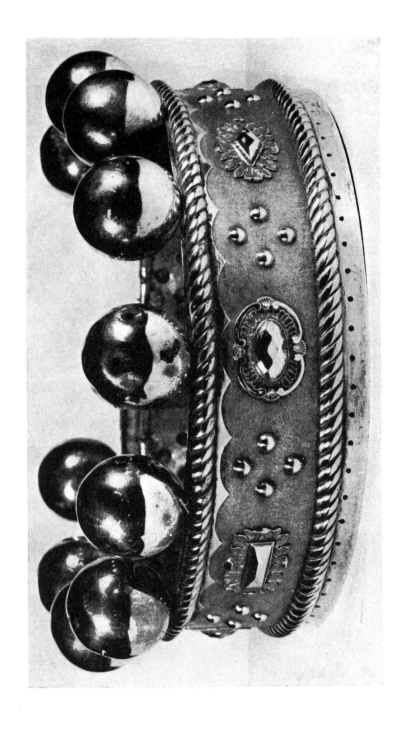

ST. PANCRAS CHURCH—ALTAR PLATE
SILVER-GILT

As mentioned in the first chapter of this work, H.R.H. Frederick Duke of York presented this church with a full set of altar plate in keeping with the Greek architectural *motifs* so prominent in the new building designed by William Inwood and his eldest son, Henry William. This noble set is in silver-gilt and originally consisted of fifteen pieces, but two of the four large cups were melted down by Storr's successors (Hunt and Roskell) in 1853 and remade as four smaller cups of simpler design. In 1827 a silver verger's wand had been presented. Thus, as the two photographs show, there are now eighteen pieces in all. The designs used by Storr can all be found on the north doorway of the Erechtheum, of which Henry William Inwood had made casts when in Athens and had already used for the doorways under the hexastyle portico on the west front of the church. Apart from the verger's wand, which really has nothing to do with the altar plate at all, the items comprise two flagons, two large and four (remade) cups, three patens, three dishes, two spoons and a knife.

We shall describe them in that order.

The Flagons

The main body of each flagon is straight-sided and plain, except for the Glory and a broad lower band of anthemion and floral scrolls on a matted ground. The Glory encloses a crown of thorns, while in the centre is the sacred emblem I H S, formed of small acanthus leaves, with the H surmounted and pierced by the cross *pattée fitchée*. The handle is formed of a reeded recurving scroll enriched at the top with acanthus leaves, while others, held together by a small frilled collar, connect it with the body just below the egg-and-dart moulding which surrounds the rim. The lower part of the handle rests on a very small reeded scroll, with an anthemion spandrel at their juncture, which is attached to the broad border by another small frilled collar. The spout, in line with the handle, is decorated with floral spirals. The domical lid is capped with applied water-leaves, and is surmounted by a finial of anthemion through which rises a cross.[1] There is an acanthus thumb-piece, the recurving portion of which forms the hinge attached to the handle. The lower part of the flagon is thistle-shaped and decorated with applied acanthus and floral vases of fruit. A gadrooned collar separates this from the spreading foot, which again is enriched with acanthus leaves which appear to be held in place by a narrow ovolo moulding. The base is quite plain.

Height: 18 in.	Weight of the other: 112 oz. 18
Diameter of base: 5⅝ in.	dwt.
Weight of one flagon: 115 oz. 8 dwt.	London date-letter for 1821–2.

[1] It is difficult to decide whether to describe this as a Maltese cross, a cross *pattée*, or cross *moline*. It appears to have no exact heraldic equivalent.

Plate LXVI

The Two Cups (as originally made)

The body is quite plain except for the Glory, which is exactly similar to those on the flagons. The sides are gently sloping and there is a moulded everted rim. The lower part of the cup is enriched with applied acanthus and floral vases of fruit. The gadrooned collar, the spreading foot and ovolo moulding are all exactly as on the flagons.

Height: 9¾ in.
Diameter of bowl: 5½ in.
Diameter of foot: 5 in.

Weight of one: 35 oz. 3 dwt.
Weight of other: 35 oz. 9 dwt.
London date-letter for 1821–2.

The Four Smaller Cups (remade from two larger ones)

The bowls are naturally much smaller and lighter. They are plain except for the Glory. The narrow stem, decorated with acanthus, has a graceful spreading foot, a flattened knop being placed at a convenient point a little below the bowl.

Height: 8¼ in.
Diameter at lip: 4½ in.
Diameter at base: 4¾ in.

Weight of two: 14 oz. 10 dwt. each.
Weight of other two: 15 oz. each.
London date-letter for 1853–4.

The Three Patens

Except for the Glory, the central part of these standing-patens is quite plain. The broad flat rims are enriched with the anthemion and floral scrolls design as before. Round the inner edge runs a narrow astragal band, while the outer edge has a much broader gadrooned moulding.

Height: 2¾ in.
Weights: 17 oz. 3 dwt., 17 oz. 4 dwt., 21 oz. 10 dwt.

Diameter: 8½ in.
London date-letter for 1821–2.

The Three Dishes

These resemble the patens in every particular, except that they have no foot. The astragal is clearly seen in the large dish, which is of very beautiful proportions.

Diameter of large dish: 24 in.
Weight: 194 oz.
London date-letter for 1821–2.

Diameter of smaller dishes: 14½ in.
Weights: 61 oz. 10 dwt. and 56 oz. 11 dwt.

The Two Spoons

One of these spoons is perforated, the cutting being of a floral design. Both of them have turned-down ends, which are decorated with acanthus leaves. A similar enrichment occurs at the juncture of the shaft with the bowl.

Length: 10 in.　　Weight: 3½ oz.　　London date-letter for 1821–2.

The Knife

This matches the spoons in decoration. It is 10¾ in. long and bears the London date-letter for 1822–3.

The Verger's Wand

This is of silver, not gilded, and has a grip of acanthus leaves. It is surmounted by a cross matching those on the flagons. For an enlarged photograph see E. Freshfield, *Communion Plate of the Parish Churches in the County of London*, 1895, Pl. VII, No. 3, "Beadles' Staves". His dates are incorrect.

Length: 28½ in.
Weight: 14 oz. 15 dwt.

London date-letter for 1827–8.

By courtesy and personal assistance of Rev. W. P. Baddeley, Vicar of St. Pancras

PLATE LXVII

SIX-BRANCH CANDELABRUM—SILVER

ON a slightly concave triangular plinth, supported by three broad acanthus legs, stand three classical maidens clad in diaphanous garments. On their heads rests a floral wreath to which their right hands extend as if to balance the six-branch candelabrum, which rises above in preponderating fashion. The branches are in the form of reeded vine-stems with acanthus scroll enrichments, and terminate in floral sockets with grease-pans to match. A large central finial is formed of upright acanthus leaves. Both branches and finial can be removed and a broad fruit basket of acanthus and floral design substituted, thus providing a centre-piece for a luncheon table or side buffet.

In later years a silver-plate stand, with silver border and three lion's-head feet, was added. It had a mirror base and a wooden sub-structure. By its use the preponderating branches of the candelabrum were counter-balanced and a better proportion given to the whole.

The piece was presented to Dr. Charles Thomas Longley, headmaster of Harrow, by his pupils on his leaving in 1836 to take up the Bishopric of Ripon. The three sides of the plinth bear record of this. One side carries a shield engraved with the following inscription:

CAROLO THOMAE LONGLEY STP
PIO · SEDVLO · INDVLGENTI
ALVMNORVM · SVORVM · INFORMATORI
EPISCOPATVM · RIPENSEM
OCCVPATVRO
HOC · GRATI · ANIMI · TESTIMONIVM
QVIBVS · PRAEFVIT · HERGENSES
DE · SVA · PECVNIA · DEDERVNT
A·S. M. DCCC. XXXVI

The Hergenses[1] gave this testimonial of their gratitude, bought with their own money, to their Head Master Charles Thomas Longley, Professor of Sacred Theology—a devout, careful and charming teacher of his pupils—on his leaving to take up the Bishopric of Ripon. The year of Our Saviour 1836.

On a second side of the plinth are the Arms of Ripon Cathedral, while on the third side are Dr. Longley's own Arms impaling those of his wife, Caroline Sophia, eldest child of Sir Henry Brook Parnell, 1st Baron Congleton. Dr. Longley had been seven years at Harrow, during which time the number of boys had risen from 115 to 165. After twenty years at Ripon he was translated in 1856 to the See of Durham, to the Archbishopric of York in 1860 and to Canterbury in 1864. He died in 1868.

Height (without added round stand) to point of finial: 2 ft. 9 in.
Circumference of base on which figures stand: 3 ft. 1 in.
Circumference of added round stand: 5 ft. 3 in.
Weight (without round stand): 400 oz. approx.
London date-letters for 1824–5 (branches and sockets), 1825–6 (the plinth), 1833–4 (the female figures) and 1835–6 (the finial and basket fitting).

The round stand, unmarked, must have been added between 1860 and 1864 as it is engraved "Archbishop of York". At the same time a large box was made to take all the pieces. It has a brass plate similarly inscribed.

Storr often made several castings of sections suitable for candelabra, centre-pieces, presentation cups, etc., which would be ready for orders which otherwise take years to complete. He had learned this during the peak mass-production years with Philip Rundell.

By courtesy of Mrs. L. M. Kaye, of Sussex

---

1 Authorities suggest that there was a temple (OE. *Hearge, Hergas, Hergan, Herges,* etc.) of ancient heathen worship on the hill site now occupied by Harrow. Its full name was originally *Gumeninga hergae,* perhaps "Temple of Guma's people". The modern Latinized "Hergenses" was formed to mean "Harrovians". See English Place-names Society, Vol. XVIII, 1942; and E. Ekwall, *Oxford Dictionary of English Place-names,* 1947, s.v.

PLATE LXVIII

THE ASCOT CUP—SILVER-GILT

THIS cup is based on the Warwick Vase, not only as to its general shape, but in the employ-ment of the "shelf" and in the arrangement of the eight horses' heads which correspond to the eight masks on the Warwick Vase. The chief differences are that the "shelf" is draped with corn instead of lions' skins, the handles are here U-shaped and not great vine branches, the grape-frieze is missing and instead of the ovolo rim we now have a hanging rim of grapes and vine leaves. This *motif* is repeated on the otherwise plain round spreading foot. The Cup rests on a plain square plinth which on one side reads "The Right Honble Viscount Anson, Steward", and on the other "Ascot Heath/1827".

Height: 10¾ in.   Greatest diameter: 11¾ in.
Weight: 122 oz.   London date-letter for 1825 or 1826
                                                (indistinct).

By courtesy of the Art Institute of Chicago

BRISTOL GLASS JARS WITH SILVER MOUNTS AND STANDS
(One of a set of four)

ON octofoil saucer-stands, with ovolo borders, fit the round hob-nail cut Bristol glass jars with silver-mounted rims surmounted by ovolo mouldings. On the plain central panelled surface are the Arms of George, 4th Earl of Aberdeen, impaling Abercorn, within the motto and collar of the Order of the Thistle: NEMO ME IMPUNE LACESSIT. George Hamilton-Gordon, 4th Earl of Aberdeen, K.G., K.T., P.C., etc. (1784–1860), had married (1st), in 1805, Catherine Elizabeth Hamilton, eldest surviving daughter of John James, 9th Earl, and 1st Marquess of Abercorn—she died in 1812: (2nd) in 1815, Harriet, daughter of the Hon. John Douglas, and widow of James, Viscount Hamilton. Thus the double relationship of the Aberdeens and Abercorns will be appreciated. In 1808 Aberdeen had been made a Knight of the Order of the Thistle, hence his use of the motto and collar (of golden thistles and sprigs of rue—the ancient insignia of the Scots and Picts) to encircle the Arms on these glass jars of 1825–9. In 1855 he was made a Knight of the Garter, and in the ordinary way would have relinquished the ensigns of the Order of the Thistle, but as a rare exception (former cases were the Duke of Hamilton and Brandon, and the Duke of Roxburghe—both in 1712) he was allowed to retain both orders. For an important article on the subject see E. A. Jones, "The Order of the Thistle", *Connoisseur*, December 1939, pp. 269–74 and 301.

Stands: 6¾ in. diameter.   London date-letters for 1825–6 (2)
Jars: 5¼ in. high.   and 1829–30 (2).

By courtesy of James Robinson, Inc., of Fifth Avenue, New York

PLATE LXIX

COMMUNION SERVICES—SILVER

Two identical services consisting of chalice, paten, standing-paten and tankard flagon, one being at St. James Sarsden and the other at All Saints, Churchill, Oxfordshire. Both villages are three miles SW. of Chipping Norton and a mile apart from each other. The pieces are quite plain, except for the Glory enclosing a crown of thorns and the sacred emblem I H S. The H on the patens is surmounted by a cross *pattée fitchée*. The flagons, with their plain moulded bases, S-shaped handles and thumb pieces, are surmounted by a cross which may be *pattée* or *moline* (cf. the similar ones on the St. Pancras flagons, Pl. LXVI, p. 211).

The pieces are inscribed "Churchill 1826" and "Sarsden 1826" respectively. They were the gift of Squire James Haughton Langston, of Sarsden House (1796–1863), who was the son of a Liverpool wine merchant (d. 1812). He was regarded as one of the best and most go-ahead squires. He built Churchill Church, many farms and good cottages, and was one of the first to use steam ploughs. He was M.P. for Oxford for some years and married Julia Frances, second daughter of the 1st Earl of Ducie of Tortworth, and his daughter, also Julia, married her first cousin the 3rd Earl Ducie.

The plate at Churchill fits into a box, which has a label on the inside of the lid as follows:

Storr and Mortimer
Successor to Mr. W. Gray
Goldsmiths, Jewellers and Silversmiths
15, New Bond Street

All the plate of both churches bears the London date-letter for 1826–7. See J. T. Evans, *Church Plate of Oxfordshire*, 1928, pp. 42, 150.

The measurements and weights are as follows:

Churchill

Chalice: height $9\frac{1}{2}$ in., diameter $4\frac{3}{8}$ in., weight 14 oz. 5 dwt.
Paten: diameter $7\frac{5}{16}$ in., weight 8 oz. 15 dwt.
Standing-paten: height $2\frac{1}{2}$ in., diameter $8\frac{3}{4}$ in., weight 16 oz.
Tankard flagon: height $13\frac{1}{2}$ in., inside diameter $3\frac{1}{2}$ in., weight 38 oz.

Sarsden

Chalice: height $8\frac{5}{8}$ in., diameter 4 in., weight 13 oz. 15 dwt.
Paten: diameter $7\frac{1}{4}$ in., weight 8 oz. 15 dwt.
Standing-paten: height $2\frac{1}{2}$ in., diameter $7\frac{1}{4}$ in., weight 12 oz. 10 dwt.
Tankard flagon: height $12\frac{3}{4}$ in., weight 32 oz. 10 dwt.

I have to thank the Rev. A. W. S. Holmes, Rector of Churchill and Sarsden, for taking great trouble over the measurements and supplying the photograph.

At St. Peter ad Vincula in South Newington, seven miles NE. of Chipping Norton, is a standing-paten by Storr, exactly similar to those described above. It is $7\frac{3}{4}$ in. high, weighs 19 oz., bears the London date-letter for 1826–7, and is inscribed "South Newington 1827". See J. T. Evans, *op. cit.*, p. 113.

PLATE LXX

VEGETABLE-DISH—SILVER

(One of a set of four)

Of oval shape. Both dishes and high sloping cover are lobed, thus producing irregular outlines to their edges. The rococo element, introduced by the broken scroll ornament on the flat edge of the dish, is continued by the projecting shell lugs, the scroll feet terminating in acanthus leaves, and the spiral medallions above. Between the dish and the lid is a flat tray for use when depth is not needed. It also has shell lugs slightly upturned to allow of easy handling. The feature of the set lies in the handles surmounting the lids which are beautifully modelled in the form of different vegetables: the tomato, pea, ridge cucumber and capsicum.

The Arms on the lid, and crest on the dish, are those of Theophilus Richard Salwey, of the Lodge, Ludlow, Salop (1757–1837), quartering those of Anna Maria, younger daughter and co-heir of Thomas Hill, M.P., of Court of Hill, Salop. (Cf. Lord Berwick's Arms on the tray of 1819, Pl. LXII, from the same collection.)

Length (including lugs): 13¼ in.	Weight: 103 oz. 10 dwt.
Width: 11½ in.	London date-letter for 1829–30.
Height to top of handles: 9½ in.	Order No. 226 of Storr & Mortimer.

By courtesy of Lord Fairhaven, 1st Bt., D.L., J.P., F.S.A.

Storr naturally shows us the "old time" ribbed tomato, as in 1829, when the dishes were made, the "smooth" variety was unknown in such size. With the advent of the tinning industry, the ribbed tomato was found to be unsuitable and so the small cherry variety was gradually cultivated larger and ultimately took its place. For further details see Sturtevant's *Notes on Edible Plants*, Ed. U. P. Hedrick, Albany, 1919, pp. 343–8; and L. H. Bailey, *Cyclopedia of American Horticulture*, 1902, Vol. IV, pp. 1813–20 (see Fig. 2520).

Plate LXXI

THE GOODWOOD CUP—SILVER-GILT

A LARGE circular, and comparatively shallow, bowl with very slightly sloping sides which form the plain background for a spirited frieze in high relief of racing quadrigae. The overhanging ovolo (egg-and-dart) moulding above acts as a cornice to the frieze. The rim of the bowl is surmounted by a pearl, or bead, border. Below the frieze the bowl is decorated with elongated gadrooning, while at three equidistant points twin bearded masks support thick reeded handles. Below the masks are three muscular lion's jambs, supporting the bowl and resting on a plain thick triangular plinth which, in turn, is supported by acanthus scroll feet on square bases.

In the centre of the plinth is the following inscription:

> The Goodwood Cup, 1829, won by His Majesty's mare, Fleur de Lis, beating Mameluke, Varna, Lamplighter and Rough Robin.

On the front of the plinth are the words "Goodwood 1829". The mare, Fleur de Lis, also won the Lincoln the same year (to celebrate which John Bridge made a cup) and was again successful at Goodwood in 1830. Storr made a cup for this victory decorated with two panels, one of the horse winning the race, and the other of "The Gods adjudging the prizes". See E. A. Jones, *Gold and Silver of Windsor Castle*, 1911, pp. 134, 135.

Height: 17½ in.   Weight: 470 oz.
Diameter: 17 in.   London date-letter for 1829–30.

From the Collection at Windsor Castle. By Gracious Permission of H.M. The Queen

PLATE LXXII

HOT-MILK JUG—SILVER

PLAIN pear-shaped jug with plain moulded rim and looped handle affixed to the body with anthemion terminals, having an acanthus-leaf decoration on the upper curve. The lip, on the opposite side, has a plain moulded edge continued from that round the rim, and a hinged cover. The domed lid is surmounted by an Earl's coronet resting on a cushion—both being gilded.

The engraved Arms are those of the 2nd Earl Spencer, K.G., impaling those of Bingham. The jug was presented to George John, 2nd Earl Spencer, and his wife Lavinia on the occasion of their Golden Wedding, 1831, by their children.

Lavinia was the eldest daughter of Charles Bingham, 1st Earl Lucan. She died later in the year (1831), her husband dying three years later.

Height: 6⅛ in.	London date-letter for 1831–2.
Weight: 13 oz. 5 dwt.	Makers: Storr & Mortimer. Order No. 214.

By courtesy of the Earl Spencer

TWO STANDING CUPS AND COVERS— SILVER-GILT

THE bowl of each cup is cylindrical in form with wide lip, and base in two stages. The drum is chased in flat relief with plain curving flutes alternating with Renaissance panels. The under part of the lip is composed of lobes with matted surrounds, the edge being of scroll and diaper work. The lower portion of the bowl has six masks and six plain bosses. The vase-shaped stem is formed with three masks and brackets leading up to a leafage disk on which the body rests. The foot, domed in two stages with hollow between, has broad convex flutes on a matted ground corresponding with those on the bottom of the bowl. The cover, slightly domed and with the same ornamentation as on the drum of the body, is surmounted by a winged boy.

Height: 14 in.	London date-letter for 1833.
Weight: 40 oz. 15 dwt. each.	

Arms on covers. 1. The first crest, that of "A swan's head erased issuant from an annulet and holding in the beak an annulet", was the crest granted in 1894 to Viscount Alverstone, then Sir Richard Everard Webster. 2. The other crest, that of Fortescue, Baron Carlingford (1874–98), is "an heraldic tiger supporting in the forepaw a plain shield argent".

Inscription: "To the Worshipful Company of Goldsmiths the gift of the Rt. Hon. Lord Alverston, G.C.M.G., Lord Chief Justice of England, Prime Warden 1893 and 1899."

(The above description is taken, with permission, from *The Plate of the Worshipful Company of Goldsmiths,* by J. B. Carrington and G. R. Hughes, Oxford, 1926, pp. 126, 127.)

By courtesy of the Worshipful Company of Goldsmiths, who have supplied the photograph

PLATE LXXIII

STATUETTE—SILVER-GILT

STATUETTE of George III in Garter robes, crowned, and holding the sceptre. It stands on a square plinth with an inscription in front, and the name of Rundell, Bridge & Rundell in Latin at the back and sides.

Height: 9⅜ in.   London date-letter for 1833–4.

By Gracious Permission of H.M. The Queen

I understand from Buckingham Palace that there are two examples of this statuette in Her Majesty's possession, one of which was presented to Queen Victoria in 1897 and the other to the present Queen on her marriage.

DOUBLE SALTS—SILVER-GILT
(Two of a set of four)

OF highly rococo form, somewhat reminiscent of the work of Nicholas Sprimont, of Liège,[1] silversmith and manager of the Chelsea porcelain factory from 1750 to 1770. Each salt consists of two open shells (*Hippopus hippopus,* a member of the Giant Clam families of tropical waters) straddled at their hinges by an oblong fringed and tasselled cushion supporting the Craven crest—on a chapeau gu. turned up ermine a griffin statant sa. wings addorsed, beaked, membered, and a semée of fleurs-de-lis or. The salts rest on a supporting frame-work of coral (apparently some species of *Stylophora* is represented) springing from a base of seaweed (*Fucus vesiculosus* Linn) and water foliage.

Height to top of shell edge (average): 3⅜ in.   Weight: 88 oz.
Height to ears of griffin: 4⅝ in.   London date-letter for 1833–4.
Greatest breadth: 5 in.

By courtesy of Francis Stonor, Esq.

[1] E. A. Jones, *Gold and Silver of Windsor Castle,* Intro., pp. xl, xli, xliv and xlvi, and p. 98, Pl. L, No. 5, and p. 100, Pl. LI, No. 1; *Connoisseur,* May 1937, pp. 253–4; Bellamy Gardner, *Antique Collector,* Aug. 1937, pp. 120–214, and Aug. 1938, pp. 206–9; R. L. Hobson, *Catalogue of the Collection of English Porcelain in the British Museum,* 1905, p. 31; W. King, *Chelsea Porcelain,* 1922, pp. 21, 39, 42, with Pl. 6, Fig. 1, and Pl. 28; and F. S. Mackenna, *Chelsea Porcelain, the Triangle and Raised Anchor Wares,* 1948, pp. 23, 24.

Plate LXXIV

EWER—SILVER

THE body of this large ewer is an inverted pyriform resting in a calyx of overlapping lanceolate leaves. Above, with an undulating frilling at the juncture, rises a deep helmet collar or neck, while the rim and spout are decorated by a gadrooned moulding. Below the calyx, and separated from it by a narrow scotia, is a gadrooned convex projecting member. The plain spreading concave, or trumpet-shaped, foot has a round moulded base. The handle consists of two reversed C-shaped scrolls, the upper, and larger, one of which meets a small acanthus scroll projecting from the back of the rim. On one side of the body is applied a square shield bearing the cipher of Ekaterina II—Catherine the Great—of Russia, surmounted by the Russian crown. The date 1787, the significance of which is discussed in Appendix B (pp. 282–4), occupies a prominent place in the centre of the shield. On the opposite side is a wreath of laurel leaves encircling a medallion which has since been lost or purposely removed. The most striking and unusual feature, however, is the finely modelled demi-horse which projects through an embattled opening in the broadest part of the body midway between the shield and medallion. These horses appear to have been already used by Storr in 1831, for in that year they are found projecting from the supporting column of an elaborately decorated gilt ewer (50 cm. in height and 8,340 grammes in weight) formerly in the Tahra Palace. See Plate VII of Sotheby's catalogue, *The Palace Collections of Egypt* (silver and silver-gilt), 25th March 1954, lot 208.

Height: 1 ft. 5¼ in.   Weight: 80 oz. 7½ dwt.
Broadest width, including horse: 10⅔ in.   London date-letter for 1833–4.[1]
Diameter of base: 5⅖ in.

From a private collection at Montpellier, France

[1] It may be mentioned here that Jackson, usually so reliable, has shown the William IV king's head marks wrongly (p. 89). He gives the heads for 1831 to 1836 truncated, when actually this form of head started only in 1834–5 (letter t). The heads for 1830–3 show the draped shoulder, like those of George IV. The leopard's head has no whiskers for this period, and here again Jackson is most misleading.

PLATE LXXV

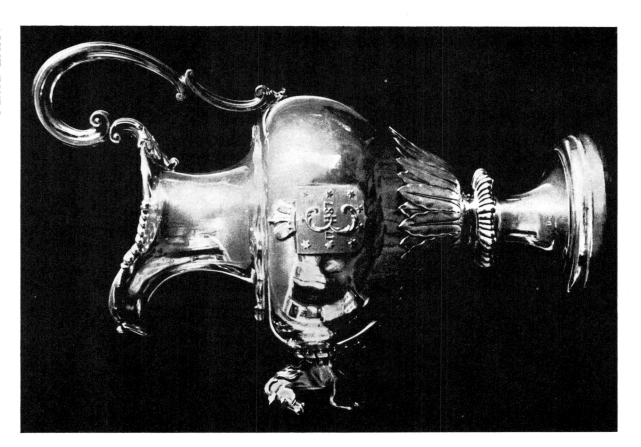

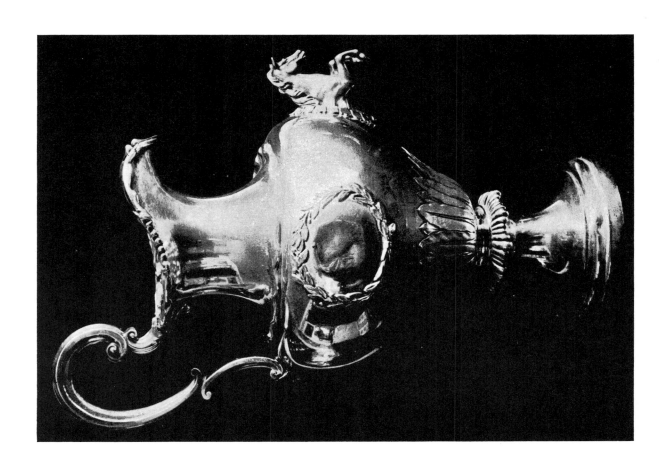

MUG—SILVER

THE gently sloping sides are enriched by a running frieze of acanthus flowers with winged amorini and baskets of fruit on stands formed of acanthus leaves. This decoration is applied to a matted ground. The plain everted lip, separated from the central section by a reeded band, matches the foot and convex base.

The handle, curving above the height of the mug, is of ribbed vine branches decorated at their juncture with acanthus leaves. It bifurcates as it drops down to meet the rim. The inside of the mug is gilt.

Height: 4 in.
Diameter: 5 in.
Weight: 11¼ oz.

Signed: Storr and Mortimer. No. 356.
London date-letter for 1834–5.

By courtesy of the Victoria and Albert Museum, London

TEA-POT—SILVER

OF round, somewhat squat, shape, divided into eight convex lobes as on a canta-loup melon. The surface is plain, save for the monogram F.C.S. engraved on one of the central lobes. The letters stand for Francis and Caroline Storr, the tea-pot being a wedding-present from Paul. The plain domed lid, fitting flush, is surmounted by a lobed finial. The spout is fluted with an acanthus-leaf decoration on the upper side near the lip. The well-proportioned handle, with the usual ivory insulating-rings, is attached to the lobe behind the flat hinge, and is decorated with a long acanthus leaf covering almost the entire upper surface. A double octofoil foot adds to the charm of a tea-pot which is as satisfying artistically as it is from a practical point of view.

Height: 5½ in.
Width (from tip of spout to outer curve of handle): 10¼ in.
Circumference: 9½ in.

Weight: 19 oz.
London date-letter for 1837–8.
Made by Paul Storr for Storr & Mortimer.

By courtesy of the Misses Storr

Made by Paul especially for the wedding of his son Francis with Caroline Holland in 1837, the tea-pot was left to their third son, Charles, Vicar of Matfield, Kent. From him it came to Colonel Lancelot Storr, and at his death in 1944 passed to his two sisters, Margaret and Freda, to whom I am indebted for its history.

PLATE LXXVI

SIX-BRANCH CANDELABRUM

On a base of seaweed, clam, nautilus and other shells rest the large heads of three dolphin-like sea monsters. Their tails twist upwards to form a support for the baluster-shaped stem which is striated and enriched with marine emblems. From the striated sconce three more sea monsters twine their tails round the six branches which are covered with coralline and oyster-shell incrustations. From the centre rises a floral knop on which three amorini, with garlands in their hands, support a mural crown.

The whole rests on a plain shaped plinth. There is an elaborate stand with mirror base, the sides of which are covered with marine devices in harmony with those on the base of the candelabrum. It is supported by the heads of monsters arranged in pairs, their tails mingle with the decoration above.

Candelabrum:

    Height: 29 in.
    Weight: 312 oz.
    London date-letter for 1835–6.

Base:

    Height: 4 in.
    Diameter: 20 in.
    London date-letter for 1822–3.

By courtesy of Messrs. Harman & Lambert

PLATE LXXVII

MILK OR CREAM JUG—SILVER

OF oval shape, with flat lobed sides engraved with conventional anthemion and acanthus at the joints of the lobes. The plain vertical edge is prolonged to form a broad lip, below which the body has a matted ground. The high curving handle, enriched with an acanthus (?) leaf, is joined to the edge of the jug by a small fluted shell. There is a plain narrow foot.

Height: $2\frac{1}{2}$ in.
Greatest length: $6\frac{1}{4}$ in.
Width: 3 in.

Weight: $7\frac{1}{2}$ oz.
London date-letter for 1835–6.

By courtesy of Dr. Anthony Storr

TEA-POT—SILVER

PLAIN oval tea-pot with straight spout, ebony loop handle fitting into silver sockets, and ebony mushroom finial with silver tip. The lid is flat and fits flush with the flat rim. Engraved on one side is "A" surmounted by a viscount's coronet for John Charles, Viscount Althorp, later 3rd Earl Spencer—1782–1845.

Length: 6 in.
Width: $4\frac{1}{4}$ in.
Height: $4\frac{1}{2}$ in.

Weight: 16 oz.
London date-letter for 1828–9.

By courtesy of the Earl Spencer

PLATE LXXVIII

MARINE DESSERT DISHES—SILVER

(Two separate sets)

1st Set

FOUR dessert dishes, each being composed of a single valve of a giant clam supported on the tails of three dolphins whose heads rest on the corners of shaped triangular plinths.

Height: 8 in.　　　　　　　　　　　　　　London date-letter for 1838–9.
Weight: 231 oz. 10 dwt.

2nd Set

Four dessert dishes formed as deep clams resting on rocky bases. To the right fish-tailed tritons blowing conches have their right hands on the edge of the shells as if to support themselves or drag the great shells along the rocky sea-bed. This is a fine and realistic piece of craftsmanship. Each dish weighs 102 oz. 9 dwt. For notes on similar marine pieces, somewhat reminiscent of Nicholas Sprimont, see the salts in the Stonor collection, Pl. LXXIVB. London date-letter for 1838–9.

Both these sets were sold at Christie's on 13th May 1953 by order of the Trustees of the Tollemache Estates (Lots 44, 45). Several other pieces by Storr were sold at the same time (see Lots 39, 41, 42, 43, 46, 47 of the catalogue). Of interest also was Lot 65, four plain sauce-boats made in 1771 by Storr's master Andrew Fogelberg; Lot 23, a pair of circular vegetable dishes, of which one was by Fogelberg and Gilbert, *c.* 1785; and, lastly, Lot 48, a pair of candelabra with sticks by John Samuel Hunt, Storr's nephew (by marriage) and successor in business. The two sets of marine dessert dishes must have been nearly the last pieces made by Storr, as 1838 was the year of his retirement from business.

By courtesy of Messrs. Christie, Manson & Woods, Ltd.

CITY MACE—SILVER-GILT

THE mace is of the usual form. The shaft, lightly engraved with acanthus foliage, is divided into three uneven lengths by gadrooned knops, with an ovolo collar at the top. The mace-head is hexagonal, all the sides being plain. To three of them are applied winged cherubic figures which end in leaf formation, while the other three sides contain respectively the crowned rose, shamrock and thistle. The open-arched crown, with the usual pearl borders to the arches, has a circlet of alternate cross pattées and fleurs-de-lis. It is surmounted by an orb and squared cross pattée. The upper section of the shaft bears the following inscription:

Presented by Sir John St. Aubyn Baronet Lord of the Manor of Stoke Damerel to the Corporation of the Borough of Devonport, Nov. 1837.

Length: 42 in.　　　　　　　　　　　　　　London date-letter for 1837–8.
Stem: 28 in. and Crown 14 in.

By courtesy of the City of Plymouth

The important maritime port and town of Devonport was formerly a portion of the "three towns" forming the "metropolis of the West", of which the others were Plymouth and Stonehouse. It was originally known as "Plymouth Dock"—being simply the Royal Dockyard, formed there in connection with Plymouth, by William III, in 1688. In 1824, by grant from George IV, the town discarded its old name of "Plymouth Dock" and assumed the more euphonious one of "Devonport", and commemorated it by the erection of the "Devonport Column".

The first mayor was Edward St. Aubyn, Esq., appointed in 1837–8, and he it was who presented the Paul Storr mace at that time. He was also mayor in 1849–50, and in 1864 he presented the mayor's chain and badge of office in gold. It records the grant of George IV in 1824.

In 1914 Devonport was amalgamated with Plymouth, and the Devonport mace then became part of the Plymouth Civic Plate. See L. Jewitt and W. H. St. John Hope, *Corporation Plate and Insignia of Office*, Vol. I, 1895, pp. 147–8, from which much of the above has been taken.

Plate LXXIX

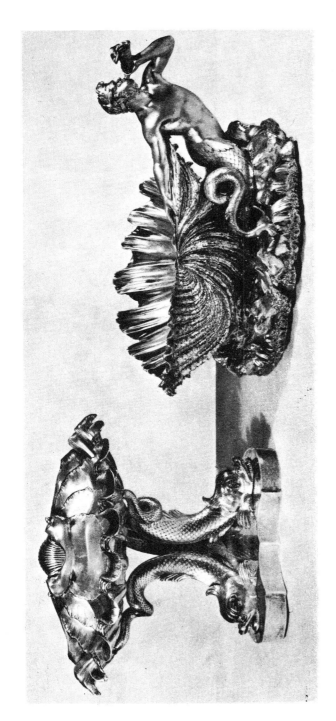

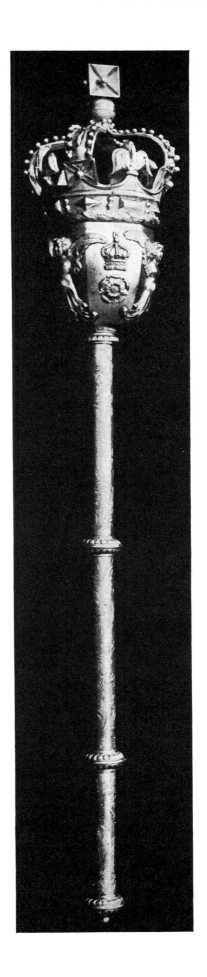

THE OTLEY CHALICE AND
STANDING-PATEN—SILVER

As already related, Francis Storr, Paul's second son, had become Rector of St. Mary's, Otley, Suffolk, in 1837. At that time the church plate consisted of an unmarked Elizabethan chalice of about 1560 and an old pewter flagon. As there was no paten, and the chalice was considered too precious for every-day use, Paul decided to make a copy of the chalice and present a standing-paten to match. According to the opinion of the present Rector, he was also responsible for the silver-plating of the flagon, but there is some doubt as to whether it is of pewter or of some other base metal. The measurements of the two chalices are identical, though the replica is heavier, weighing 10 oz., while the original weighs only 8 oz. 15 dwt. They are plain except for a double band of typical Elizabethan strapwork, the section of the foot being concave without any knop. The replica is inscribed:

The Gift of Paul Storr Esqu. 1841.

Height: 6½ in.
Diameter: 3½ in.
Weight: 10 oz.
London date-letter for 1840–1.

Makers: IM over ISH, for John Mortimer and John Samuel Hunt. Order No. 523. Paul had retired in 1838, so Mortimer and Hunt's mark is used, but I have little doubt that Paul made both chalice and paten with his own hands.

The standing-paten was designed by Storr to match the chalice and is similarly decorated.

Height: 3¼ in.
Diameter: 6½ in.

Weight: 11 oz. 10 dwt.
Makers' names and date as on chalice above.

The two chalices and the standing-paten fit into an oak case especially made for them—doubtless by Paul Storr. Apart from the plate, Paul also presented the church with a beautiful east window of three lights, surmounted by Gothic tracery. Francis must have felt great affection for this church and all his father had done to beautify it, for it was here that he set up a memorial tablet on the south wall of the sanctuary to the memory of his father and mother.

I have to thank the present Rector of St. Mary's, Otley, the Rev. D. G. R. Taylor, for all the trouble he has taken in answering my many questions about the connection of Paul and Francis with his church, for welcoming me to the rectory and allowing me to measure and weigh the plate, and for having both it and the memorial tablet photographed.

PLATE LXXX

RELIQUARY—SILVER-GILT

Of ciborium form. The bowl is round and shallow, and rests in a calyx of applied acanthus foliage, the main decoration being of small sheaves of corn arranged laterally on a matted ground—the stalks hidden by foliage. The upper edge is unevenly scalloped and stops short of the rim, which is reeded, and into which fits an ornate and elaborate lid. The sloping lower part is embossed with acanthus leaves, above which is a high dome enriched with massed floral decoration from which project four small cherubs' heads. From the top of this is an open vase-shaped member with scrolls attached. This is surmounted by a somewhat large cross with a circular stepped base. Below the bowl, and separated from it by a flattened reel-like member, is a highly ornate knop enriched with foliage and cherubs' heads as before. The stem is of baluster form, the pear-shaped section ornamented with cherubs' heads above and foliage below. An ovolo collar surmounts a spool-shaped section which is surrounded by four small female torso brackets. The domical foot, embossed with acanthus foliage, has an upper member of flowers and foliage from which again cherubs' heads project. A torus of oak leaves forms the base, below which runs the following Portuguese inscription:

ESTA' RELIQVIA DO PRECIOSISSIMO · SANGVE · DE CHRISTO · SNÕR · N⁰ · FOI · DE HṼ · CARDEAL · EVEIO · AMAÕ · DO Pᴱ · FREI · SEBASTIAM · SOTO · MAIOR · Q̃ · A DEV A ESTE · REAL MOSTᴿᴼ · DES · Mᴬ · DE ALCOBᴬ · AN⁰ 1690 *

The literal translation (kindly checked by Prof. J. B. Trend, of Christ's College, Cambridge) of this is as follows:

> This Relic of the most precious Blood of Christ our Lord was (the property) of a Cardinal and came (in) to the hand(s) of (the) Father Brother Sebastian Soto Maior who gave it to this Royal Monastery of St. Maria of Alcobaça in the year 1690.

Height: 17 in.	Maker's mark: MRE.[1]
Diameter of bowl: 6 in.	Repaired and partly remade by
Diameter of base: 5⅜ in.	Paul Storr in 1836–7, as ex-
Mark of Lisbon: c. 1670.	plained below.

From Lambeth Palace. By courtesy of the Archbishop of Canterbury

The history of the Reliquary seems to be quite unknown. It has been at Lambeth Palace for some seventy-five years, but there is no record of its donor. In his article on the "Church Plate of Surrey" (*Surrey Arch. Coll.*, Vol. XIV, 1899, pp. 75–6), T. S. Cooper suggested that it might have been given by Dr. Manners-Sutton, Archbishop of Canterbury from 1805 to 1828. This seems unlikely as its condition during that period must have been very bad, for in 1836 the whole thing had to be

---

[1] The seventeenth-century hanging lamp quoted by Rosenberg, *Goldschmiede Merkzeichen*, Vol. IV, p. 456, No. 8059, may be by the same maker, although in this case only MR is distinct.

PLATE LXXXI

remade by Storr. This modern work was not suspected by Cooper, nor when shown at the Exhibition of 17th Century Art in Europe, Royal Academy of Arts, London, 1938 (see *Catalogue*, No. 992; *Illustrated Souvenir*, Plate on p. 121; and *Connoisseur*, February 1938, p. 71). At a later date, however, Mr. Oman, of the Victoria and Albert Museum, took it to pieces and discovered the marks of Paul Storr and the date-letters for 1836–7.[1] In February 1953 I was permitted to make a detailed examination at Lambeth, and was at once struck by the difference in colour of certain portions of the silver-gilt—the whole of the bowl and the sloping portion of the lid. On taking it to pieces and removing the sleeve, or inner lining of the bowl, a full set of 1836–7 marks was revealed, with Paul Storr's initials as fresh as if stamped the previous day. But this was not all. Inside the dome of the lid Storr had scratched with a graver, or some such tool, right across the uneven back of the repoussé work, the following words in a spidery and almost illegible script:

> 7 Jany 1837. This rim weighing 4 oz. 8 dwt. made to receive a chased top of unknown assay weighing 5 oz. 9 dwt.

Thus the entire bowl as well as the lower part of the lid (for that is marked too) is the work of Storr. It is, of course, impossible to say if any of the original design remained for him to copy, or whether the introduction of the corn was his own idea. All that can be said is that whereas the influence of the florid Manoellian style is noticeable in the massed background which covers the knops, such work is *not* evident on the bowl. However that may be, the result *in toto* is excellent and the English work has remained unrecognized for over a hundred years! It is interesting to note that the introduction of cherubs' heads on English standing cups of the early seventeenth century is not uncommon, and several fine examples have been recorded.[2] As the inscription states, the Reliquary was obtained from an unnamed cardinal by the Father Brother (Padre Frei) Sebastian Soto Maior of the famous Abbey (Mosteiro de Santa Maria) of Alcobaça in 1690. Soto Maior was a native of Braga, a city of northern Portugal, formerly included in the province of Entre Minho e Douro, and famous as one of the great centres of ecclesiastical architecture. The Sé, or Cathedral, is Romanesque, with Gothic additions, while the Rennaissance interior, especially the West End, is one vast mass of rococo, as are also the two huge organs with their writhing dolphins, mermen, tritons, etc. In the Sacristy, Soto Maior would have been familiar with the fine collection of plate, which included the eleventh-century chalice of St. Geraldus and a magnificent one of 1509 in the Manoellian style.[3] The date of Soto Maior's arrival at Alcobaça is uncertain, but the esteem in which he was

---

[1] See "Portuguese Silver in the possession of English Churches", *Apollo*, July 1951, p. 16.

[2] See Jackson's *History of English Plate*, p. 202 (Figs. 215, 216); the ostrich-egg cup of 1623 and that of 1619 on the Plate facing p. 212; also Fig. 490 on p. 434, Fig. 499 on p. 439 and Fig. 886 on p. 679. The silver-gilt and rock-crystal cup from Yateley Church, Hants, shown in Jackson, p. 202, has two sets of female torso brackets on the stem somewhat similar to those on the Reliquary.

[3] See Joaquim de Vasconcellos, *Arte Religiosa em Portugal*, Vol. I, 1914–15, Braga Section; and Alberto Pereira de Almeida, *Portugal Artistico e Monumental*, Vol. II, Lisboa (?1930), pp. 674, 677. Both these works contain numerous reproductions and descriptions of the goldsmiths' art in the churches, monasteries and museums of Portugal.

held is shown by the fact that, contrary to the usual practice, he was abbot for two three-year periods—1675–8 and 1687–90. It was at the end of the second period of administration that he presented the Reliquary to the Abbey. Soto Maior took the greatest interest in the decoration of the Abbey ("apaixonado entusiasta e protector das oficinas de imaginária de Abadia") and personally designed and supervised the carvings of the monks in the Abbey workshops. To his enthusiasm are due the carvings in the reredos of the presbytery, the statues in the Sala dos Reis, and, above all, the lovely painted terra-cotta group of the death of St. Bernard in the right transept opposite the chapel, containing the famous Gothic tombs of D. Pedro I and Inez de Castro. Of particular interest to us is the upper part of this great work consisting of the Virgin in glory, surrounded by cherubs and seraphs such as appear on the Reliquary. To appreciate the extraordinary beauty of the faces of the cherubs reference should be made to the excellent photographs in Barata Feyo's *A Escultura de Alcobaça*, Lisboa, 1945, to which I am indebted for much of the above.[1] A word must be said about Alcobaça itself. Situated in a thriving region of orchards at the juncture of the Alcoa and Baça rivers (whence its name) in the district of Leiria, sixty miles north of Lisbon, lies the Cistercian Abbey (Mosteiro de Santa Maria), formerly one of the richest in Portugal and nearly the largest in the world. It was founded by D. Afonso Henriques to celebrate the capture of Santarem from the Moors in 1147. According to W. C. Watson (*Portuguese Architecture*, 1908, p. 59) the first stone was laid in 1158. It was dedicated in 1220, but the monastic buildings were not ready until 1223. The Abbey was immensely wealthy and became one of the first centres of learning in Portugal. The church is by far the largest in the country and resembles the Cistercian buildings of France, particularly that of Clairvaux. The interior, with its two long lines of tall clustered white columns stretching away into the distance, is most impressive, but early English travellers such as Lord Strathmore[2] and William Beckford[3] dwell more on the luxurious life of the monks, their great hospitality and, above all, the amazing kitchen about a hundred feet square with a riverlet of fish running through it. Beckford described it (p. 37) as "the most distinguished temple of gluttony in all Europe" and proceeds to enumerate the incredible masses of food assembled. But he also tells us (p. 49) of several golden reliquaries which he inspected. One cannot help wondering if they included that now at Lambeth Palace. But the glory of those days was soon to depart, and the Abbey was sacked by Napoleon's soldiers in 1810. The loot taken at that time doubtless included the Reliquary.

For further details of Alcobaça reference should be made to *Guia de Portugal*, Vol. II [1927], Bib. Nac. de Lisboa, pp. 611–26; Manuel Vieira Natividade, *O Mosteiro*

1 For the "Altar da Morte de São Bernardo" see Pl. 64, and Pls. 40–4, 57–63 for the cherubs and seraphs. Of particular value is the Bibliography on pp. 39, 40.

2 From a MS. formerly in the possession of Martin Hume. See his *Through Portugal*, 1907, pp. 173–4, and his own description of Alcobaça, pp. 188–97.

3 *Recollections of an Excursion to the Monasteries of Alcobaça and Batalha*, by the author of "Vatek", London, 1835. It was reprinted in *The Travel Diaries of William Beckford*, Vol. II, 1928, p. 255 to end.

de Alcobaça, 1885, and similar work by his son Joaquim Vieira Natividade, 1929 and (2nd edit.) 1937; "Alcobaça" in the *Grande Encic. Port. e Brasileira*, Vol. I, pp. 800–5. English travel books contain only brief accounts (i.e. those by James Murphy, W. M. Kinsey, G. B. Loring, P. S. Marden, Douglas Goldring, Aubrey Bell, etc.), but reference may be made to *The Selective Traveller in Portugal* by Ann Bridge and Susan Lowndes, London, 1949, for their short description on pp. 139–41 and especially the good Bibliography on pp. 275–6 and series of excellent maps.

APPENDICES

RECORD OF PIECES BY PAUL STORR SOLD BY MESSRS. CHRISTIE, MANSON & WOODS

THE following list, arranged alphabetically by object, and then in chronological order under each object, has been prepared specially for this work by Mr. A. G. Grimwade from his valuable card-index at Christie's. In a few cases items from private or public collections have been added which otherwise would have remained unrecorded.

Except for certain rearrangements, a few additions and an odd annotation here and there, the material is exactly as received from Mr. Grimwade.

Baskets

Four dessert-baskets, gilt, circular. 10¼ in. diam. 1798. 147 oz., lot 55 of 17th July 1917 (The Hope Heirlooms). Illustrated in Thomas Hope's *Household Furniture and Interior Decoration*, 1807, Pl. 52.

Pair of bread-baskets, gilt, circular, trellis border. Royal Arms. 1801 and 1806. 81 oz. 5 dwt., lots 254/5 of 6th June 1904 (Duke of Cambridge). Also lot 131 of 26th Jan. 1944.

Cake-basket, circular, pierced trellis border. 12¼ in. diam. 1802. 31 oz. 5 dwt., lot 63 of 10th Dec. 1946.

Cake-basket, circular, pierced trellis border, gadrooned rim and reeded handle. 12½ in. diam. 1803. 33 oz. 2 dwt., lot 133 of 16th Nov. 1949.

Cake-basket, oblong, gadrooning, shell and foliage. 1806. 73 oz. 15 dwt., lot 32 of 4th Nov. 1919 (Duke of Hamilton Collection).

Cake-basket, oblong, fluted, gadroon, shell and foliage rim. Width 13 in. 1812. 40 oz. 11 dwt., lot 13 of 13th June 1947.

Biggin.   See under COFFEE-POTS, etc. (first item)

Bowls.   See also under PUNCH-BOWLS, SUGAR BOWLS and VASES.

Circular bowl, quilted fluting, moulded rim, gadrooned foot. 10½ in. diam. 1812. 53 oz. 8 dwt., lot 98 of 17th Dec. 1947.

Fruit bowl, gilt, panels of flowers, stand of dish-form. 11½ in. diam. 1812. 99 oz. 15 dwt., lot 141 of 19th Feb. 1947 (Earl of Lonsdale Collection).

Pair of parcel gilt bowls, ivy foliage, matted ground, 9 in. diam. 1817. 46 oz. 4 dwt., lot 130 of 16th May 1949.

Silver-gilt strawberry bowl and cover, three shell feet, body chased strawberries and leaves, foliage finial. 6 in. diam. 1821. 27 oz., lot 135 of 16th May 1949.

Pair of bowls, fluted borders, each with four doves, cylindrical pedestals 21 in. high. 1838. 490 oz., lot 94 of 19th May 1944 (Duke of Sutherland Collection).

Bread-baskets.   See under BASKETS

Butter-dish

Butter-dish, cover and stand. Cow finial. 1802. 23 oz. 8 dwt., lot 78 of 28th April 1948.

Cake-baskets.   See under BASKETS

Candlesticks.   See also under CHAMBER CANDLESTICKS

Twelve candlesticks, gilt, masks, shells, scale-work. 9¼ in. high. 1811–12. Gross weight 397 oz. 5 dwt., lot 151 of 19th Feb. 1947 (Earl of Lonsdale).

Four candlesticks, probably similar, 9 in. high, 1811–13. 117 oz., lot 61 of 3rd Oct. 1940. Arms of Viscount Lismore.

Pair of candlesticks, square plinths, foliage, scales, masks. 1814. 56 oz. 12 dwt., lot 202 of 6th June 1904 (Duke of Cambridge). Lot 565 of 19th Jan. 1951 at Parke-Bernet Galleries, New York—as from above collection.

Eight candlesticks, gilt, foliage, fruit, masks of Seasons. 1816. 390 oz. 15 dwt., lot 109 of 17th March 1920.

Pair of candlesticks, flowers and foliage, baluster stems. 8¾ in. high. 1832. 29 oz. 13 dwt., lot 92 of 14th March 1951.

Candelabra

Two pairs of two-light candelabra, trellis work, shells, scale-work panels, entwined serpent loop-handles between lights. 24¾ in. high. 1807. 318 oz. 11 dwt. and 322 oz. 14 dwt., lots 117–18 of 14th June 1950 (Duke of Bedford).

Six three-light candelabra, circular plinths, foliage. 19½ in. high. 1809 and 1816. 540 oz. 15 dwt., lot 206 of 6th June 1904 (Duke of Cambridge).

Six four-light candelabra, scale-pattern and trellis work. 25 in. high. 1810. 1127 oz. 15 dwt., lot 33 of 4th Nov. 1919 (Duke of Hamilton).

Pair of three-light candelabra, triangular stems with ivy, tortoises and three busts. 25 in. high. 1810. 409 oz., lot 155 of 8th Dec. 1944. As from Collection of Ninth Earl of Coventry.

Four-light candelabrum, chased dolphins, owls' heads, lions' masks. 23 in. high. 1813. 244 oz. 5 dwt., lot 34 of 14th May 1914 (Coutts Heirlooms).

Pair of ten-light candelabra, stems with three figures of Apollo, tripod bases decorated with foliage, on claw feet; the upper part of bases supported on three stags. The Cavendish Arms are applied on each side. London, 1813–14. Total height 40 in. From the collection of the Duke of Devonshire, who has kindly lent one of the two existing copies of the Catalogue made in 1931 by E. Alfred Jones, from which the above has been taken.

Pair of four-light candelabra, three female caryatid figure stems. 1814. 303 oz. 5 dwt., lot 262 of 20th Feb. 1947 (Earl of Lonsdale).

Ten-light candelabrum, palm-tree stem, Highland figures. 40 in. high. 1814. Gross: 845 oz., lot 43 of 18th June 1951.

Six candelabra—two of four-lights, and four of three-lights. 1814. Corporation of Dover. See L. Jewitt and W. H. St. John Hope, *Corporation Plate and Insignia of Office*, Vol. 1, 1895, p. 378, with an illustration on p. 325. As with the punch-bowls, by Storr, the candelabra were presented by Mr. Fector.

Candelabra—*continued*

Pair of four-light candelabra, three female caryatid stems. 31½ in. high. 1816. 599 oz. 15 dwt., lot 261 of 20th Feb. 1947 (Earl of Lonsdale). See also lot 80 of 6th Oct. 1948 (one only).

Pair of candelabra and centre-piece, gilt, lions on tripod base, Amorini friezes. 1816. 2,106 oz., lot 83 of 22nd July 1903.

Four four-light candelabra, gilt, foliage stems, triangular bases. 29 in. high. 1816. 863 oz., 10 dwt., lot 64 of 18th June 1924.

Five-light candelabrum, baluster stem, lions, dolphins and flowers. 29 in. high. 1816. Gross weight: 301 oz. 10 dwt., lot 148 of 26th Feb. 1947.

Nine-light candelabrum, military trophy finial, triangular base, equestrian figures and horses. 46 in. high. 1837. 530 oz., lot 188 of 24th July 1946.

Centre-pieces.   See under DESSERT-STANDS

Chamber Candlesticks

Four circular chamber candlesticks, gadrooned borders, detachable nozzles and extinguishers. 1817. 53 oz., 3 dwt., lot 3 of 14th Dec. 1938 (W. R. Hearst, St. Donat's Castle, Wales).

Coffee-pots, etc.   See also HOT-WATER JUGS

Coffee-biggin, plain, cylindrical, 7¼ in. high. 1793. 13 oz. 17 dwt., lot 100 of 14th March 1951.

Coffee-jug, plaited borders, mask on handle. 1802. (Stand and lamp. 1820.) 43 oz. gross, lot 53 of 2nd Jan. 1946.

Coffee-pot, gilt, stand and lamp, basket-work borders. 1805. 52 oz. 10 dwt., lot 79 of 6th June 1904 (Duke of Cambridge).

Coffee-jug, fluted border, stand and lamp. 1806. 48 oz. 7 dwt., lot 11 of 19th Jan. 1921.

Coffee-jug, gilt, honeysuckle fluting, serpent handle, tripod stand and lamp. 1808. 59 oz., lot 9 of 17th Dec. 1930, and lot 11 of 16th Dec. 1931.

Coffee-pot, gadroon and shell borders, fluted, stand and lamp. 1810. 60 oz. 10 dwt., lot 71 of 30th May 1911.

Pair of vase-shaped coffee-pots, spiral fluting, serpent ivory handles—one with lamp and stand. 1813. Gross: 83 oz., lot 48 of 5th July 1949.

Coffee-pot on circular stand with lamp, partly fluted, gadroon, shell and foliage borders, serpent handle, honeysuckle on spout. 1813. 54 oz., lot 77 of 11th July 1912 (J. E. Taylor Collection). See further Tea Service of 1813 *en suite*.

Pear-shaped coffee-pot, stand and lamp, chased flowers, scrolls and trellis, stand on bearded mask and shell feet. 1820. Gross: 67 oz. 3 dwt., lot 100 of 19th Dec. 1951.

Cream-jugs

Gilt, bucket-shaped, with chain and ladle attached, Queen Charlotte's cipher. 1793. 7 oz. 11 dwt., lot 62 of 3rd April 1903. This is probably a cream-pail.

Gilt, Medusa masks, rosettes and foliage. 1813. 25 oz. 16 dwt., lot 93 of 5th Dec. 1917, and lot 44 of 13th July 1926—24 oz. 5 dwt.

Gilt, branches of flowers, branch handle, scroll feet. 1820. 10 oz. 18 dwt., lot 239 of 6th June 1904 (Duke of Cambridge).

With branch handle, chased flowers, three feet. 5 in. high. 1820. 9 oz. 17 dwt., lot 278 of 29th April 1902 (Dunn Gardner Collection).

Cream-jugs—*continued*

Classical ewer form, handle with two goats, winged figure below. 1837. 13 oz. 2 dwt., lot 46 of 9th May 1949.

Cruets

Pair, with silver necks and rims. 1810–11, and pair of glass mustard pots. 1811–21; lot 37 of 18th Oct. 1950.

Square frame, shell feet, gadrooned border, eight bottles. 1822. 44 oz. 17 dwt.; lot 148 of 21st Dec. 1949.

Cups (including VASES and WARWICK VASES, but see also under SUGAR BOWLS AND VASES and WINE-COOLERS)

Cup and cover, vase-shaped, shallow fluting, palm leaves on cover, cone finial. 18 in. high. 1792. 71 oz. 15 dwt., lot 116 of 13th Jan. 1947.

Cup and cover, gilt, two-handled, Campana form. 1798. 172 oz. 14 dwt. Merchant Taylors' Company (The White Cup). See Fry & Tewson's *Illustrated Catalogue*, p. 54 and pl. 20.

Cup and cover, vase-shaped, palm leaves, festoons and plaques. Helmet handles, Victory figure finial. 19¾ in. high. 1799. 161 oz., lot 79 of 28th April 1948.

Cup and cover, vase-shaped, 15 in. high. 1800. 78 oz. The Hon. Society of the Middle Temple, presented by H.R.H. Albert Edward, Prince of Wales, K.G. See Jackson, *History of English Plate*, Vol. I, pp. 321–2, and B. Williamson, *Catalogue of Silver Plate . . . of the Middle Temple*, 1930, p. 44 and Pl. XVII.

Cup and cover, vase-shaped, palm leaves, laurel wreaths, fluted border, cone finial. 15¼ in. high. 1801. 84 oz. 8 dwt., lot 138 of 2nd June 1948.

Pair of vases, classical design, acanthus and palm. One by Paul Storr, 1803, the other by Thomas Robins, 1805. 248 oz. 6 dwt., lot 94 of 21st Nov. 1934.

Cup and cover, gilt, medallion of Diana, fluting and arabesque foliage. 14½ in. high. 1805. 160 oz. 8 dwt., lot 69 of 1st May 1912.

Cup and cover, gilt, flowers and fruit, eagle's-head handles, liners for use as ice-pail. 21 in. high. 1808. 281 oz. 5 dwt. See J. Starkie Gardner, *Old Silver-Work chiefly English . . . exhibited at St. James Court, 1902*, p. 174 (Case Q. No. 7). Duke of Newcastle. Lot 52 of 7th July 1921.

Cup and cover, fluting, vine foliage, Satyrs' masks as handles. 1809. 120 oz. 10 dwt., lot 41 of 22nd May 1946.

Cup and cover, Campana form, three horses, Satyrs' heads. "Given by H.I.H. the Grand Duke of Russia to be run for on the Hippodrome Steeplechase, Saturday, May 25. 1839." 1809. 111 oz. 15 dwt., lot 61 of 5th July 1911.

Cup and cover, fluted, chased horses, Satyrs' masks to handles. 16½ in. high. 1809. 120 oz. 5 dwt., lot 68 of 24th Jan. 1917.

Vase, cover and stand, gilt, Bacchanalian figures, anthemion, mask handles, cone finial, stand on claw feet. 17 in. high. 1809. 231 oz., lot 15 of 25th Sept. 1946.

Cup and cover, fluted, horses, laurel and vines. 1810. 137 oz. 13 dwt., lot 48 of 1st July 1931.

Cup and cover, gilt, Campana form, laurel rim, low cover, cone finial. 12¼ in. high. 1810. 99 oz., lot 129 of 19th Feb. 1947 (Earl of Lonsdale Collection).

Warwick vase, gilt, 10¾ in. high. 1811. 225 oz. 18 dwt., lot 45 of 10th Feb. 1938.

Warwick vase, 10 in. diam. 1811. 161 oz. 5 dwt., lot 142 of 27th April 1938.

Cups—*continued*

Vase and cover, gilt, amphora shape, serpent handles, foliage, elephant's head feet. 22½ in. high. 1811. 379 oz. 10 dwt., lot 93 of 6th Aug. 1942.

Of Warwick vase form, applied anchors and military trophies. 17 in. high. 1811. 270 oz. 17 dwt., lot 64 of 5th July 1939.

Vase, gilt, figures and vines on matted ground, acanthus. 1811–12. 143 oz. 17 dwt., lot 110 of 1st June 1908.

Vase and cover, oviform, fluting, laurel, oak wreaths. 18 in. high. 1812. 109 oz. 6 dwt., lot 84 of 25th March 1919.

Cup and cover, fluted, honeysuckle, racehorse finial, gadroon, shell and foliage borders. 1812. 98 oz. 5 dwt., lot 30 of 26 Oct. 1943.

Vase and cover, gilt, eagles'-head handles, festoons. 20 in. high. 1812 and 1814. 280 oz. 14 dwt., lot 269 of 6th June 1904 (Duke of Cambridge).

Cup and cover, gilt, gadrooned, masks on handles, horse finial. 1813. 125 oz. 5 dwt., lot 62 of 2nd July 1935.

Cup and cover, gilt, Campana form, racing scene, honeysuckle. 1814. 101 oz. 7 dwt., lot 65 of 25th Feb. 1931.

Warwick vase, gilt, with cover, chased ivy, square plinth. 19¼ in. high. 1815. 300 oz. 10 dwt., lot 124 of 23rd Oct. 1946.

Cup and cover. Goodwood Cup for 1817, gilt, Campana form, oak, acorns and hops. 15 in. high. 1816. 114 oz., lot 57 of 23rd June 1915.

Cup and cover, vase-shaped, gilt, fluted, oak handles, racehorse finial. 17¼ in. high. 1816. 120 oz. 3 dwt., lot 100 of 14th Feb. 1951. The Monaghan Course Cup.

Pair of cups, Campana form, hop foliage. 1817. 30 oz., lot 280 of 29th April 1902 (Dunn Gardner Collection).

Cup and cover, Campana form, Bacchanalian figures, mask handles (with square stand of 1820). Lambton Park races, 1822. 1817. 195 oz. 17 dwt., lot 59 of 23rd June 1915.

Cup and cover, gilt, fluted, horses, vines and grapes. 15 in. high. 1817. 108 oz. 10 dwt., lot 32 of 27th Feb. 1946.

Cup and cover, military trophies, Pegasus handles, pedestal on sphinx feet. "By Paul Storr and Philip Rundell" (?) 1818. 301 oz. 5 dwt., lot 46 of 23rd Sept. 1942.

Vase, triangular pedestal bay wreath finial. "Presented to John Philip Kemble by his admirers." 1818. 291 oz. 10 dwt., lot 141 of 14th Dec. 1905, and lot 92 of 9th Aug. 1917.

Vase and cover, oviform, vine branches, grapes and foliage. 17 in. high. 1819. 128 oz., lot 32 of 24th April 1929 (Capt. Adrian Bethell Collection).

Cup and cover, vase-shaped, gilt, square plinth, fluted and vine decoration, berry finial. 12 in. high. "Burdrop races 1821." 1819. 136 oz. 15 dwt., lot 142 of 28th Jan. 1948.

Cup and cover, gilt, oak, and laurel, palm, grapes and vine. 1820. 117 oz. 5 dwt., lot 36 of 10th Dec. 1930.

Warwick vase, gilt, square pedestal with arms. 17 in. high. 1820. 248 oz. 8 dwt., lot 113 of 23rd July 1919.

Warwick vase, gilt, square pedestal, 17½ in. high. 1820–1. 248 oz. 17 dwt. Presented by the Goldsmiths' Company to Thomas Lane, Clerk for thirty-five years. 1821, lot 88 of 17th July 1950.

Cups—*continued*

Cup, gilt, Campana form, vines, grapes and tendrils. 12 in. high. 1824. 108 oz. 14 dwt., lot 106 of 3rd May 1933.

Cup and cover, chased Juno, Mercury and Cupid on dolphin. 1835. 336 oz., lot 79 of 6th Jan. 1920.

Cup and cover, gilt, cherubs and vines, infant Bacchus on cover. 12½ in. high. 1837. 41 oz. 15 dwt. "To Lady Victoria Leveson Gower from her Godmother Victoria R. 1838." Lot 56 of 26th Feb. 1947.

Decanter-stands. See under WINE-COASTERS

Dessert-baskets. See under BASKETS

Dessert-stands (including "centre-pieces" and "plateaux")

Dessert-stand, basket, ivy border, three figures of nymphs. 1808. 68 oz., lot 79 of 24th April 1929.

Pair of dessert-stands, gilt, caryatid figures of leopards, triangular bases. 1808. 128 oz., lot 29 of 4th Feb. 1946.

Pair of dessert-stands, pierced baskets, female figure stems, triangular plinths. 20 in. high. One by Paul Storr 1809, the other by Philip Rundell, 1820. Weight, with four smaller ditto *en suite*, 849 oz. 5 dwt., lot 205 of 6th June 1904 (Duke of Cambridge).

Pair of dessert-stands, gilt, fluted baskets, classical figures. 1810. 259 oz. 8 dwt., lot 104 of 20th Jan. 1920.

Three dessert-stands, circular baskets, figures of nymphs, triangular bases, chased flowers and fruit. 1810. 514 oz., lot 154 of 8th Dec. 1944. (From the Collection of the 9th Earl of Coventry.)

Pair of dessert-stands, gilt, circular baskets, triangular stems, classical figures. 1812–13. 250 oz. 5 dwt., lot 52 of 10th June 1926.

Centre-piece, circular wire basket, three caryatid figures as stem, dolphin feet, plinth with guilloche border. 19 in. high. 1813. 231 oz. 18 dwt., lot 102 of 19th Dec. 1951.

Pair of dessert-stands, gilt, shells supported by Tritons, circular plinths, crowned monograms. 1815. 346 oz. 2 dwt., lot 103 of 6th June 1904 (Duke of Cambridge), and lot 132 of 25th Feb. 1930 (Barnet Lewis's Collection).

Centre-piece, gilt, twelve lights, circular basket, lions and Amorini. 36 in. high. 1816. 1357 oz., lot 83 of 22nd July 1903.

Pair of centre-pieces, gilt, six lights, central basket, female figures, dolphins and shells, triangular bases. 1816. 712 oz., lot 50 of 15th Nov. 1944.

Pair of dessert-stands, gilt, shells supported by tritons. 1816. 346 oz. 5 dwt., lot 103 of 6th June 1904 (Duke of Cambridge).

Pair of centre-pieces, gilt, circular baskets, Bacchanalian figures, adaptable to six-light candelabra. 1816. 1,233 oz. 5 dwt., lot 63 of 14th May 1914 (Coutts Heirlooms).

Centre-piece, gilt, six lights, alternating with circular basket, Pan, Bacchante, etc. 1816. 615 oz., lot 51 of 15th Nov. 1944.

Centre-piece, triangular plinth, fluted stem, circular bowl, basket work and vines, three branches. 19 in. high. 1816. 336 oz. 15 dwt., lot 107 of 7th May 1947 (Earl of Wemyss) and lot 64 of 6th Dec. 1950.

Dessert-stands—*continued*

Centre-piece, triangular plinth, foliage and shell borders, six glass dishes or candle nozzles, 1817. 274 oz. 10 dwt., lot 138 of 3rd July 1905.

Centre-piece, formed as tree with two figures, base with three leopards, bowl chased laurel. 19 in. high. 1818. 542 oz., lot 156 of 19th March 1947.

Plateau, four sections, mirror centre, vine, grapes and foliage rim. Eight feet in length. 1819. Lot 67 of 28th May 1943. Red Cross Sale.

Four dessert-stands, ivy baskets, infant Bacchanals and leopard stems, triangular bases. 1820. 450 oz., the liners are 1852. Lot 67 of 19th Nov. 1943.

Centre-piece, boys and panther stem, trellis basket. 19½ in. high (with plinth). 1821. 120 oz. 12 dwt., lot 85 of 20th July 1949, and lot 145 of 30th July 1951.

Dinner Services. See also under PLATES

Seventy-two plates, six oval dishes, four circular dishes, gadrooned. 1797. 1,825 oz. 10 dwt., lot 94 of 18th March 1942 (Earl of Desborough Collection). Of the above plates, forty-eight were sold as lot 98 of 7th Dec. 1943. 866 oz. 10 dwt.

Soup tureen, cover and liner; four sauce tureens and covers, and four salt-cellars, oval tub form, reeded loops and handles, covers foliage ring handles. 1800. 222 oz. 5 dwt., lot 116 of 20th July 1949.

Service of 201 pieces (apart from covers to entrée-dishes and liners to soufflé-dishes), with shaped gadrooned, shell and foliage borders, 1804–19, consisting of:

72 dinner plates. 1804 ⎫
24 dinner plates. 1808 ⎬ By W. Sumner.
24 dinner plates. 1816. ⎭

18 soup plates. 1804 ⎫ By W. Sumner.
 6 soup plates. 1808 ⎭

16 oval meat-dishes. 12 in. to 21½ in. long. 1805.
 2 oval meat-dishes. 15½ in. long. 1807.
 2 oval meat-dishes. 21½ in. and 24 in. long. 1808.
 6 oval meat-dishes. 14 in. to 17 in. long. 1816.
 2 oval strainers. 16 in. and 18 in. long. 1805.
 4 circular dishes. 12½ in. diam. 1805.
 4 oblong dishes. 13½ in. long. 1805.
 2 venison-dishes. 21 in. and 23½ in. long. 1805.
 2 venison-dishes. 18½ in. and 20 in. long. 1805.
 4 oblong entrée-dishes and covers. 1805.
 4 oval dish-covers. 14 in. to 19 in. long. 1805.
 2 oval dish-covers. 14 in. long. 1816.
 3 soufflé-dishes and liners, 1818 (2 liners Victorian).
 4 oblong heaters for entrée-dishes—made to match. 1819.

Total weight: 6,704 oz.

Engraved with Arms: Quarterly—Egerton and Grey, with Haynes in pretence. John William, 8th Earl of Bridgwater, had married Charlotte Haynes. He left his estates to John Hume-Cust, first son of the 1st Earl Brownlow, who had married Sophia, daughter of Sir Abraham Hume, granddaughter of John Egerton, Bishop of Durham, and great-granddaughter of Henry Grey, Duke of York.

Lot 42 of 13th March 1929. From the Belton Collection of Lord Brownlow.

Dinner Services—*continued*

Service of 191 pieces (apart from covers, stands and liners), with gadrooned shell and foliage borders, 1804–29, including twenty-four pieces of 1749 and 1775 by makers other than Paul Storr:

2 oval soup-tureens, covers, stands and liners, 1814 and 1815.
4 oblong entrée-dishes and covers, 1814, with top plates, 1829, on plated heaters.
2 oblong vegetable-dishes and covers, 1815, on plated heaters.
4 oblong entrée-dishes. 1809 and 1810.
4 circular entrée-dishes and covers, 1814 and 1829—on plated heaters.
6 oval sauce-tureens and covers, 1815, with liners made in Edinburgh.
2 oval meat-dishes. 15 in. long. 1810.
2 oval meat-dishes. 17 in. long. 1810.
2 oval meat-dishes. 17½ in. long. 1804 and 1807.
2 oval meat-dishes. 19½ in. long. 1810.
2 oval meat-dishes. 20½ in. long. 1810.
2 oval meat-dishes. 22 in. long. 1810.
4 circular dishes. 11½ in. diam. 1829.
3 oval dish covers. 12½in., 14 in. and 19 in. long. 1814 and 1816.
2 oval mazarins. 17 in. and 18½ in. 1810.
80 dinner plates. 1810.
26 dinner plates, made to match (no date given).
18 soup plates, 1749—maker ?—with borders added.
6 soup plates, 1775—maker ?—with borders added.
10 soup plates, made to match (no date given).
1 cruet-frame, with four cut-glass cruets. 1815.
1 soy-frame, with six cut-glass bottles. 1815.
1 oblong bread-basket. 1814.
1 oval two-handled tea-tray. 27 in. long. 1814.
1 oval two-handled tea-tray. 20½ in. long. 1814.
2 oval salvers. 12 in. long. 1814.
1 tea-urn. 1815.

Total weight: 7,284 oz.

To the above were added:

2 vegetable-dishes and divisions, with plated covers and heaters.
1 plated venison-dish, cover and mazarin.
2 oval plated dish-heaters.
1 toasted-cheese dish on plated beater.

Engraved with the Arms of Balfour impaling Maitland. The service was made for the grand-father of the late Earl of Balfour; James Balfour, who married Lady Eleanor Maitland, daughter of James 8th Earl of Lauderdale, and died in 1845. Lot 45 of 16th July 1930. From the Balfour Collection.

Service of 278 pieces (apart from certain covers and stands), partly fluted, with gadrooned, shell and foliage borders, the handles supported by lions' masks, 1806, consisting of:

4 soup-tureens, covers and stands.
1 oval venison-dish. 26 in.
14 oval dishes. 15 in. to 23 in.
14 circular dishes. 12 in. to 15 in. diam.
5 circular covers.

Dinner Services—*continued*

  4 fish strainers. 14 in. to 18 in.
  6 sauce tureens, covers and liners.
 144 dinner plates.
  36 soup plates.
  8 circular plated dish-covers, with silver handles.
  24 oval ditto.
 10 oval plated dish-heaters.
  4 oblong ditto.
  4 circular ditto.
Total weight: 9,513 oz.

From the Collection of the late Duke of Hamilton, sold by the Trustees, 4th Nov. 1919, lot 31.
Service of 126 pieces (apart from covers, stands, etc.). The following twelve lots were sold together. 4th May 1932. All pieces were engraved with the Arms of Prince Henry of Battenburg, K.G., *accollé* with those of H.R.H. Princess Beatrice:

 116. Twenty-four soup plates, with gadrooned edges. 1810 (six), 1811 (remainder). 558 oz. 4 dwt.
 117. Seventy-two dinner plates, with gadrooned borders. 1808, 1810 and 1811. 1,581 oz. 12 dwt.
 118. Set of four circular entrée-dishes with domed covers, with gadrooned rims and handles rising from lions' heads. 1811; with four plated stands with hot-water receptacles on claw feet. 218 oz. 7 dwt.
 119. Set of four oblong entrée-dishes and covers, with gadrooned borders, with plated stands with hot-water receptacles, on claw feet. 1810, one dish 1811. 322 oz. 6 dwt.
 120. Set of six two-handled oval sauce tureens and covers, on four scroll and foliage feet, the whole enriched with bands of gadrooning, the handles at the sides and on the covers rising from lions' heads. 1811. 277 oz. 19 dwt.
 121. Pair of large oval soup-tureens and covers, similar. 1811, the stand of one tureen 1807. 563 oz. 13 dwt.
 122. Set of four circular wine-coolers, similar, 1810 and 1811 (two each). 484 oz. 17 dwt.
 123. Pair of candelabra, three-light, on circular bases, baluster-stems and vase-shaped holders, chased with gadroons, lattice-work and foliage, branches scrolled and richly decorated. 1811. 369 oz. 7 dwt.
 124. Pair of oval meat-dishes, with shaped gadrooned borders. 15 in. 1811. 85 oz. 8 dwt.
 125. Ditto. 16¾ in. 1811. 121 oz.
 126. Ditto. 18 in. 1811. 138 oz. 17 dwt.
 127. Ditto. 19 in. 1811. 160 oz. 19 dwt.
    Total weight: 4,882 oz. 9 dwt.

Dish-cover

 Gadrooned border, fluted centre, 16½ in. wide. 1803. 62 oz. 8 dwt., lot 32 of 7th July 1948.

Dishes. See also under BUTTER-DISH

Breakfast dishes

 Three breakfast dishes and covers, gadrooned rims, two 1797, one by John Edwards, 1798. 127 oz. 15 dwt., lot 119 of 18th March 1942 (Lord Desborough's Collection).

Dishes—*continued*

Circular dishes.   See also under SECOND-COURSE DISHES

Pair of circular dishes on tripod stands, with covers which have radiating leafage and a seeded fruit in the centre. Round the rims is a Greek fret. The stems are slender and balustered with three female figures in classic drapery holding each other by wreaths. The bases are triangular with concave sides. The linings, lifted by two small cockle shells, bear the Royal Crest and Garter. Height 11½ in., diam. 11⅛ in. 1808. See J. Starkie Gardner, *Old Silver-work chiefly English . . . exhibited at St. James Court, 1902*, p. 173 (Case Q. Nos. 1 and 2). Lent by J. E. Taylor. Also, lot 117 of 11th July 1912.

Pair of circular dishes, with covers, stands and liners. Covers with vines, triangular stands with female figures. 11½ in. diam. 1808–10. 304 oz., lot 153 of 19th March 1947.

Circular dish and cover, fluted, 1816. 42 oz. 10 dwt., lot 64 of 16th July 1941.

Entrée-dishes

Pair, oval with covers, reeded borders. 1793. 73 oz. 17 dwt., lot 85 of 17th Dec. 1930.

Four oblong, with reed-and-tie borders. 10 in. wide. 1794. 184 oz. 10 dwt. With Victorian covers, lot 123 of 2nd Oct. 1946.

Pair, with covers, oblong, gadrooned. 1797. 92 oz., lot 105 of 21st Sept. 1943.

Four, plain oval, reeded rims. 12 in. wide. 1798. 60 oz., lot 132 of 26th Jan. 1949 (plated covers).

Pair, with covers, oblong, gadrooned, domed covers. 10½ in. wide. 1799. 144 oz. 8 dwt., lot 114 of 27th June 1934.

Pair, with covers, oblong, corded borders. 12 in. wide. 1800. 106 oz., lot 49 of 16th Nov. 1938.

Four, with covers, octagonal, beaded borders, fluted covers. 1800–2. 268 oz. 5 dwt., lot 25 of 10th July 1918.

Four, with covers, oblong, reeded borders. 11¾ in. wide. 1801. 214 oz. 6 dwt., lot 41 of 10th May 1934.

Pair, with covers, octagonal, gadrooned borders. 10¾ in. wide. 1801. 111 oz. 3 dwt., lot 117 of 5th July 1950.

Pair, with covers, oblong. 1802. 102 oz. 3 dwt., lot 38 of 28th June 1927.

Pair, with covers, circular, gadrooned. 1802. 107 oz. 8 dwt., lot 20 of 23rd July 1930.

Four, with covers, oblong, gadrooned. 1802. 260 oz. 15 dwt., lot 22 of 23rd July 1930. Ditto, lot 23, 1802. 290 oz. Lot 24, 4 dishes only, 1802. 108 oz. 18 dwt.

Pair, with covers, oblong, gadrooned. 12 in. wide. 1802. 104 oz. 10 dwt., lot 45 of 11th June 1951.

Pair, with covers, circular, gadrooned rims and drop ring handles. 9 in. diam. 1803. 96 oz. 10 dwt., lot 28 of 15th Feb. 1939.

Four, with covers, oblong, gadrooned-fruit basket finials. 1803–4. 218 oz. 10 dwt., lot 63 of 10th May 1944.

Four, with covers, oblong, gadrooned. 1805. 227 oz. 18 dwt., lot 100 of 16th March 1932.

Four, with covers, circular, gadrooned. 1805. 199 oz. 5 dwt., lot 90 of 3rd May 1933.

Four, with covers, octagonal, gadroon and shell borders. 1806. 285 oz. 15 dwt., lot 27 of 2nd June 1919.

Dishes—*continued*

Entrée-dishes—continued

Four, with covers, oblong, gadroon, shell and scroll borders. 1806. 276 oz., lot 82 of 1st July 1931.

Four, with covers, octagonal, gadroon, shell and foliage rims. 1806. 304 oz. 18 dwt., lot 133 of 23rd June 1926.

Four, with covers, cushion-shaped, gadroon, shell and foliage rims. 11¼ in. wide. 1806. 142 oz. 13 dwt., lot 146 of 25th Feb. 1948 (Duke of Hamilton's Trustees).

Eight, and four covers, cushion-shaped, gadroon, shell and foliage, lion's-mask handles. 12 in. wide. 1808. 481 oz. 5 dwt., lot 100 of 3rd Nov. 1948.

Pair, with covers, oblong, gadrooned, lions'-mask and ring handles. 12½ in. wide. 1809. 142 oz. 10 dwt., lot 96 of 5th Dec. 1934.

Pair, with covers, circular, gadroon and foliage rims, lions'-mask and ring handles. 10½ in. diam. 104 oz. 18 dwt., lot 71 of 16th May 1935.

Pair, with covers, oblong, gadroon and foliage rims, lions'-mask and ring handles. 12½ in. long. 1809. 140 oz. 13 dwt., lot 72 of 16th May 1935.

Four, with covers, gadroon, shell and foliage rims, Coronet finials. 1810. 261 oz., lot 116 of 25th Feb. 1920 (Earl of Methuen Collection).

Eight, with covers, circular, reed-vine-and-tie borders. 11 in. diam. 1810. 505 oz. 10 dwt., lot 52 of 19th Feb. 1947 (Earl of Lonsdale Collection).

Four, with covers, cushion-shaped, reed-vine-and-tie borders. 10½ in. wide. 1810. 143 oz. 5 dwt., lot 50 of 19th Feb. 1947 (Earl of Lonsdale Collection).

Pair, with covers, oblong, gadroon, shell and foliage rims, lions' mask handles. 12½ in. wide. 1810. 163 oz. 10 dwt., lot 98 of 14th March, 1951.

Four, with covers, oblong, gadrooned. 1811. 246 oz. 7 dwt., lot 60 of 16th July 1919.

Four, with covers, circular, gadrooned rims. 1812. 243 oz. 3 dwt., lot 37 of 28th June 1927.

Four, with covers, oblong, plain. 1813. 248 oz., lot 99 of 6th June 1901.

Four, with plated covers, shaped gadroon and shell rims, lions' mask handles. 10½ in. wide. 1813. 151 oz. 10 dwt., lot 211 of 13th June 1941.

Pair, with one cover, circular, gadrooned rims, lions'-mask and foliage handles. 10½ in. diam. 1814–15. 75 oz. 13 dwt., lot 122 of 27th June 1951 (Earl of Harewood's Collection).

Pair, with covers, shaped oblong, lion's-mask and foliage handles. 1815. 122 oz. 19 dwt., lot 80 of 27th July 1932.

Four, with covers, oblong, gadroon rims, foliage handles. 1815. 274 oz. 5 dwt., lot 114 of 15th Oct. 1946.

Pair, with covers, oblong, gadrooned, lions'-mask handles. 12½ in. wide. 1815. 131 oz. 15 dwt., lot 79 of 11th Oct. 1951.

Four, with covers, gadroon, shell and foliage rims. 1816. 292 oz. 15 dwt., lot 42 of 15th Feb. 1905.

Pair, with covers, oblong, vine leaves and grapes. 13 in. wide. 1816. 154 oz. 5 dwt., lot 88 of 16th Dec. 1936.

Pair, with covers, cushion-shaped, vine and grape borders. 11 in. wide. 1816. 148 oz. 17 dwt., lot 89 of 16th Dec. 1936.

Pair, with covers, cushion-shaped, vine and reeded rims, foliage handles. 11 in. wide. 1816. 147 oz. 10 dwt., lot 150 of 26th Feb. 1947; lot 151, one similar, 75 oz. 10 dwt.

Dishes—*continued*

Entrée-dishes—*continued*

Pair, with covers and stands, oval, shells and foliage, oak branches and acanthus handles. 1817. 429 oz. 5 dwt., lot 68 of 14th May 1914 (Coutts Heirlooms). Other similar lots at same sale and of same date: lot 69, two oval, 294 oz. 10 dwt.; lot 70, four oblong, 341 oz. 5 dwt.; lot 71, four oblong, 357 oz. 10 dwt.; lot 72, four oblong, 390 oz. 10 dwt.

Four, with covers, oblong, gadroon, shell and foliage borders, lions'-mask handles. 1817–18. 303 oz., lot 125 of 22nd May 1946.

Four, with covers, oblong, gadroon, shell and foliage rims. 12 in. wide. 1820 (2 covers by Emes and Barnard). 223 oz., lot 70 of 2nd Oct. 1946.

Pair, with covers, oblong, gadroon, shell and foliage rims. 12 in. wide. 1820. 61 oz. 15 dwt., lot 39 of 8th Oct. 1947.

Four, with covers, circular, shaped gadrooned rims, 10½ in. diam. 1822. 229 oz. 3 dwt., lot 21 of 7th June 1937.

Single, with cover, bands of flowers, rose finial, 11½ in. wide. 1826–7. 70 oz. 18 dwt., lot 76 of 16th June 1948.

Four, with covers, circular, shaped gadrooned rims. 1828. 163 oz. 16 dwt., lot 44 of 7th July 1943.

Four, with covers and liners, circular, gadroon, shell and scroll borders, phoenix-crest handles. 1830. 343 oz. 5 dwt., lot 20 of 23rd Feb. 1911.

Pair, with covers, octafoil. 11¼ in. diam. 1831. 105 oz. 4 dwt., lot 95 of 14th March 1951.

Four, with covers, oval, shaped outline, arm-crest handles. *c.* 1815 (?) 247 oz. 12 dwt., lot 21 of 4th June 1896.

Mazarines

Pair of mazarines, 19 in. wide. 1808. 132 oz. 15 dwt., lot 133 of 3rd Dec. 1947.

Single mazarine, oval, diaper piercing, 18¼ in. wide. 1812. 56 oz. 8 dwt., lot 39 of 18th Oct. 1950.

Two mazarines, pierced diaper work, one 19 in. wide. 1814; the other 22½ in. wide. 1815. Gross weight 153 oz. 12 dwt., lot 39 of 28th Jan. 1948.

Meat-dishes

Ten, oval, reed-and-tie decoration. 15 in. to 22½ in. wide. 1794. 524 oz., lot 114 of 2nd Oct. 1946.

Three, oval-shaped and gadrooned, 13, 15 and 20 in. wide. 1795. 178 oz. 5 dwt., lot 76 of 20th Dec. 1939.

Eleven, oval, gadrooned. 13½–23 in. long. 1796. 565 oz. lot 51 of 25th Feb. 1920 (Earl of Methuen Collection).

Four, oblong, ball feet, shaped gadrooned rims. 20¼ and 21 in. wide. 1805. 551 oz., lot 33 of 10th May 1934. Also two similar 16½ in. wide. 1805. 168 oz. 8 dwt., lot 34 same sale.

Pair, oval, shaped gadrooned rims. 22½ in wide. 1805. 265 oz. 10 dwt., lot 121 of 19th Jan. 1948.

Four, oval, gadroon, shell and foliage rims, two 13 and two 17 in. wide, 1806. 226 oz. 5 dwt., lots 134–5 of 23rd June 1926.

Ten, oval, gadroon, shell, and foliage rim, Arms of George III. 13 to 19 in. wide. 1806. 569 oz. 18 dwt., lot 83 of 1st July 1931.

Dishes—*continued*

Meat-dishes—continued

One, with plated cover, shaped gadroon, shell and foliage rim. 20¾ in. wide. 1806. 103 oz. 11 dwt., lot 92 of 3rd Dec. 1947.

Pair, oval, gadroon and foliage rims. 14¾ in. wide. 1808. 93 oz. 15 dwt., lot 130 of 3rd Dec. 1947; also pair similar 17 in. wide, 1808. 130 oz. 5 dwt., lot 131 of same sale; pair similar 18¾ in. wide. 1808. 182 oz. 10 dwt., lot 132 of same sale.

Twelve, reed, vine and ribbon rims. 14½–22 in. wide. 1809. 992 oz., lots 43–45 of 19th Feb. 1947 (Earl of Lonsdale Collection).

Three, oval, gadroon, shell and foliage rims. 17, 19½ and 22½ in. wide. 1811. 266 oz., lot 9 of 17th April 1940.

One, oval, shaped and gadrooned, 18¼ in. wide. 1811. 73 oz. 16 dwt., lot 79 of 9th Nov. 1949.

One, gadrooned, 22 in. wide. 1812. 115 oz. 4 dwt., lot 44 of 28th June 1927.

One, shaped and gadrooned. 18 in. wide. 1813. 54 oz. 5 dwt., lot 75 of 28th Oct. 1942.

One, gadroon and foliage rim. 25 in. wide. 1813. 156 oz., lot 46 of 19th June 1946.

Pair, gadroon, shell and foliage rims. 17½ in. wide. 1815. 123 oz. 10 dwt., lot 61 of 14th March 1951.

Four, gadroon, shell and foliage rims. 1815–16. About 350 oz., part of lot 128 of 22nd May 1946.

Twelve, vine and grape rims. 16 in. to 22½ in. wide. 1816. 999 oz., lot 26 of 12th Dec. 1928.

Pair, oval, gadroon and shell rims. 14¼ in. wide. 1816. 79 oz. 8 dwt., lot 152 of 1st Feb. 1950.

Pair, oval, gadroon and shell rims. 15¼ in. wide. 1818. 94 oz., lot 92 of 16th May 1940.

One, shaped, gadrooned. 22 in. wide. 1819. 107 oz. 10 dwt., lot 142 of 29th Jan. 1947.

Five, oval, shell and foliage rims. 12½, 13¾, 17¾ in. wide. 1819. 258 oz. 10 dwt., lot 97 of 14th March 1951.

Ten, oval, gadroon, shell and foliage rims. 1820, lots 66–8 of 2nd Oct. 1946; also two similar 22 in. wide. 1820. 216 oz. 8 dwt., lot 69 of same sale.

One, oval, shaped gadrooned rim. 17 in. wide. 1826. 76 oz. 11 dwt., lot 76 of 9th July 1947.

Three, oval-shaped, gadrooned rims. 17, 18 and 21 in. wide. 1828. 194 oz. 5 dwt., lots 39–41 of 7th July 1943.

Oval dishes (so-called, probably meat-dishes)

Four oval dishes, gadrooned, rose, thistle and shamrock. Crown and Garter motto. 14¼ in. wide. 1801. 173 oz., lot 142 of 13th June 1945; also one similar. 16 in. wide. 1801. 45 oz. 12 dwt., lot 143 of same sale.

Second-course dishes

Four circular dishes with reed-and-tie rims, 12 in. diam. 1794. 99 oz., lot 113 of 2nd Oct. 1946.

Pair, circular, shaped gadrooned rims. 16 in. diam. 1822. 139 oz. 13 dwt., lot 22 of 7th July 1937.

Four circular dishes with gadroon, shell and foliage rims. 11½ in. diam. 1820. 110 oz., lot 65 of 2nd Oct. 1946.

Dishes—*continued*

Soufflé-dishes

With liner, gadrooned rim, foliage handles. 8¾ in. diam. 1825. 40 oz. 18 dwt., lot 158 of 11th July 1951.

Vegetable-dishes

Plain, circular, with cover, drop-ring handles. 1794. 8¼ in. diam. 46 oz. 13 dwt. (with stand and lamp), lot 81 of 18th June 1951.

Pair, with covers, gadrooned rims, ring handles. 8½ in. diam. 1795. 108 oz. 18 dwt., lot 131 of 26th Jan. 1949.

Circular, with lining, gadrooned rim. 12¾ in. diam. 1796. 107 oz. 10 dwt., lot 114 of 19th Jan. 1948.

Pair, with covers, circular, gadrooned rim. 8½ in. diam. 1797. 84 oz. 11 dwt., lot 126 of 15th June 1938.

Pair, with covers and liners, circular, rams' heads. 1801. 142 oz., lot 42 of 17th July 1917 (Hope Heirlooms). See Thomas Hope, *Household Furniture and Interior Decoration*, 1807, Pl. 47.

Four, gadroon, shell and foliage rims. Royal and Hamilton crests. 11 in. diam. 1806. 181 oz. 16 dwt., lot 145 of 25th Feb. 1948 (Duke of Hamilton Trustees).

Pair, with covers, circular, gadrooned rims, serpent ring handles to covers. 10½ in. diam. 1807. 116 oz. 4 dwt., lot 150 of 17th Dec. 1948. (Modern partitions.)

Oval, with cover, divisions and heater, gadrooned borders. 1809. 152 oz. 5 dwt., lot 124 of 10th July 1918.

Trefoil, with cover, gadrooned rim, fluted cover. 13 in. wide. 1825. 83 oz. 19 dwt., lot 96 of 14th March 1951.

Trefoil, with cover, gadrooned. 13¼ in. wide. 1825. 79 oz. 3 dwt., lot 125 of 27th June 1951 (Earl of Harewood Collection.)

Venison-dishes

Oblong, ball feet, shaped gadrooned rim. 16½ in. wide. 1805. 84 oz. 10 dwt., lot 151 of 1st Feb. 1950.

Dressing Service

Silver-gilt dressing service, consisting of coffee-pot, stand and lamp; hot jug; cream-jug, sugar-basin; box cover and stand; fourteen glass bottles and boxes, shaving brush and case. The whole fitting in rosewood case. 1837. 98 oz. 14 dwt., lot 105 of 22nd Oct. 1947.

Ewers.   See under JUGS

Flagons

Cylindrical flagon and cover, oak and hop foliage, acanthus spout, fluted cover, shell thumb-piece. 7 in. high. 1816. 40 oz. 11 dwt., lot 101 of 19th Dec. 1951.

Fruit Bowl.   See under BOWLS

Honey-pots

Beehive of skep shape, with stand, the cover with disc handle engraved with crest, stand with reed-and-tie border, similarly engraved. 1793. 10 oz. 16 dwt., lot 45 of 29th April 1936.

Beehive, with cover, handle formed as crest. 1798. 8 oz. 3 dwt., lot 41 of 8th June 1932.

Honey-pots—*continued*

Beehive, with cover and stand, reed-and-tie border. 1798. 14 oz. 13 dwt., lot 117 of 17th June 1936.

Beehive, gilt, with cover and stand surmounted by a bee. 1799. 15 oz. 17 dwt., lot 56 of 10th April 1929 (R. Astley Collection).

Beehive, with stand. 1799. 14 oz. 18 dwt., lot 13 of 28th June 1933; and Sotheby's lot 66 of 17th Nov. 1937 (W. R. Hearst Collection).

Beehive, with stand, reed-and-tie border, bee finial. 1799. 14 oz. 13 dwt., lot 45 of 5th April 1938.

Beehive, gilt. 1799. 9 oz. 16 dwt., lot 53 of 18th April 1934.

Beehive, with cover and stand. 1803. 13 oz. 16 dwt., lot 80 of 16th June 1948.

Hot-water Jugs

Gilt, on three feet, the finial formed as a Royal Coronet, engraved with the Arms of George III and those of the 7th Earl of Elgin. 1799. No. 200 of "The Four Georges" Loan Exhibition at 25 Park Lane, 1931. Lent by Crichton Bros.

Of classical form with stand and lamp, the stand has three legs with claw feet, handle is S-shaped scroll with a female terminal head on its upper socket, projecting spout embossed with acanthus leaf. 1800. C. J. Jackson, *History of English Plate*, p. 962, fig. 1287.

Gilt, vase-shaped, with stand and lamp, with chased bands round body and honeysuckle lip. 1803. Given to Adolphus Frederick, Duke of Cambridge, by his sisters and brothers—Elizabeth Landgravine of Hesse Homburgh; Augusta Sophia; Edward, Duke of Kent; Augustus, Duke of Sussex; Sophia, and Mary, Duchess of Gloucester. Lent by H.M. Queen Mary for the "Loan Exhibition of Old English Plate", at 25 Park Lane, 1929, No. 8. See Pl. 1 middle shelf. With stand and lamp, gadrooned, claw feet, pendent rings to stand. 12½ in. high. 1803. 42 oz. 10 dwt., lot 86 of 3rd March 1937.

Vase-shaped, with stand and lamp, gadrooned, stand has claw feet and rings. 1803. 45 oz., lot 111 of 4th March 1936.

With stand and lamp, gadrooned, stand has claw feet and rings. 1803. 43 oz., lot 115 of 19th April 1939.

Vase-shaped, with stand and lamp, claw feet, ring handles. 11½ in. high. 1805. 47 oz. 10 dwt. gross, lot 247 of 20th Feb. 1947 (Earl of Lonsdale Collection).

With stand and lamp, ovolo border, triangular stand, ring handles. 1806. 52 oz. 10 dwt. gross, lot 28 of 5th July 1950.

With stand and lamp, ovolos on shoulder, acorn finial, stand with claw feet and ring handles. 11 in. high. 1807. 46 oz. 10 dwt., lot 134 of 25th May 1938.

With stand and lamp, fluted borders. 1807. 49 oz. 13 dwt., lot 9 of 12th June 1923.

With stand and lamp, ovolo border, stand with claw feet and ring handles, urn-shaped lamp. 11¾ in. high. 1807. 52 oz., lot 27 of 15th Feb. 1939.

With stand and lamp, fluted border, tripod stand and lamp. 1808. 47 oz. 15 dwt., lot 24 of 20th March 1923.

With stand and lamp, basket-work and ovolo border, serpent ivory handle, triangular stand, drop ring handles. 1808. 56 oz. 6 dwt. gross, lot 43 of 3rd Nov. 1948.

With stand and lamp, claw feet and ring handles to stand. 1809. 48 oz. 7 dwt., lot 10 of 27th July 1932.

Hot-water Jugs—*continued*

With stand and lamp, honeysuckle border, serpent handle. 1809. 54 oz. 10 dwt., lot 28 of 18th June 1941; also lot 49 of 1st Nov. 1944, 54 oz. 12 dwt. gross.

Vase-shaped, with stand and lamp, gadrooned shoulder, ivory serpent handle, claw feet to stand. 11¼ in. high. 1809. 57 oz. 5 dwt. gross, lot 118 of 16th Dec. 1946.

With fluting, shell and anthemion ornament, serpent handle. 11 in. high. 1812. 40 oz. 13 dwt., lot 144 of 28th May 1951.

With stand and lamp, fluted, serpent ivory handle, anthemion lip, berry finial, ring handles to stand. 1813. 56 oz. 17 dwt. gross, lot 102 of 14th March 1951.

With bands of shells, serpent handle, fluting. 1814. 32 oz. 10 dwt. gross, lot 44 of 5th May 1944.

Vase-shaped, gilt, fluted, anthemion decoration, double serpent handle. 10¾ in. high. 1814. 40 oz. gross, lot 75 of 28th June 1950.

Ice-pails.

See under WINE-COOLERS (the name familiar in the sale-rooms).

Inkstands

Oblong, gadroon and foliage border, with taper-stick and two glass bottles. 1813. 33 oz., lot 51 of 5th Dec. 1945.

Oblong, classical foliage border, nymphs at altar in centre. 1817. 150 oz. 3 dwt., lot 44 of 17th Dec. 1912.

Oblong, shell and foliage feet, shell border, two bottles. 16 in. long. 1817. 57 oz. 13 dwt., lot 31 of 6th Dec. 1933 (Earl Howe Collection).

Oblong, foliage rim, flowers, two glass bottles, oblong box surmounted by dragon. 11 in. wide. 1826. 38 oz. 1 dwt., lot 108 of 24th Nov. 1948.

Oval, gilt, chased waves, Triton handle. 12 in. wide. 1833. 25 oz. 3 dwt., lot 7 of 25th Sept. 1946.

Jardinière

Oval, with fluting and foliage, satyr's head, handles. 14 in. wide. 1808. 128 oz. 5 dwt., lot 116 of 9th July 1929.

Jugs (including EWERS).

See also under COFFEE-POTS, ETC., and HOT-WATER JUGS

Jug, of classical design with honeysuckle and shells. 1809. 59 oz. 5 dwt., lot 157 of 14th July 1911.

Ewer, fluted and plaited border, honeysuckle ornament. 1809. 65 oz. 4 dwt., lot 81 of 17th April 1928.

Pair of ewers, gilt, trefoil lips, Egyptian masks on handles. 13½ in. high. 1816. 127 oz., lot 163 of 6th March 1935 (Sir H. Clayton Collection). Also lot 150 of 20th May 1936.

Mustard-pots

With fluting, gadroon, shell and foliage rim. 1817. 9 oz. 10 dwt., lot 93 of 26th July 1948; also similar, 1817. 9 oz. 1 dwt., lot 42 of 27th April 1949.

Plateaux.

See under DESSERT-STANDS

Plates. See also under DINNER SERVICES

Dessert

Thirty-six dessert plates, gilt, laurel wreath borders. 1798. 547 oz. 5 dwt., lots 65–67 of 17th July 1917.

Dinner

Seventy-two, reed-and-tie rims. 9¾ in. diam. 1794. 1,298 oz., lot 110 of 2nd Oct. 1946.

Twelve, gadrooned. 1797. 217 oz., lot 56 of 31st Jan. 1945.

Twenty-four, gadrooned. 1800. 407 oz., lot 7 of 9th March 1943.

Twelve, gadrooned. 9¾ in. diam. 1801. 217 oz. 10 dwt., lot 100 of 30th June 1948.

Thirty-six, gadroon, shell and foliage rims. 1805. 877 oz. 5 dwt., lot 55 of 14th May 1914 (Coutts Heirlooms).

Thirty-six, and eighteen soup plates, gadrooned rims. 1806. 1,084 oz., lot 11 of 17th Dec. 1930.

Thirty-six, and twenty-four soup plates, gadroon and foliage rims (six of the soup plates are 1820). 1807. 1,193 oz., lots 37–41 of 28th Nov. 1917.

Twenty-four, reed vine and ribbon rims. 10¼ in. diam. 1809. 598 oz., lot 40 of 19th Feb. 1947 (Earl of Lonsdale Collection).

Seventy-two, gadroon and foliage rims. 10¼ in. diam. 1810. 1,637 oz. 16 dwt., lots 30, 31 of 10th May 1934.

Four, gadroon, shell and foliage borders. 10½ in. diam. 1811. 96 oz. 14 dwt., lot 100 of 10th May 1950.

Eleven, shell and foliage rims. 1815. 302 oz., lot 73 of 10th May 1944.

Ninety-six, gadroon, shell and foliage rims. 10½ in. diam. 1820. 2,254 oz. 10 dwt., lot 64 of 2nd Oct. 1946.

Sixty, gadroon and foliage rims. 10 in. diam. 1828. 1,177 oz. 3 dwt., lot 62 of 9th Oct. 1946.

Soup. (For soup tureens see under TUREENS)

Eighteen (also thirty-six dinner plates), gadrooned rims. 1806. 1,084 oz., lot 11 of 17th Dec. 1930.

Twenty-four (also thirty-six dinner plates), gadroon and foliage rims. 1807 (including six of 1820). 1,193 oz., lots 37–41 of 28th Nov. 1917.

Twenty-four, threaded vine and grape rims. 1809. 614 oz., lot 73 of 6th Dec. 1933 (Earl Howe Collection).

Eighteen, gadroon and foliage rims. 1810. 456 oz. 16 dwt., lot 32 of 10th May 1934.

Twelve, shell and foliage rims. 1818. 325 oz., lot 78 of 14th May 1914 (Coutts Heirlooms).

Eighteen, shaped gadrooned rims. 1824. 363 oz. 10 dwt., lot 50 of 15th March 1946.

Fourteen, shaped gadrooned rims. 10 in. diam. 1829. 295 oz. 5 dwt., lot 63 of 9th Oct. 1946.

Eighteen, gadrooned, Arms of Duke of Clarence. 1830–3. 365 oz. 15 dwt., lot 126 of 22nd July 1936.

Venison

Eighteen, gadrooned, with hot-water compartments. 9¾ in. diam. 1819. Engraved with the Cavendish Crest and a Ducal coronet. 1819–20. (From the Duke of Devonshire. *Catalogue* by E. A. Jones, p. cxli.)

Punch-bowls.   See also under BOWLS

Melon-shaped, with reeded riband and beaded border. 11 in. diam. 1800. 32 oz., lot 49 of 27th Oct. 1941.

Plain, with classical frieze, handles rest on bold lion's masks, supported on three goats' heads and feet. Edge of circular foot is gadrooned. A flame-like ornament is fixed under the bowl. Height 9¾ in.; diam. 11¼ in. 1806 (Emperor of Russia Collection). See E. A. Jones, *Old English Plate of the Emperor of Russia*, 1909, p. 102, Pl. L, where it is merely described as a "large bowl".

Lion's-mask ring handles joined by swags of foliage, with cartouches either side—one inscribed "To Oscar Browning, in kindly remembrance of many years spent together at Eton from his friends and colleagues. Eton. Decr. 1875". Foot decorated with ovolos and swags below. Diam. 11¾ in. Height 8¼ in. See E. A. Jones, *Catalogue of the Plate . . . at King's College, Cambridge*, 1933, p. 50. King's College, Cambridge.

Salt-cellars

Four, double, gilt, with laurel borders and fluted legs. 1798. 28 oz. 8 dwt., lot 69 of 17th July 1917 (The Hope Heirlooms).

Six, plain, circular, with straight sides and gadrooned rims. 1798. 23 oz. 2 dwt., lot 107 of 14th June 1950 (Duke of Bedford's Collection).

Four, oval, gadrooned rims, bifurcated scroll handles. 1800. 22 oz. 12 dwt., lot 18 of 27th April 1949.

Sixteen, circular, with chased fruit, lions' masks and paw feet. 1808. 213 oz. 5 dwt., lot 13 of 6th June 1904 (Duke of Cambridge Collection).

Eight, circular, gilt, festoons of flowers, lions' masks and paw feet. 1809. 99 oz. 15 dwt., lot 256 of 13th June 1941.

Four, double shell, coral and seaweed stands, with twelve spoons. *c.* 1810. 98 oz. 3 dwt., lot 24 of 2nd July 1895.

Four, shells, supported by Tritons. 1811 (1), 1813 (3). 84 oz. 6 dwt., lot 153 of 16th May 1890; also lot 14 of 31st May 1933 (with four spoons of 1818). 84 oz. 3 dwt.

Four, shells supported by two mermen, liners. 1813. About 132 oz., lot 252 of 7th Jan. 1939. The W. R. Hearst Collection at Parke Bernet Galleries, New York.

Eight, gilt, with festoons of flowers, lions' masks and paw feet. 1814. 108 oz. 10 dwt., lot 90 of 24th Feb. 1910. Acquired by the Goldsmiths' Company. See J. B. Carrington and G. R. Hughes, *The Plate of the Worshipful Company of Goldsmiths*, p. 140 and Pl. 83.

Six, circular, flowers, lions' masks and claw feet. Royal Crown, Garter motto. 1814. (With six spoons by Eley and Fearn.) 91 oz., lot 94 of 14th March 1951.

Four, partly fluted, serpent handles, liners. 1815. 49 oz. 14 dwt., lot 82 of 9th Jan. 1946.

Pair, gilt, serpent handles and feet, beaded borders, liners. 1815. 24 oz. 12 dwt., lot 25 of 16th April 1913.

Eight, circular, flowers, lions' masks and paw feet. 1815. (With eight spoons.) 117 oz., lot 36 of 16th July 1930.

Four, gilt, fluted bowls on serpent stems. 1815. About 47 oz., lot 14 of 19th March 1943.

Twelve, gilt, gadroon and foliage, with spoons. 1820. 121 oz., lot 81 of 6th June, 1904 (Duke of Cambridge Collection). Of these, four formed lot 150 of 20th March 1947 (Knight, Frank and Rutley: Sir A. Bailey Collection).

Salt-cellars—*continued*

Four, gilt, palm leaves (with twelve spoons), Garter motto and crown. 1820. 56 oz. 3 dwt., lot 33 of 15th Feb. 1922.

Four, double shell, on sprays on coral and seaweed bases, gryphon-crest handle. 1833. 87 oz. 7 dwt., lot 110 of 24th Nov. 1948.

Four, double shell, coral and seaweed bases. 1833, with Victorian spoons. 84 oz. 13 dwt., lot 121 of 29th March 1950.

Pair, double, chased gryphons and scrolls, figures of children. 1835. 69 oz. 12 dwt., lot 116 of 16th May 1916.

Four, shell, with shell feet. 1836. 17 oz., lot 93 of 14th March 1951.

Salvers (all circular).   See also under WAITERS

Four, shaped gadroon and foliage borders. Royal Arms. 10 in. diam. 1815. 100 oz. 14 dwt., lot of 8th May 1946 (Marquess of Cambridge Collection).

Gilt, shell and foliage border. 10 in. diam. 1815. 30 oz., lot 74 of 10th May 1944.

Pair, shell and foliage rims. 8¾ in. diam. 1819. 40 oz. 10 dwt., lot 112 of 6th Nov. 1946.

Gilt, vine border, with six heads. 23 in. diam. 1821 (Duke of Devonshire). Engraved with the Arms of Boyle and Clifford. It is described on p. lxii of the Private Inventory by E. A. Jones.

Mask and scroll border, chased signs of the Zodiac. 25 in. diam. 1827. *c.* 178 oz., lot 166 of 30th Oct. 1947. J. P. Morgan's Collection at Parke Bernet Galleries. See the *Catalogue* of that sale, p. 34, with illustration.

Sauce-boats

Pair, dolphin handles, lions' masks and paw feet. 1811. 37 oz. 10 dwt., lot 11 of 7th March 1917.

Six, with shells, dolphin handles, serpents on feet. 1812. 193 oz. 10 dwt., lot 33 of 14th May 1914 (Coutts Heirlooms).

Pair, with lions' masks and paw feet, interiors gilded. 9¼ in. 1817. *c.* 72 oz., lot 390 of 1st Nov. 1947. J. P. Morgan's Collection at Parke Bernet Galleries. See the *Catalogue* of that sale, p. 104, with illustrations on p. 105.

Pair, three lions' masks and claw feet, festoons of flowers, trellis-work. 1818. 59 oz. 3 dwt., lot 99 of 14th March 1951.

Pair, shell-shaped, oval feet, serpent stems, dragon handles. 1819. 69 oz., lot 129 of 16th Nov. 1949.

Four, with festoons of fruit. No date. 134 oz. 5 dwt., lots 139/140 of 16th May 1890; one pair, lot 360 of 17th May 1892.

Four, with serpents and dragons. No date. 130 oz., lot 152 of 4th June 1896.

Saucepan

With cover, plain, lip chased with shell. 1825. 39 oz. 10 dwt., lot 86 of 4th March 1947.

Sauce-tureens.   See under TUREENS

Seal Boxes

With Arms of George III, oak foliage border. 1815 (inkpot later). 21 oz. 15 dwt., lot 5 of 17th April 1940.

Shield

Circular, with equestrian warriors on matted ground, reeded and riband borders. 28 in. diam. 1833. 342 oz., lot 65 of 27th Feb. 1946.

Sideboard Dish

Gilt, Bacchanalian chariot, border of masks, trophies and vines. 31 in. diam. 1817. 357 oz. 10 dwt., lot 76 of 15th Nov. 1944.

Soy-frames

Pair, oval, gadrooned and beaded border, six bottles each. 1808–9. 68 oz. 15 dwt., lot 116 of 3rd Dec. 1947.

Gadrooned rim, six bottles. 1810. 37 oz. 17 dwt., lot 27 of Oct. 6th 1948.

Oblong, gadroon, shell and foliage rim, six bottles. 1816. 27 oz. 8 dwt., lot 136 of 5th July 1950.

Strawberry Bowl. See under BOWLS

Sugar Bowls and Vases

Gilt, octagonal, panels of Chinese flowers. 6¾ in. diam. 1812. 22 oz. 2 dwt., lot 53 of 3rd June 1935 (Sir John Noble Collection).

Sugar bowl (or sweetmeat bowl), fluted foot, anthemion border, laurel festoons and medallions. 6¼ in. diam. 1814, lot 206 of 30th Oct. 1947. J. P. Morgan's Collection at Parke Bernet Galleries. See the *Catalogue* of that sale, p. 44, and centre of lower row of Plate on p. 45.

Four, with covers, gilt, fluting, acanthus and foliage on matted ground, with two sifters. 1816. 126 oz., lot 68 of 10th July 1935.

Four two-handled vases and covers, vertical gadroons and running foliage, cone finials—inscription. 1816. 104 oz. 3 dwt., lot 68 of 10th July 1935.

Table-services

Thirty-three table-forks and thirteen table-spoons, the stems chased with panels of shells and foliage. 1811. 152 oz. 3 dwt., lot 82 of 14th Oct. 1947.

A large table-service, the handles chased at the front with a stag hunt, and on the reverse with hunting trophies, the backs of the bowls with shell and mask, engraved with a crest. From the Collection of the Rt. Hon. the Viscountess D'Abernon. The service was sold in three lots as follows, 28th June 1950:

129. Forty-eight table-spoons, ditto table-forks, thirty dessert-spoons, thirty-four tea-spoons, six sauce-ladles, a cream-ladle, a sugar-sifter, two cheese-scoops, two skewers, a butter-knife, eight salt-spoons, and thirty-six dessert-forks similar (1834), six dessert-spoons (1834), one tea-spoon and eighteen oyster-forks. 1815 and 1816. 597 oz.

130. Forty-eight table-knives with silver handles, similarly chased with a stag hunt, 1816, four carving-knives and forks, and a steel similar, four Victorian.

131. Thirty-six cheese-knives, similar, 1834.

Twenty-four table-spoons, ditto table-forks, twelve dessert-spoons, ditto dessert-forks, eleven table-spoons, four sauce-ladles, two gravy-spoons, a soup-ladle and six salt-spoons—with twelve table-forks by Eley and Fearn (1824). Shell and hour-glass pattern, engraved with a crest. 1816, etc. 237 oz. 19 dwt., lot 34 of 6th Dec. 1950.

Table-services—*continued*

Service chased with hunting and Bacchanalian subjects and trophies, masks etc. after Flaxman's design. Similar to a service in the possession of Her Majesty the Queen. Dec. 19th 1893, lots 81–97, as follows:

81. Twelve table-forks. 48 oz. 4 dwt.
82. Twelve table-forks. 48 oz. 5 dwts.
83. Twelve table-spoons. 47 oz. 10 dwt.
84. Twelve table-spoons. 47 oz. 3 dwt.
85. Twelve dessert-forks and twelve dessert-spoons. 53 oz. 17 dwt.
86. Pair of sauce-ladles. 6 oz. 16 dwt.
87. Salad fork and spoon. 14 oz. 6 dwt.
88. Fish-slice. 7 oz. 5 dwt.
89. Pair of sugar-sifters and butter knife. 6 oz. 16 dwt.
90. Six egg-spoons and four salt-spoons. 9 oz. 18 dwt.
91. Six dessert-knives.
92. Set of four circular salt-cellars on lions' mask and claw feet, richly chased with groups of shells in high relief. 34 oz. 10 dwt.
93. Vase-shaped mustard-pot, flowers and scrolls. 6 oz.
94. A ditto muffineer. 2 oz. 5 dwt.
95. Six tea-spoons, vine branches and grapes. 10 oz.
96. Pair of asparagus-tongs; and a skewer. 9 oz.
97. Pair of silver-gilt grape-scissors, with vine-branch handles. 4 oz. 5 dwt.
        Total weight: 366 oz.

No dates given.

Tazze

Pair, gilt, circular, lion stems on triangular bases. 9½ in. diam. 1808. 127 oz. 15 dwt., lot 56 of 17th July 1917 (The Hope Heirlooms).

Gilt, Arms of St. Albans and Coutts, stand with supporters in relief. 1834. 103 oz., lot 61 of 14th May 1914 (Coutts Heirlooms).

Tea-caddy

Casket tea-caddy, fluting, gadroon and shell rim. 1820. 21 oz. 4 dwt., lot 101 of 14th March 1951.

Tea-kettles

Fluting and foliage, serpent handle, dolphin tap, with stand and lamp. 1802. 191 oz. gross. Lot 24 of 10th May 1944.

Gilt, basket-work borders, with stand and lamp. Possibly by Paul Storr. 1802. 109 oz. 15 dwt., lot 80 of 6th June 1904 (Duke of Cambridge).

Circular, palm leaves, serpent handle, dolphin tap, with stand and lamp. The stand has claw and wing feet, quatrefoils and guilloche ornament. 15 in. high. 1802. 190 oz. gross. Lot 38 of 16th March 1949 (Duke of Manchester); also lot 138 of 28th Oct. 1953.

Oval, fluted, dolphin tap, stand and lamp, four reeded and claw feet. 1811. 121 oz. 8 dwt. gross. Lot 99 of 20th Nov. 1950.

Circular, fluted, with stand and lamp, lion's-mask spout, laurel and reed-and-tie borders, claw feet to stand on shaped plinth, initials of William and Adelaide as Duke and Duchess of Clarence. 1818. 142 oz. 15 dwt. gross. Lot 62 of 16th June 1948.

Tea-kettles—*continued*

With flowers, shells and fluting, stand and lamp. 1823. 88 oz. 15 dwt. gross. Lot 46 of July 7th, 1943.

Melon-shaped, with lamp and stand, rustic spout and handle, acorn finial, bracket stand. 1832. 81 oz. 7 dwt. gross. Lot 142 of 1st Feb. 1950.

Melon-shaped, gilt, with stand and lamp, chased flowers and fruit. 1833. (With tea-service by another maker, 1824.) Lot 72 of 14th June 1950 (Duke of Bedford).

Melon-shaped, gilt, flowers and scrolls, serpent handle. 1836. Stand and lamp 1847. 44 oz. gross. Lot 107 of 19th Jan. 1948; also lot 115 of 28th Oct. 1953.

Tea-pots

Compressed spherical, rosettes round shoulder. 1808. 29 oz. 5 dwt., lot 26 of 7th June 1937.

Circular, gadroon and foliage collar, serpent handle. 1808. 30 oz. 6 dwt., lot 22 of 30th Nov. 1938.

Gilt, with stand, plaited border, honeysuckle, serpent handle. 1808. 39 oz. 15 dwt. gross. Lot 145 of 8th Dec. 1944.

Circular, gadrooned foot and collar, anthemion spout, ivory serpent handle. 1812. 29 oz. 5 dwt. gross. Lot 248 of 20th Feb. 1947 (Earl of Lonsdale Collection); also lot 145 of 15th Dec. 1953.

Circular, serpent handle, fluted and shell bands. 1812. 34 oz. 8 dwt. gross. Lot 8 of 21st Sept. 1943.

Circular, gadroon shell and foliage rim, ivory serpent handle. 1814. Lot 721 of 10th Nov. 1951. Parke Bernet Galleries, New York.

Hemispherical, anthemion and flowers. 1814. 29 oz., lot 61 of 25th Feb. 1948.

With stand, gadrooned border, honeysuckle spout, serpent handle. 1815. 39 oz. 15 dwt., lot 23 of 20th March 1923.

Pair, circular, vertical acanthus leaves, diaper work on lids, ivory handles. 1816. 59 oz. gross. Lot 240 of 20th Feb. 1947 (Earl of Lonsdale Collection).

Circular, plain, fluted collar, ivory handle. 1818. 25 oz. gross. Lot 86 of 27th July 1943.

Melon-shaped, panel, of flowers. 1829. 24 oz. 5 dwt., lot 46 of 10th March 1948.

Tea Services

Tea-pot and stand, sugar-basin and cream-jug. Tea-pot 1808, others 1806. 77 oz. 10 dwt., lot 158 of 6th June 1904 (Duke of Cambridge Collection).

Gilt, tea-pot and stand, basket-work border, 1808, with sugar-basin and cream-jug—similar. 74 oz. 12 dwt., lot 78 of June 6th, 1904 (Duke of Cambridge Collection).

Gilt, tea-pot, coffee-jug with stand and lamp, sugar-basin and cream-jug, key-pattern borders, female head handles. 1808. 133 oz., lots 50, 51 of 17th July 1917 (The Hope Heirlooms).

Gilt, honeysuckle bands, gadrooned rims, serpent handles, oval tray 29 in. long, urn on a square plinth, coffee-pot and stand, tea-pot, and tea-caddy. 1809–11. 621 oz. 10 dwt., lot 6 of 18th June 1902.

Tea-pot, sugar-basin, cream-jug, hot-water jug, stand and lamp (or coffee-pot), partly fluted, serpent handles. 1810. 128 oz. 15 dwt., lot 3 of 12th July 1922. Also tea-pot, sugar-basin and cream-jug—similar. No date or maker given. 66 oz. 12 dwt., lot 4 of same sale (Earl of Eglinton).

Tea-pot, sugar-basin, cream-jug, hot-water jug, stand and lamp. Circular, gadrooned border, serpent handle, spouts of antique lamp form. 1810. 121 oz. gross. Lot 124 of 3rd Dec. 1947.

Tea Services—*continued*

Circular, tea-pot, sugar-basin and cream-jug, gadroon, shell and foliage rims. 1810–11–14. 67 oz. gross. Lot 29 of 10th Dec. 1946; also lot 152 of 15th Dec. 1953.

Tea-pot, sugar-basin and cream-jug. Gadroon shell and foliage, serpent handles. 1811. 74 oz. 10 dwt., lot 12 of 19th Jan. 1921.

Gilt, tea-pot, sugar-basin and cream-jug. Satyr's masks and serpents. 1812–13. 70 oz. 8 dwt., lot 23 of 13th May 1925.

Tea-pot, sugar-basin and cream-jug, honeysuckle, gadrooned borders, serpent handles. 1813. 60 oz. 10 dwt., lot 76 of 11th July 1912 (J. E. Taylor Collection).

Circular, with sugar-basin and cream-jug, quilted fluting, gadroon and shell rim, serpent handle. 1813. 64 oz. 16 dwt. gross. Lot 103 of 14th March 1951.

Tea-pot, sugar-basin and cream-jug, circular, fluted bodies, anthemion shoulder, tea-pot handle as serpent. 1814. 63 oz. 13 dwt. gross. Lot 63 of 30th June 1948.

Tea-pot, sugar-basin and cream-jug, bands of shells and anthemion, gadroon and shell rims. 1815. 75 oz. 5 dwt. gross. Lot 90 of 26th Feb. 1947.

Tea-pot and stand, hot-water jug, sugar-basin and cream-jug, gadrooning, anthemion ornament, serpent handles. 1816–17. 117 oz. gross. Lot 4 of 14th Dec. 1938 (W. R. Hearst Collection).

Tea-pot, sugar-basin and cream-jug, chased flowers and foliage, circular. 1823. 55 oz. 15 dwt. gross. Lot 69 of 28th July 1947.

Tea-trays. See under TRAYS

Tea-urns

Pair, lions' mask handles, dragon spout, gadroon borders. 1800. 375 oz. 14 dwt., lot 13 of 19th Jan. 1921.

Vase-shaped, gilt, lion's head spout. 15 in. high. 1801. 176 oz. 15 dwt., lot 54 of 17th July 1917 (The Hope Heirlooms). Illustrated in Hope's *Household Furniture and Interior Decoration*, 1807, Plates 49 and 52.

Flat vase form, square plinth, paw feet, lion's-mask handles. 15 in. high. 1805. "The Backhouse Urn" at Lloyds. See Wright and Fayle, *History of Lloyd's*, pp. 181–2, and Plate facing p. 182; Warren R. Dawson, *Treasures of Lloyd's*, 1930, p. 157; and *Catalogue of the Historic Plate of the City of London*, 1951. No. 265.

Gilt, key-pattern and Egyptian ornament. 1805. 212 oz. 10 dwt., lot 52 of 17th July 1917 (The Hope Heirlooms).

Vase-shaped, circular, square plinth, claw feet, lion's-mask handles, gadrooned rim, cone finial. 15 in. high. 1806. 193 oz. 15 dwt. gross. Lot 120 of 3rd Dec. 1947.

Fluting and honeysuckle, lion's-mask handles and spout. 1809. 212 oz., lot 84 of July 18th 1923 and lot 75 of 11th May 1927.

Honeysuckle border, gadrooning, shells and foliage. 1809–10. 210 oz. 15 dwt., lot 75 of 15th Nov. 1944.

Pair, dolphin spouts, lion's-mask handles, gadrooned. 1810. 415 oz., lots 5 and 6 of 12th July 1922.

Circular, square plinth, claw feet, fluted body, lion's-mask handles, dolphin tap, cone finial. 1810. 200 oz., lot 142 of 9th Nov. 1949.

Circular, square plinth, claw feet, fluted, dolphin tap, lion's-mask handles, gadrooned rim, cone finial. 14½ in. high. 1810. 202 oz. 5 dwt., lot 65 of 16th Nov. 1949. Identical model to the preceding.

Tea-urns—*continued*

Lions' mask handles, square plinth. 14 in. high. 1812. 198 oz. 10 dwt., lot 116 of 11th Feb. 1903.

Vase-shaped, partly fluted, honeysuckle borders, lion's-mask tap. 1813. 175 oz. 8 dwt. gross. Lot 123 of 31st July 1946.

Vase-shaped, bearded masks and serpent handles, square plinth, claw and foliage feet. 14½ in. high. 1813. 200 oz. gross. Lot 108 of 7th May 1947 (Earl of Wemyss Collection).

Trays

Pair, gadroon, shell and foliage borders. 30 in. long. 1808. 215 oz. and 216 oz. 15 dwt., lots 59 and 60 of 6th June 1904 (Duke of Cambridge).

Oval, gadroon and foliage borders. 30 in. long. 1809. 195 oz. 8 dwt., lot 42 of 10th March 1920.

Oval, gadroon, shell and foliage rim. 26 in. long. 1809. 187 oz. 10 dwt., lot 141 of 27th April 1938.

Pair, oval, gadroon, shell and foliage. 20 in. long. 1810. 181 oz. 5 dwt., lot 140 of 27th April 1938.

Oval, gilt, Royal Arms, shell, foliage and gadroon rim. 32 in. long. 1812. 241 oz. 10 dwt., lot 67 of 25th March 1919.

Oblong, engraved hunting scenes, fox's-mask handles. "To George Osbaldeston Esqu. from the Gentlemen of the Burton Hunt, 1812." 30 in. long. 1812. 216 oz. 6 dwt., lot 38 of 3rd July 1946. For George Osbaldeston (1787–1866), known in sporting circles as the "Squire", and his great feats of riding endurance, his duel with Lord Bentinck, etc., see the *Dictionary of National Biography*.

Oval, shaped gadrooned rim, reeded and foliage handles. 24 in. long. 1812. 155 oz. 10 dwt., lot 55 of 27th July 1950.

Pierced vine and grape border, serpent handles, Royal Arms. 30 in. long. 1813. 271 oz. 10 dwt., lot 62 of 28th Feb. 1923.

Oblong, gadroon and shell rim. 19 in. long. 1813. 98 oz. 9 dwt., lot 121 of 4th Nov. 1936.

Oval, with border of openwork and applied vine leaves and grapes, entwined snake handles, on four chased feet. 25½ in. long. Royal Arms. 1814. Presented to H.R.H. the Duke of York, K.G., on the occasion of his marriage, 26th April 1923. See *Catalogue of the Loan Exhibition of Old English Plate, at 25 Park Lane*, 1929, No. 442 and Plate XLVII. This item may possibly be the same as that described two items above—with the date given as 1814 by mistake, and the length including the handles.

Oval, gadroon and foliage rim. 24 in. long. 1814. 118 oz. 12 dwt., lot 194 of June 6th 1904 (Duke of Cambridge).

Oval, gadroon, shell and foliage border, four palm-leaf feet. 24 in. long. 1815. 152 oz. 3 dwt., lot 104 of 14th March 1951.

Oval, engraved flowers, shells and scrolls, with foliage and shell rim. 32 in. long. 1816. 263 oz., lot 39 of 3rd July 1946.

Pair, oval, vine and grape borders, foliage handles, 28 in. long. 1816. 364 oz. 18 dwt., lots 32, 33 of 12th Dec. 1928.

Oval, gadroon and foliage rim, with foliage handles. 21 in. long. 1816. 89 oz., lot 66 of 5th Dec. 1945.

Trays—*continued*

Oval, shell and foliage rim, oak and acanthus handles. 28 in. long. 1817. 179 oz., lot 79 of 14th May 1914 (Coutts Heirlooms).

Oval gadroon, shell and foliage rim. 24 in. long. 1817. 177 oz. 16 dwt., lot 97 of 25th April 1933.

Oval, gilt, vine and grape border, serpent handles. 1818. 289 oz. 10 dwt., lot 69 of 15th Nov. 1944.

Oval, gadroon and shell rim. 22¾ in. long. 1819. H.M. the Queen (wedding present from Cheshire).

Oval, gadrooned rim, foliage handles. 28½ in. long. *c.* 1810. 153 oz. 8 dwt., lot 110 of 17th July 1890 (Marquis of Normanby Collection).

Tureens

Sauce

Four, with covers, boat-shaped, gadrooning, urn finials. 1792–5. 66 oz. 11 dwt., lot 135 of 20th June 1934.

Six, with covers and six ladles, oval, reed-and-tie borders. 1794. 193 oz. 14 dwt., lots 121 and 122 of 2nd Oct. 1946.

Pair, with covers, boat-shaped, reeded. 1795. 33 oz., lot 64 of 2nd July 1935.

Pair, octagonal, with covers, panels of fluting, ring handles to covers. 1796. 38 oz. 16 dwt., lot 72 of 5th Oct. 1949.

Four, oval, with covers, gadrooned feet and rims, crest and coronet finials. 1797. 78 oz. 13 dwt., lot 140 of 17th Dec. 1947.

Pair, plain oval, reeded rims. 1798. 26 oz. 15 dwt., lot 224 of 20th Feb. 1947 (Earl of Lonsdale Collection).

Pair, plain oval, gadrooned rims, crest finial. 1799. 50 oz. 18 dwt., lot 26 of 12th Dec. 1907.

Pair, with covers, gadrooned, drop-ring handles. 1799. 45 oz. 16 dwt., lot 33 of 27th March 1935.

Pair, with covers, oval, gadrooned, drop-ring handles. 1799. 45 oz. 10 dwt., lot 76 of 10th July 1935.

Pair, with covers, gilt, mask handles, serpent handles to covers, gadroon and foliage rims. 1799. 73 oz. 7 dwt., lot 44 of 13th June 1929.

Pair, oval, with covers, gadrooned rims, ring handles. 1799. 50 oz. 10 dwt., lot 50 of 15th July 1947.

Pair of circular (sauce?) tureens "Presented to Vice Admiral Lord Nelson by the Committee for managing a Subscription made for the Wounded and Relatives of the Killed at the Battle of the Nile". 1800. 91 oz. 3 dwt., lot 66 of 28th June 1905.

Four, with covers, boat-shaped, gadrooned, "Presented to . . . Nelson . . . by the Committee appointed to manage the Subscription made for the benefit of the wounded . . . in the glorious Victory obtained off Copenhagen on the 2 of April 1801". 84 oz. 7 dwt., lots 163 and 164 of 12th July 1895; lot 89 of 10th July 1913; and lot 64 of 10th May 1916.

Pair, with covers, oblong, gadrooned, lion's-mask handles. 1803. 70 oz. 16 dwt., lot 97 of 19th Dec. 1945.

Pair, with covers, oblong, fluted and gadrooned, lion's-mask handles, with crest finials. 1805. 70 oz. 5 dwt., lot 134 of 16th May 1949.

Tureens—*continued*

Sauce—*continued*

Pair, with covers, circular, lion's-mask handles. 1805. 68 oz., lot 74 of 10th July 1935.

Six, with covers, circular, fluted and gadrooned, sea-horse crest finials. 1806. 211 oz. 10 dwt., lot 8 of 18th June 1902.

Pair with covers and stands, panels of anthemion, lion's-mask handles, gadroon, shell and foliage rims. 1806. (Stands by B. & J. Smith 1810.) About 140 oz., lot 89 of 3rd Dec. 1947. *En suite* with soup tureen, 1806, presented to Sir Matthew Wood, see later.

Four, with covers, oval, leopards' heads on handles, shell feet. 1807. 209 oz., lot 120 of 28th June 1905.

Four, honeysuckle and palm borders in beading. 1807. 115 oz. (With four plain covers—date uncertain.) Lot 28 of 12th Dec. 1945.

Four, with covers, oval, fluting, gadrooned rims, lion's-mask handles. 1808. 171 oz. 10 dwt., lot 4 of 9th March 1943.

Four, with covers, oval, fluted, gadrooned rims, shell and scroll feet, lion's-mask handles, liners. 7½ in. wide. 1808. 201 oz. 15 dwt., lot 134 of 3rd Dec. 1947.

Oval, gadrooned rim and gadrooned calyx, scroll feet on acanthus leaf bases, reeded handles, 6¾ in. high, 10 in. long. 1810. See C. J. Jackson, *History of English Plate*, p. 826 and fig. 1067.

Four, with covers, half-fluted, lion's-mask handles, gadroon and foliage. 1811. 156 oz. 16 dwt., lot 76 of 12th June 1941.

Pair, with covers, circular, fluted and gadrooned, foliage feet, lion's-mask handles. 1812. 81 oz. 10 dwt., lot 84 of 22nd July 1942.

Pair, with covers, circular, gadrooned, shell feet. 1813. 76 oz. 15 dwt., lot 106 of 21st Sept. 1943; also lot 151 of 15th Dec. 1953.

Pair, with covers, oval, reeded rims, urn finials. 1813. 35 oz. 10 dwt., lot 58 of 15th Feb. 1933.

Four, circular, lion's-mask handles, gadrooning. 1815. 172 oz. 18 dwt., lot 96 of 6th July 1932.

Six, partly fluted, oak branches, acanthus. 1817. 409 oz., lot 67 of 14th May 1914 (Coutts Heirlooms).

Four, with covers, oval, bands of fluting, lion's-mask handles. 1817. 153 oz. 10 dwt., lot 113 of Oct. 15th 1946.

Pair, with covers, oval, fluted, foliage feet, lion's-mask handles. 1817. 72 oz. 13 dwt., lot 70 of 16th Nov. 1951.

Four, with covers, partly fluted, gadrooned rims, foliage handles. 1819 (four stands of 1826). 225 oz., lot 35 of 13th June 1918.

Four, with covers, gilt, claw and foliage feet, gadrooned bodies. 1822. 160 oz. 2 dwt., lot 104 of 5th July 1933.

Four, with covers, gilt, oval, fluted, claw feet, lion's-mask handles. 1822. 160 oz., lot 144 of 1st Feb. 1950.

Four, oak branches, acanthus and shell, fluted covers. 1827. 196 oz. 10 dwt., lot 59 of 16th April 1913.

Six, oval, two handled, fluting, gadroon and shell rims, handles of lion's masks. 7½ in. long. 1828. 168 oz. 15 dwt., lot 63 of Oct 2nd 1946.

Tureens—*continued*

Soup

Oval, with cover, fluted, reeded border. 13½ in. wide. 1792. 74 oz. 14 dwt., lot 81 of 16th Nov. 1951.

Pair, with covers, oval, reed-and-tie borders, oblong bases. 1794. 235 oz. 15 dwt., lot 120 of 2nd Oct. 1946.

Oval, with cover, plain, gadrooned rim, crest finial. 1799. 109 oz. 12 dwt., lot 25 of 12th Dec. 1907.

Oval, with cover, four scroll and foliage feet, gadrooned rim, bifurcated scroll handles. 13 in. wide. 1800. 124 oz. 12 dwt., lot 61 of 20th May 1947.

With cover, stand and liner, oval, boat-shaped, fluted and gadrooned. 1801. 251 oz. 8 dwt., lot 79 of 14th May 1902 and lot 108 of 8th July 1902.

Circular, naval trophies "Presented by Old Madras Insurance Company to Captain Collier". 1802. 129 oz. 5 dwt., lot 38 of 11th Dec. 1916.

Pair, with covers, stands and liners, circular, seahorse crest finials. 1806. 602 oz. 10 dwt., lot 7 of 18th June 1902.

Circular, with cover and stand, panels of anthemion, lion's-mask handles, gadroon, shell and foliage rim. 19 in. wide. 1806. 289 oz. 10 dwt., lot 88 of 3rd Dec. 1947. Inscribed: "To Matthew Wood from his Fellow Britons . . . for his Exertions in the cause of Queen Caroline . . . ". This is Sir Matthew Wood (1768–1843), municipal and political reformer. Received baronetcy from Queen Victoria in 1837, her first bestowal. See further, *Dictionary of National Biography*.

Circular, with cover and stand, acanthus and lions' masks. 1806–7. 280 oz. 15 dwt., lot 78 of 8th July 1902.

Four, with covers and stands, half-fluted, lion's-mask handles. 1807. Two 669 oz. and two 427 oz. 11 dwt., lots 75 and 76 of 12th June 1941 (Sir Lionel Faudel Phillips).

Pair, with covers and stands, oval, partly fluted, lion's-mask handles, liners. 1807. 629 oz., lot 172 of 1st May 1946.

Oval, fluted, lion's-mask handles. 1807. 200 oz., lot 30 of 6th May 1903.

Oval, with cover, fluting and gadroons, leopard's-mask handles, shell feet. "To Captain I. F. Timins . . . " 1807. 170 oz. 17 dwt., lot 119 of 28th June 1905.

Pair, with covers, stands and liners, oval, claw feet to stands, body with shell and tulip border, coronet finials. 17 in. wide. 1807. 530 oz. 10 dwt., lot 114 of 20th July 1938 (Duke of Richmond & Gordon Collection).

Oval, lion's-mask handles, shells and scrolls. 1808. 186 oz. 8 dwt., lot 83 of 21st Dec. 1942 (Red Cross Sale).

Circular, gadrooned borders, lion's-mask handles. 1809. 173 oz., lot 46 of 27th Feb. 1917.

Pair, oval, with covers, fluted, gadroon rims, foliage and lion's-mask handles. 13¾ in. wide. 1809. 378 oz. 10 dwt., lot 109 of 7th May 1947 (Earl of Wemyss Collection).

Oval, part fluted, lion's-mask handles and feet. 1810. 189 oz., lot 495 of 10th April 1916 (Red Cross Sale).

Pair, oval, with covers, fluted, gadroon rims, lion's-mask handles, coronet finials. 13 in. wide. 1810. 322 oz. 15 dwt., lot 73 of 13th June 1947.

With four entrée-dishes, lion's-mask handles, gadroon and foliage borders. 1811. 487 oz. 10 dwt., lot 70 of 7th Dec. 1917.

Tureens—*continued*

Soup—*continued*

Oval, with cover, fluted, lion's-mask handles. 13½ in. wide. 1811. 174 oz. 18 dwt., lot 164 of 11th July 1951.

Circular, with cover, gadrooning, four feet, lion's-masks to handles. 11 in. diam. 1812. 152 oz. 14 dwt., lot 95 of 6th July 1932.

Circular, with cover, fluted and gadrooned, foliage feet, lion's-mask handles. 1812. 158 oz. 15 dwt., lot 83 of 22nd July 1942.

Pair, with covers, Warwick vases, covers chased ivy, with Cupid and panther finial. 12½ in. diam. 1813. 605 oz., lot 154 of 19th March 1947.

Oval, with cover, gadroon, shell border, lion's-mask handles. 1814. 153 oz., lot 55 of 22nd July 1903.

Pair, with covers and liners, oval, fluted bodies, vine borders, oak handles. 13½ in. wide. 1816. 324 oz., lot 149 of 26th Feb. 1947.

Two pairs, partly fluted, oak branches and acanthus. 1817. Lot 64 of 14th May 1914 (Coutts Heirlooms), 713 oz. 10 dwt.; lot 65 of same sale, 713 oz. 15 dwt.

Pair, with covers and stands, fluted, oak foliage, shell feet, thread and vine borders. 1817. 686 oz. 10 dwt., lot 86 of 6th Dec. 1933 (Earl Howe Collection). Also lot 34 of 1st July 1953.

With cover, stand and liner. St. George and the dragon on cover and Royal Arms. 1818. 640 oz., lot 42 of 6th June 1904 (Duke of Cambridge).

Gilt, as preceding lot, 1818. 649 oz., lot 43 of 6th June 1904 (Duke of Cambridge); also lot 70 of 10th May 1916.

With cover and stand, shell and foliage feet and rims, lion's-mask handles. 21½ in. wide. 1818. 337 oz. 4 dwt., lot 56 of 15th June 1938.

With cover, gadroon and shell, lion's-mask handles. 13½ in. long. 1818. 142 oz. 4 dwt., lot 76 of 31st Jan. 1941.

Pair, oval, fluted, eagle handles, four eagle feet. 1820. 590 oz. 10 dwt., the Cavendish Arms on each side (Duke of Devonshire Collection). See E. A. Jones's private catalogue of the collection, p. cl, Nos. 3a, b.

Pair, on shell-like stands, finial of lobster and foliage, merman and mermaid handles, body of rocaille work, stem formed of four dolphins. 1821. One weighs 525 oz. (Duke of Devonshire Collection). See E. A. Jones's catalogue, p. cl, Nos. 2a, b.

Oval, with cover, lion's claw feet, mask handle. 1821. 124 oz., lot 45 of 7th July 1943.

Pair, circular, with covers and liners, gadrooned rims, claw and foliage feet. 11¼ in. diam. 1822. Stands by Garrard, 1825. 601 oz. 10 dwt., lot 20 of 7th June 1937.

Circular, with cover, foliage feet, scroll handles. 11½ in. diam. 1824. 112 oz., lot 89 of 19th Feb. 1947 (Earl of Lonsdale Collection).

Vegetable-dishes.   See under DISHES

Waiters

Two, circular, claw feet, gadroon rims. 5¼ and 6 in. diam. 1812. 16 oz. 15 dwt., lot 281 of 20th Feb. 1947 (Earl of Lonsdale Collection).

Circular, scroll and foliage rim, flowers and scrolls. 7¼ in. diam. 1824. About 10 oz., lot 48 of 30th Nov. 1949.

Wine-coasters

Ten, with amorini, leopards and vines. 1815–17, lot 92 of 14th May 1914 (Coutts Heirlooms). Also, six similar (possibly from the above set). 1817, lot 125 of 10th March 1920.

Six, with reed, vine and ribbon rims, chased vines and laurel. 1817, lot 58 of 19th Feb. 1947 (Earl of Lonsdale Collection).

Wine-coolers

Pair, with liners, barrel-shaped, reeded hoops. 1798. 126 oz. 16 dwt., lot 79 of 9th Dec. 1913, also lot 148 of 10th Dec. 1948 (Parke Bernet Galleries, New York).

Pair, with covers and liners, partly fluted, shell feet, leopard-head handles. 1807. 245 oz. 5 dwt., lot 121 of 28th June 1905.

Six, gilt, fluted, frieze of shells, lion's-mask handles, shell feet. 1807. 948 oz., lot 71 of 4th Nov. 1919 (Duke of Hamilton Collection).

Pair, barrel-shaped, reeded hoops, gadrooned rims. 1808. 203 oz., lot 31 of 7th May 1917.

Pair, with stands, gilt, Bacchanalian frieze, fluted and honeysuckle borders. Liners. 1809. 482 oz., lot 16 of 9th March 1943.

Pair, lion's-mask handles, shell and foliage feet. 1809. 250 oz. 5 dwt., lot 359 of 11th March 1907.

Pair, with stands, Bacchanalian friezes, vines and acanthus. 1809–10. 496 oz. 10 dwt., lot 58 of 4th April 1922. Park Lane 1929 Exhibition, *Catalogue*, No. 443 and Pls. XLV and XLVI. H.R.H. The Duke of York, K.G.

Pair, gilt, Warwick Vases. 1810. 443 oz. 5 dwt., lot 70 of 13th June 1918.

Four, honeysuckle and foliage. 1810. 705 oz., lot 153 of 8th Dec. 1944 (from the Collection of 9th Earl of Coventry).

Pair, classical chariots on matted ground, vine wreaths, acanthus borders. 1810. 352 oz., lot 36 of 12th Dec. 1945.

Pair, partly fluted, lion's-mask handles, scroll and foliage feet, liners. 9¼ in. high. 1811. About 250 oz., lot 91 of 7th Dec. 1951 (W. R. Hearst Collection, Parke Bernet Galleries, New York).

Two pairs of Warwick Vase design. 1811. 377 oz. and 372 oz., lots 203 and 204 of 6th June 1904 (Duke of Cambridge).

Four, gilt, acanthus and vine, goat's-mask handles. 1811 (3) and 1834 (1). 756 oz. 13 dwt., lot 84 of 26th July 1939.

Pair, gilt, vase-shaped, Bacchanalian frieze, vines "after Flaxman". 11½ in. high. 1812. Duke of Beaufort. Red Cross Exhibition, Garrards, 1915, p. 16. No. 28.

Pair, with liners, partly fluted, lion's-mask handles. 1812. 242 oz. 12 dwt., lot 48 of 28th June 1927.

Pair, gilt, vine wreaths, coat of arms. 1812. 299 oz. 3 dwt., lot 88 of 1st July 1931.

Warwick Vase design. 1812. 268 oz. 15 dwt., lot 46 of 8th July 1931.

Four, partly fluted, lion's-mask handles, gadroon, shell and foliage rims. 1812. 488 oz. 10 dwt., lot 52 of Feb. 27th 1946.

Four, classical vases, partly fluted, vines and berries on matted ground. 1813. 663 oz., lot 42 of 19th June 1946.

Pair, gilt, fluted, Triton and mermaid, dolphin and shell plinths. 1813. 474 oz. 15 dwt., lot. 12 of 12th May 1922; also lot 26 of 26th June 1935.

Wine-coolers—*continued*

Pair, foliage feet, lion's-mask handles, gadrooned. 10 in. high. 1814. 246 oz. 5 dwt., lot 83 of 26th June 1935.

Pair, Warwick Vase shape. 1814. 599 oz., lot 97 of 5th Dec. 1917.

Pair, partly fluted, lion's-mask handles, claw feet, feet, gadroon, shell and foliage borders. 1814. 215 oz. 10 dwt., lot 158 of 7th Nov. 1945.

Pair, partly fluted, lion's-mask handles, gadroon, shell and foliage rims. 1814. 244 oz., lot 53 of 27th Feb. 1946.

Pair, classical figures and vines, matted ground, (1) Storr 1814 (1) P. Rundell 1820. 181 oz., lot 43 of 31st Oct. 1945.

Pair, gilt, fluted, applied figures of Phoebus and Diana in chariots. 9 in. high. 1815. 203 oz. 8 dwt. "Waterloo June 18th 1815" and "A Memento from Field Marshal von Blücher, Prince of Wahlstadt", with Royal Crest. Lot 39 of 7th October 1946; also lot 146 of 15th Dec. 1953.

Pair, Campana shaped, fluted, vine handles. 1815. 318 oz., lot 115 of 11th July 1912 (John E. Taylor Collection). Probably the same as Case Q, Nos. 3 and 4, p. 173 of *Old Silver-Work . . . Catalogue of the . . . collection exhibited in 1902 at St. James Court*, London, 1903, where they are described as Warwick Vases.

Pair, fluted, vine and grape borders, and liners. 1816. 218 oz., lot 30 of 12th Dec. 1928.

Pair, Warwick Vase shape. 9½ in. high. 1816–17. 392 oz. 5 dwt., lot 80 of 14th May 1914 (Coutts Heirlooms); also lot 97 of 29th Jan. 1919.

Pair, shallow liners (also Fruit coolers), vines on matted ground, two alternative rims. 1817. 308 oz. 8 dwt., lot 89 of 17th March 1920.

Pair, with stands, fluted, oak branches, shells and foliage. 1819. 369 oz. 5 dwt., lot 27 of 10th July 1918.

Pair, fluted, shell and oak feet, shell and foliage rims. 9¼ in. high. 1819. 273 oz. 15 dwt., lot 145 of 16th April 1947.

Four "Ice Pails or Wine Coolers . . . massive and elaborate, with Cavendish Arms applied to the sides in relief". 11½ in. high. 1820. 824 oz. 10 dwt. Duke of Devonshire. See E. A. Jones's catalogue, p. cxviii, Nos. 1a–d.

Four, vines and grapes on matted ground, palm leaves. 10¼ in. high. 1821. 550 oz. 10 dwt., lot 121 of 31st July 1918.

Pair, vines and grapes, gryphons in relief on foot. 1825. 310 oz. 10 dwt., lot 9 of 12th May 1922 (Burdett-Coutts Collection).

Pair, gilt, as above. 1825. 316 oz. 9 dwt., lot 10 of 12th May 1922.

Pair, hooped buckets, gadrooned rims, swing handles. 6¾ in. high. 1829. 75 oz. 18 dwt., lot 130 of 6th Oct. 1948.

"A Large Wine Cooler", 1834. Given to Dr. Keate on his retirement by subscription from Eton boys. Presented to the College by the family in 1947 as a memorial to Lt.-Col. E. des Graz, Rifle Brigade, Killed in Action, 1942. See *Eton Quincentenary Exhibition*, 1947, Section A, p. 39, No. 16.

Two pairs, Warwick Vase design. *c.* 1810. 800 oz. 15 dwt., lots 103 and 104 of 20th July 1893.

Pair, tub-shaped. *c.* 1810. 120 oz. 2 dwt., lot 104 of 28th Feb. 1895.

This comprises pieces sold by Messrs. Christie, Manson & Woods 1952–53, arranged in similar order to the main record.

Baskets

Cake-basket, circular, pierced trelliswork band, reeded swing handle. 12¼ in. diam. 1802. 36 oz. 10 dwt., lot 148 of 22nd Dec. 1952 and lot 87 of 18th Feb. 1953.

Cake-basket, oblong, bands of fluting, gadrooned shell and foliage rim. 13 in. wide. 1814. 45 oz. 19 dwt., lot 148 of 15th Dec. 1953.

Cake-basket, oblong, bands of fluting, gadrooned rim, reeded handle. 13 in. wide. 1815. 41 oz. 18 dwt., lot 147 of 15th Dec. 1953.

Candlesticks

Six gilt, shaped square bases, masks of the Seasons and shells, octagonal baluster stems with panels of scales and husks. 9 in. high. Four 1812, two 1814. 173 oz. 13 dwt., lot 110 of 1st July 1953 (Earl Howe Collection). These are the same model as the set of twelve of 1811 from the Lonsdale Collection. See Appendix A.

Pair, circular bases with paw feet, cylindrical stems chased acanthus and ivy foliage, Royal Arms and inscription "The Gift of His Majesty King William the Fourth to the Honble Nigel Kennedy 1836". 12¼ in. high. 1815. 77 oz. 5 dwt., lot 128 of 4th Nov. 1953.

Candelabrum

Nine lights, rockwork base with figures of mermaid, Neptune and triton, water-lily stem, three double coral branches entwined by dolphins and three single ditto, Neptune figure finial, with circular mirror plateau on dolphin feet. 45 in. high without plateau. 1838. Total weight 715 oz. 10 dwt., lot 43 of 13th May 1953.

Chamber Candlesticks

Three circular chamber candlesticks, gadrooned shell and foliage borders, detachable nozzles and extinguishers. 1809. 60 oz. 8 dwt., lot 154 of 15th Dec. 1953.

Coronet

Viscount's coronet, gilt jewelled circlet and twelve silver balls. 8¼ in. diam. 1820. 24 oz. 6 dwt., lot 35 of 25th March 1953. See Plate LXV.

Cruets

Oval cruet, gadrooned rim with scroll ends, eight glass bottles and mustard-pots. 1803. 39 oz. 13 dwt., lot 94 of 18th Feb. 1953.

Cups

Gilt, campana form, body chased foliage, laurel wreaths enclosing race scene and inscription, cover with palm-leaf rosette. 14¾ in. high. 1808. 122 oz. Beverley Races 1808. Lot 33 of 28th Oct. 1953.

Vase and cover, campana form, applied groups of Victory, trophies and cavalry officers, horse's-head handles, laurel wreath on cover. 17¾ in. high. 1818. 150 oz., 14 dwt., lot 88 of 5th March 1952.

Gilt vase and cover, chased acanthus foliage, vine-tendril handles encircling neck, foliage finial, later arms and inscription. 17 in. high. 1820 (cover 1843). 128 oz., lot 140 of 30th July 1952.

Dessert-stands

Centre-piece, on triangular base, shell and vine feet and shamrock border, applied arms and inscription, palm foliage stem, fluted central bowl and three double branches for candle sockets or cut-glass dishes. 20½ in. high. 1817. 274 oz. 3 dwt. Presented to Maj.-Gen. Sir Denis Pack, K.C.B., etc., by the County and City of Kilkenny. Lot 100 of 15th April 1953. See Plate LXI.

Four dessert-stands, shell shape, on three dolphin figure supports and shaped triangular plinths. 18 in. high. 1838. 231 oz. 10 dwt., lot 44 of 13th May 1953.

Four dessert-stands, formed as large shells supported by kneeling tritons blowing conches, oval rockwork bases. 1838. Weight of one 102 oz. 9 dwt., lot 45 of 13th May 1953.

Dish-covers

Pair, oval, fluted borders and centres, foliage ring handles. 15 in. wide. 1800. 108 oz. 16 dwt., lot 86 of 18th June 1952.

Dish-stands

Four vase-shaped, on square plinths, drop-ring handles at the sides. 9½ in. diam. 1838, with weighted silver discs. 163 oz. 5 dwt., lot 39 of 13th May 1953

Dishes

Dessert-dishes

Pair, gilt, circular, borders repoussé with spiral fluting and beading. 9½ in. diam. 1824. 30 oz. 16 dwt., lot 95 of 1st July 1953 (Earl Howe Collection).

Pair, oval, similar to above. 12¾ in. wide. 1824. 37 oz. 3 dwt., lot 96 of 1st July 1953.

Entrée-dishes

Four octagonal entrée-dishes and covers, gadrooned borders, covers reeded and foliage ring handles, engraved coat-of-arms and crests. 11½ in. wide. 1793, each with plated two-handled hot-water stand on four feet. 159 oz. 12 dwt., lot 161 of 15th Dec. 1953.

Two-handled oval, reeded border, stand and oval lamp. 12¼ in. wide. 1797. 75 oz. 18 dwt., lot 75 of 20th Feb. 1952.

Pair oblong and covers, gadrooned borders, domed covers with reeded and foliage ring handles, engraved coat-of-arms in mantling. 11½ in. wide. 1805. 119 oz. 15 dwt., lot 21 of 15th Dec. 1953.

Four octagonal, reed-and-tie borders, 9½ in. diam. 1814, and two by B. & J. Smith 1810. 145 oz. 18 dwt., lot 30 of 1st July 1953 (Earl Howe Collection).

Four oblong and covers, gadrooned rims, leaf corners, foliage ring handles to covers. 12¼ in. wide. 1813. 229 oz. 11 dwt. Plated stands, lot 49 of 17th Dec. 1952.

Four oblong, shell and foliage borders, fluted covers, foliage handles. 11½ in. wide. 1817. 357 oz. 10 dwt., lot 92a of 8th July 1953. Identical with set of four, lot 71 of 14th May 1914, recorded in Appendix A.

Meat-dishes

Pair oval, shaped gadrooned rims, arms. 20½ in. wide. 1796. 174 oz. 3 dwt., lot 118 of 17th June 1953.

Pair oval, shaped gadrooned rims, shells and foliage, 19 in. wide. 1807. 172 oz. 5 dwt., and plated covers, lot 87 of 15th Dec. 1953.

Mazarine

Oval, pierced diapers and arabesque, engraved Royal Ducal Coat-of-Arms. 18¼ in. wide. 1812. 45 oz., lot 35 of 15th Dec. 1953.

Vegetable-dishes

Pair circular and covers, gadrooned rims, ring handles. 9¼ in. diam. 1799. Covers with later chasing and finials. 90 oz. 12 dwt., lot 166 of 9th July 1952.

Egg-stand

Oblong, gadrooned rims, shell corners. Six egg-cups 1815 and five modern spoons. 42 oz., lot 142 of 12th Nov. 1952.

Flagons

Pair cylindrical, scroll handles, horse's-head crest finials, applied names "Ale" and "Beer". 13¼ in. high. 1838. 93 oz. 6 dwt., lot 41 of 13th May 1953.

Honey-pot

Gilt, skep beehive, stand with reed-and-tie rim, engraved Royal Crown and Monogram of Queen Charlotte. 1798. 13 oz. 11 dwt., lot 86 of 9th Dec. 1953.

Hot-water Jugs

Plain vase-shaped, gadrooned shoulder and rim, ball finial to cover. 1800. Gross weight 17 oz. 10 dwt., lot 112 of 13th May 1953 (Marquess of Sligo Collection).

Gilt, vase-shaped, band of basket-work, ivory handle ending in female mask, anthemion foliage below lip, Arms of 1st Earl Howe. 8½ in. high. 1800. Gross weight 35 oz. 2 dwt., lot 118 of 1st July 1953 (Earl Howe Collection).

Vase-shaped, stand and lamp, fluted shoulder, band of husks round neck, stand on three paw feet, curved triangular plinth, circular lamp, drop-ring handles. 11 in. high. 1805. Gross weight 46 oz. 15 dwt., lot 157 of 15th Dec. 1953.

Inkstand

Oblong, four sphinx feet, sides with engine-turned panels, lion's-mask and ring handles, drawers at the ends, two cylindrical vases and tripod vase on female-bust and paw feet, cover with amorino. 12¼ in. wide. 1802. 125 oz. 8 dwt., lot 132 of 17th June 1953.

Plates

Dinner

Pair, gadrooned shell and foliage rims, arms and crest. 10½ in. diam. 1811. 48 oz. 18 dwt., lot 66 of 17th June 1953.

Eighteen circular, shaped gadrooned and foliage rims. 10 in. diam. 1814. 342 oz. 17 dwt., lot 177 of 1st Dec. 1952

Soup

Eight, shaped gadrooned rims. 9½ in. diam. 1810. 149 oz. 5 dwt., lot 100 of 25th March 1953

Salt-cellars

Four plain circular, paw feet, gadrooned rims, crest. 1803. 17 oz. 3 dwt., lot 159 of 15th Dec. 1953.

Six circular, on three lion's-mask and paw feet, bodies chased quilted fluting, ovolo and shell rims, two crests. Four 1813, two 1827, with six shell-and-rosette pattern saltspoons by Eley and Fearn 1823. 73 oz. 8 dwt., lot 150 of 15th Dec. 1953.

Four oval, four scroll foliage feet, fluted bodies, shell and foliage rims, crest. 1818. 36 oz. 14 dwt., lot 141 of 15th Dec. 1953.

Four plain circular, three foliage feet, knurled rims, crest. 1825. 16 oz. 12 dwt., lot 140 of 15th Dec. 1953.

Eight shell-shaped, supported by kneeling tritons on oval bases chased shells and scrollwork. 1838. Gross weight 135 oz. 18 dwt., lot 46 of 13th May 1953.

Salvers

Circular salver, gadrooned shell and foliage rim. 9¼ in. diam. 1813. 17 oz. 18 dwt., lot 69 of 18th Feb. 1953

Salvers—*continued*

Pair, circular, shell and vine feet, shell and foliage rims, engraved arms and chased shells, flowers and foliage. 14 in. diam. 1820. 85 oz. 18 dwt., lot 76 of 28th Oct. 1953.

Circular, four shell feet, rim chased masks, animals, birds, centre flowers and foliage. 12½ in. diam. 1829. Later monogram and date. 34 oz. 4 dwt., lot 107 of 18th Feb. 1953.

Table-services

Dessert Service

Gilt, shell-and-rosette pattern. 1812. Comprising twenty-four dessert-spoons, twenty-four dessert-forks, six table-forks, sugar-spoon, sugar-tongs, six table-knives, twenty-four dessert-knives, steel blades. Weight without knives, 112 oz. 17 dwt., lot 49 of 1st July 1953 (Earl Howe Collection).

Tankards

Cylindrical, with cover and spout, base chased foliage, fluted cover, laurel scroll handle. 9 in. high. 1816. 64 oz. 6 dwt., lot 53 of 13th Oct. 1952

Cylindrical, double scroll handle, crest finial to cover, engraved arms. 9½ in. high. 1835. 39 oz. 13 dwt., lot 42 of 13th May 1953.

Tea-kettle

Melon-shaped, upright serpent handle, shoulder chased flowers. 1837, with stand and lamp 1847. Gross weight 44 oz. 2 dwt., lot 115 of 28th Oct. 1953.

Tea-pots

Large circular, fluted foot, body chased band of shells and anthemion foliage, gadroon and shell collar, handle terminating in serpent's mask and tails, engraved coat-of-arms. 1810. Gross weight 40 oz. 13 dwt., lot 153 of 15th Dec. 1953.

Plain circular, shell and foliage rim. 1812. Gross weight 29 oz. 12 dwt., lot 79 of 22nd June 1953.

Small, circular, partly fluted body and fluted foot, collar chased gadrooning, shells and foliage. 1815. Gross weight 20 oz. 13 dwt., lot 144 of 15th Dec. 1953.

Compressed spherical, body engraved bands of foliage, acorn finial. 1831. Gross weight 22 oz. 10 dwt., lot 164 of 22nd June 1953.

Melon-shaped, chased panels of flowers, cover with thistle finial. 1836. Gross weight 19 oz. 11 dwt., lot 68 of 11th March 1953.

Tea-services

Circular tea-pot, sugar-basin and cream-jug, each on fluted foot, gadrooned shell and foliage rims, handles to tea-pot and cream-jug formed as serpents, sugar-basin with rising loop handles, engraved crest. 1810, 1811 and 1814. Gross weight 66 oz. 18 dwt., lot 152 of 15th Dec. 1953.

Double breakfast service. 1812. For full description see text to Plate XXIX, p. 136, lot 139 of 1st July 1953 (Earl Howe Collection).

Oblong tea-pot, sugar-basin and cream-jug, each on four ball feet, lower parts of bodies chased curved fluting, gadroon, shell and foliage rims, tea-pot handle formed as a double serpent, other pieces with chased foliage handles. 1813. Gross weight 58 oz. 11 dwt., lot 149 of 15th Dec. 1953.

Tea-urns

Two-handled circular vase-shaped, square plinth, four paw and foliage feet, reed-and-tie handles rising from lions' masks, similar spout, cover with writhen cone and foliage finial. 15¼ in. high. 1808. Gross weight 186 oz. 5 dwt., lot 155 of 15th Dec. 1953.

Circular vase-shaped, square plinth and paw feet, partly fluted body, lion's-mask tap, female-mask handles, cone finial to cover. 15½ in. high. 1814. Gross weight 19 oz. 13 dwt., lot 156 of 28th Jan. 1953.

ADDENDUM TO APPENDIX A

Toast-rack

Oval seven-bar, on four feet with ring handle. 1793; and another of shaped oblong form, pierced scroll feet, wires and handles chased foliage. 1831. 22 oz. 7 dwt., lot 139 of 15th Dec. 1953.

Trays

Two-handled oblong, foliage feet, reeded rim, arms. 24 in. wide. 1808. Chased later with flowers, shells and scrolls. 185 oz. 18 dwt., lot 34 of 2nd Dec. 1953.

Two-handled oval, on four shell-and-vine feet, border and handles chased shells and foliage, centre engraved coat-of-arms and chased with band of shells, flowers and foliage. 24½ in. wide. 1816. 164 oz. 5 dwt., lot 143 of 15th Dec. 1953.

Two-handled oval, similar design, centre engraved coat-of-arms. 22½ in. wide. 1818. 150 oz. 10 dwt., lot 142 of 15th Dec. 1953.

Tureens

Sauce

Pair, oval, beaded feet and rims, band of foliage. 1793. 52 oz. 15 dwt., lot 66 of 25th June 1952.

Four two-handled and covers, each on four scroll foliage feet, bodies with bombé centres, gadrooned rims and bifurcated reeded and foliage handles, ring handles to covers. 6¼ in. wide. 1802. 115 oz. 7 dwt., lot 160 of 15th Dec. 1953.

Four two-handled and covers, each on circular gadrooned feet, bodies with fluted borders, ovolo rims and reeded and tie handles rising from lions' masks, covers with serpent ring handles on foliage rosettes in beaded borders, engraved crest. 6½ in. diam. 1806. 151 oz. 10 dwt., lot 156 of 15th Dec. 1953.

Soup

Pair circular, gadrooned borders, partly fluted bodies. 10¼ in. diam. 1801. 240 oz. 2 dwt. Arms of Earl St. Vincent., lot 141 of 30th July 1952.

Oval, four scroll-and-foliage feet, reeded handles rising from lions' masks, cover fluted border and lions'-mask and foliage handle. 13 in. wide. 1809. 183 oz. 8 dwt., lot 93 of 12th Nov. 1952.

Wine-coolers

Four gilt, vase-shaped, 1811, similar to pair of 1809, illustrated Plate XXIX, lot 107 of 1st July 1953 (Earl Howe Collection).

Pair, similar to above, with stands, 1809. See Plate XXIX, lot 108 of 1st July 1953.

Pair, hooped and staved bucket form, gadrooned rims and swing handles. 7 in. high. 1829. 75 oz. 19 dwt., lot 164 of 15th April 1953.

NOTES ON THE HORSE'S-HEAD EWER

THE history of the ewer is quite unknown, though it is said to have belonged at one time to members of the Galitsin family. There are, however, certain deductions which may be made when we consider on the one hand the style of the ewer, which is mid-eighteenth century, and, on the other hand, the date of its manufacture, which is 1833. Style and date are incongruous. Except for occasional uses at state banquets or in college halls, where ancient tradition still lingers, the ewer, with its accompanying rosewater bowl, had long since disappeared with the introduction of forks in the early seventeenth century. We can conclude, therefore, that when Paul Storr produced this work in 1833 he was either making a pair to an existing ewer of 1787 or 1788, or else he was copying one which had been damaged beyond repair and so needed replacing. However this may be, no companion piece appears to be recorded, so any deductions must be made solely from the nineteenth-century example before us. The goldsmith who made the original might well have copied an early-seventeenth-century ewer with its vase-shaped body and narrow neck, but he has preferred to base his work on the inverted pyriform cream jug which in England, at least, was in vogue from about 1740 till 1780. It is clear that such an object with its horse, its royal cipher with the date 1787 so prominently displayed, and its medallion encircled by laurel leaves had been specially made to celebrate some event which figured largely in the lives of Catherine of Russia and of the person represented on the missing medallion. The cipher is clearly that of Ekaterina Alexeyevna, Catherine II Empress of Russia. It is a large capital E formed of acanthus, or similar leaves with the numeral entwined at the centre. It occurs both on coins[1] and also on porcelain[2] made at the Imperial factory at St. Petersburg from 1762 to 1796, the date of Catherine's death.

That the cipher was also used on plate is shown in Baron A. de Foelkersam's fine

---

[1] U. Brückner, *Katharina die Zweite* (Allgemeine Geschichte, III, Hauptabth. X, Theil) Berlin, 1883, Plate facing p. 119; Baron de Chaudoir, *Aperçu sur le Monnaies Russes*, 1836–7, Pls. 38, 39, 41; V. I. Petrov, *Catalogue des Monnaies Russes de tous les princes Tscars et Empereurs 980–1899*, Moscow, 1899, 2nd edit., Pls. 39, 40; and T. F. de Schubert, *Monnayes Russes*, Atlas, Leipzig, 1857, Taf. XXVII, XXVIII, XXIX.

[2] V. I. Petrov, *Marques des porcelaines . . . russes . . .* Moscow, 1904, pp. xi, xii; *The Imperial Porcelain factory: 1744 to 1904*, (in Russian, with summary in French), St. Petersburg, 1904–6; J. Folnesics, "Petersburger Porzellan" in *Kunst. u. Kunsthandwerk*, X, 1907, p. 387 (review); G. Lukomsky, *Russiches Porzellan.*, Berlin, 1924; A. Rozembergh, *Les marques de la porcelaine russe*, Paris, 1926; D. Roche and T. Issaievitch, *Musée Céramique de Sèvres: Expos. de cér, russes anciennes: Cat.*, Paris, 1929; E. Hannover and B. Rackham, *Pottery & Porcelain. III. European Porcelain*, 1925, XIX, Russia, pp. 471–81 (esp. p. 477, see bib. on p. 553); Chaffers, *Pottery and Porcelain*, 14th edit., 1932, p. 544; E. Alfred Jones, "Old Russian Porcelain – Imperial Factories and Collections", *The Times Russian Supplement*, 26th Feb. 1916, p. 7. The Imperial cipher was continued in use by Nicholas I (1825–55) as may be seen on a cup and saucer in the Victoria and Albert Museum, and on a large vase, dated 1844, at Windsor Castle.

work on the Russian Imperial Collections[1] where are included (Vol. 1, No. 46) specimens of a large set of silver-gilt tableware, each piece bearing the Imperial cipher. The set in question had been presented to Catherine in 1782 by Prince Potemkin, and had been made in Paris in 1778–9 by "CA", now recognized as Claude Aubry,[2] and subsequently known as the "Sèvres" service. In Plate 51 Foelkersam shows a selection of tea- and coffee-pots by J. F. Köpping (1748–80) and J. J. Blohm (1766–86) on some of which Catherine's cipher can be seen. We now pass on to a consideration of the dated shield bearing the cipher of Catherine the Great.

The date 1787 is famous in Russian history as marking the year in which Catherine undertook her amazing journey to the Southern Provinces as planned by Prince Potemkin after the annexation of the Crimea in 1783. The trip—often referred to as the Tauric Journey—had taken years to prepare, and was designed as a kind of triumphant progression to impress the world in general, and Catherine in particular, with the splendour and flourishing condition of the conquered lands and to exhibit in no uncertain manner the power and riches of Russia. The guests included the Emperor Joseph, the vassal King of Poland, the Prince de Ligne, the Comte de Ségur, Count Cobenze, the British Envoy Alleyne Fitz-Herbert and a host of lesser officials, secretaries, etc. As explained by George Soloveytchik in his interesting work *Potemkin*,[3] the part Catherine wanted them to play in connection with this trip was threefold: as representatives of their respective countries they were to carry on their diplomatic duties during the trip and inform their governments of what they had seen; as courtiers they were to contribute to her entertainment during so long and exhausting a journey, and, finally, as prolific letter writers—like all the cultured people of the day—they were to spread the news of Russia's glory throughout the world. Except for that section which was made on the Dnieper on painted Roman galleys, the journey was made by sleigh and the all-important factor was the horse. The number employed was enormous. In all there were 178 sleighs drawn by horses varying in numbers from two in the smallest to thirty in Catherine's own sledge which consisted of four separate rooms.[4] At each station where they stopped 560 fresh horses were waiting. It is not surprising, then, to find a demi-horse represented on a gift given in commemoration of this great ride. But if this is not the symbolism intended, there still remain several other possibilities where the horse would figure as a compliment to Catherine. For instance, the House of Romanov traced its descent from one

---

[1] *Inventaire de l'Argentaire conservée dans les garde-meubles des Palais Impériaux: Palais d'Hiver, Palais Anitchkov et Château de Gatchino*, St. Petersbourg, 2 vols., 1907.

[2] Henry Nocq, *Le Poinçon de Paris*, Vol. I, Paris, 1926, p. 26, where the marks on one of the Russian forks are reproduced. It appears that although the official report of the registration reads "étoile" between the initials, it is a mistake for "une crosse"—the crozier being clearly shown in the pieces under discussion.

[3] See p. 276 of the 1938 edition (which contains thirteen illustrations besides the map) or p. 117 of the 1949 edition (which has only six illustrations but shows Leberecht's medallion of Potemkin on the plate between pp. 96 and 97).

[4] See U. Brückner, *op. cit.*, p. 351, and G. Soloveytchik, *Potemkin*, 1938 edition, plate facing p. 276, with folding map of route in preliminaries of volume.

Andrei, surnamed Kobyla, which means a horse.[1] The Arms of Russia are borne on the breast of the crowned Imperial double-headed eagle. The central shield displays the Arms of Moscow with St. George on a prancing horse killing the dragon. Finally, mention might be made of the famous bronze statue of Peter the Great at St. Petersburg, executed in 1766 for Catherine by the French sculptor Étienne Falconet. Here the horse is the most striking part of this undoubted masterpiece. Peter the Great is represented ascending a hill—a huge block of granite—at full gallop pointing with his right hand to the Neva on which the city stands.

On the completion of the trip valuable presents were exchanged and Catherine bestowed upon Potemkin the title of "Prince of Taurida". She also ordered Timothei Iwanoff (1729–1802)[2] to strike a medal showing herself on the obverse and a map of the journey on the reverse. There was another medal by Wassili Besrodny (1783–1806)[3] showing Potemkin, but of more interest was one by Carl Leberecht (1749–1827)[4] with Potemkin on the obverse and a map of the Crimea on the reverse. Leberecht had also struck a medal of Potemkin previously, and in 1791 we find one by his hand in celebration of the conclusion of peace with Turkey. In fact, in all events of national importance or whenever it was necessary to honour a national hero or visiting royalty it was to Leberecht that the work was usually entrusted. It seems probable, then, that the missing medallion may have been by Leberecht and Potemkin the subject represented.

[1] The horse figures also in the families of Skorniakoff (1743) and Kozodavleff (1798)—see L. Loukomsky "L'art heraldique en Russie", *Staryé Gody*, Feb. 1911, pp. 15, 26–7.

[2] L. Forrer, *Biographical Dict. of Medallists*, Vol. III, 1907, pp. 37–9. There is a copy in the British Museum.

[3] L. Forrer, *op. cit.*, Vol. I, 1902, p. 81.

[4] L. Forrer, *op. cit.*, Vo. III, pp. 353–5; and U. Brückner, *op. cit.*, pp. 348–9.

INDEX

The roman numerals refer to the plate numbers of the illustrations